John Tyler

John Tyler, by Alonzo Chappel (oil on paper). Photograph courtesy of the Virginia Historical Society, Richmond.

John Tyler
A BIBLIOGRAPHY

Compiled by
Harold D. Moser

Bibliographies of the Presidents of the United States, Number 10
Mary Ellen McElligott, Series Editor

GREENWOOD PRESS
Westport, Connecticut • London

Library of Congress Cataloging-in-Publication Data

Moser, Harold D.
    John Tyler : a bibliography / compiled by Harold D. Moser.
      p. cm.—(Bibliographies of the presidents of the United States,
      ISSN 1061–6500 ; no. 10)
    Includes indexes.
    ISBN 0–313–28168–8 (alk. paper)
    1. Tyler, John, 1790–1862—Bibliography. I. Title. II. Series.
Z8896 .M67 2001
[E397]
973.5′8′092—dc21
[B]   00–061034

British Library Cataloguing in Publication Data is available.

Library of Congress Catalog Card Number: 00–061034
ISBN: 0–313–28168–8
ISSN: 1061–6500

First published in 2001

Greenwood Press, 88 Post Road West, Westport, CT 06881
An imprint of Greenwood Publishing Group, Inc.
www.greenwood.com

Printed in the United States of America

The paper used in this book complies with the
Permanent Paper Standard issued by the National
Information Standards Organization (Z39.48–1984).

10 9 8 7 6 5 4 3 2 1

For Angie Allen Moser

and

In Memory of Walter G. Moser

Contents

Foreword

Nothing in the American constitutional order continues to excite so much scholarly interest, debate, and controversy as the role of the presidency. This remains the case in spite of the complaint, so common in the historical profession a generation ago, about the tyranny of "the presidential synthesis" in the writing of American history.

This complaint had its point. It is true enough that the deep currents in social, economic, and intellectual history, in demography, family structure, and collective mentalities, flow on without regard to presidential administrations. To deal with these underlying trends, the "new history" began, in the 1950s and 1960s, to reach out beyond traditional history to anthropology, sociology, psychology, and statistics. For a season social-science history pushed politics and personalities off the historical stage.

But in time social-science history displayed its limitations. It did not turn out to be, as its apostles had promised, a philosopher's—or historian's—stone. "Most of the great problems of history," wrote Lawrence Stone, himself as distinguished practitioner of the new history, "remain as insoluble as ever, if not more so." In particular, the new history had no interest in public policy—the decisions a nation makes through the political process—and proved impotent to explain it. Yet one can reasonably argue that, at least in a democracy, public policy reveals the true meaning of the past, the moods, preoccupations, values, and dreams of a nation, more clearly and trenchantly than almost anything else.

The tide of historical interest is now turning again—from deep currents to events, from underlying trends to decisions. While the history of public policy requires an accounting of the total culture from which national decisions emerge, such history must center in the end on the decisions themselves and on the people who make (and resist) them. Historians today are returning to the insights of classical history—to the recognition that the state, political authority, military power, elections, statutes, wars, the ideas, ambitions, delusions and wills of individuals make a difference to history.

This is far from a revision to "great man" theories. But it is a valuable corrective to the assumption, nourished by social-science history, that public policy is merely a passive reflection of underlying historical forces. For the ultimate fascination of history lies precisely in the interplay between the individual and his environment. "It is true," wrote Tocqueville, "that around every man a fatal circle is traced beyond which he cannot pass; but within the wide range of that circle he is powerful and free; as it is with man, so with communities."

The *Bibliographies of the Presidents of the United States* series therefore needs no apology. Public policy is a powerful key to an understanding of the past; and in the United States the presidency is the battleground where issues of public policy are fought out and resolved. The history of American presidents is far from the total history of America. But American history without the presidents would leave the essential part of the story untold.

Recent years have seen a great expansion in the resources available for students of the presidency. The National Historical Publications Commission has done superb work in stimulating and sponsoring editions, both letterpress and microform, of hitherto inaccessible materials. "Documents," as President Kennedy said in 1963, "are the primary sources of history; they are the means by which later generations draw close to historical events and enter into the thoughts, fears and hopes of the past." He saluted the NHPC program as "this great effort to enable the American people to repossess its historical heritage."

At the same time, there has been a rich outpouring of scholarly monographs on presidents, their associates, their problems, and their times. And the social-science challenge to narrative history has had its impact on presidential scholarship. The interdisciplinary approach has raised new questions, developed new methodologies, and uncovered new sources. It has notably extended the historian's methodological arsenal.

This profuse presidential literature has heretofore lacked a guide. The *Bibliographies of the Presidents of the United States* series thus fills a great lacuna in American scholarship. It provides comprehensive annotated bibliographies, president by president, covering manuscripts and archives, biographies and monographs, articles and dissertations, government documents and oral histories, libraries, museums, and iconographic resources. The editors are all scholars who have mastered their presidents. The series places the study of American presidents on a solid bibliographical foundation.

In so doing, it will demonstrate the wide sweep of approaches to our presidents, from analysis to anecdotes, from hagiography to vilification. It will illustrate the rise and fall of presidential reputations—fluctuations that often throw as much light on historians as on presidents. It will provide evidence for and against Bryce's famous proposition "Why Great Men Are Not Chosen Presidents." It will remind us that superior men have somehow made it to the White House but also that, as the Supreme Court said in *ex parte Milligan*, the republic has "no right to expect that it will always have wise and humane rulers, sincerely attached to the principles of the Constitution. Wicked men, ambitious of power, with hatred of liberty and contempt of law, may fill the place once occupied by Washington and Lincoln."

Above all, it will show how, and to what degree, the American presidency has been the focus of the concerns, apprehensions, and aspirations of the people and the times.

The history of the presidency is a history of nobility and of pettiness, of courage and of cunning, of forthrightness and of trickery, of quarrel and of consensus. The turmoil perennially swirling around the White House illuminates the heart of American democracy. The literature reflects the turmoil, and the *Bibliographies of the Presidents of the United States* supply at last the light that will enable scholars and citizens to find their way through the literature.

Arthur Schlesinger, Jr.

Editor's Preface

Individuals who rise to the highest elected office offered by the American people hold a special fascination. Their backgrounds, their philosophies over time, the way they "rise" are matters of enduring observation, commentary, and analysis. The *Bibliographies of the Presidents of the United States,* splendidly begun by the late Carol Fitzgerald in 1988, provides to both the specialist and generalist a comprehensive guide to every aspect of those unique individuals.

Each volume records the mundane and the critical—from early education, to contemporary news and political analysis, family reminiscences, scholarly analysis and revision, partisan attacks, official papers, personal manuscripts, visual records, and, for administrations of our day, the film and video record.

The Greenwood series offers the possibility of complete access to every instant of the Chief Executive's career or preparation. Taken together, the volumes provide chronological, precise, and detailed accounts of how each President has risen, administered, and withdrawn—and how scholars, pundits, and the American people have weighed that progress.

Mary Ellen McElligott
Series Editor

Introduction and Acknowledgments

O n April 6, 1841, John Tyler, former Virginia state legislator, governor, congressman, senator, and vice president, took the oath of office of president of the United States. Elected on the Whig ticket with William Henry Harrison in 1840, he succeeded to the post upon the death of Harrison on April 4, one month after the first Whig administration had been inaugurated.

Whigs generally had given Tyler's political principles and sympathies with the party little consideration when they named him to the ticket. But questions abounded about Tyler, concerns arising from his past record. His political alliances had been highly irregular, marked more by idolatry to states' rights than a commitment to either Jacksonian or Whig principles and programs. Tyler's accession to the presidency, and his claim to the full responsibilities of the executive office, thus created something of a crisis for the Whig leadership in Congress, who had envisioned an opportunity to implement a national program for economic recovery and progress under Harrison. It was not long, however, before both Whigs and Jacksonian Democrats learned what course the tenth president would steer, and it was a course unacceptable to both.

Tyler's life and presidency came at a crucial time in the history of the American nation. From its early beginnings along the Atlantic seaboard, the young republic had expanded across the continent into Texas, the Oregon country, and into California. Large increases in population and rapid expansion altered the character of the nation. Sectional tensions, Indian conflicts, and social disharmony erupted. Revolutions in industry and transportation transformed business, labor, and professional organizations. Money, banking, internal improvements, the tariff, public land disposition, and the moral questions involving slavery and Indian removal became commonplace subjects of politics. Nationalism emerged as a dominant mood, but sectionalism and slavery soon reached crisis proportions, threatening the young republic. Party structure, practices, and procedures changed drastically; a new style of electioneering emerged; and voter participation rose as the first American party system succumbed to the second.

Tyler was at the forefront of the new party system pitting Whigs against Jacksonian Democrats. A defender of the status quo in Virginia politics and a die-hard states' righter devoted to the concept of the right of instruction, Tyler had first attracted national attention by speaking out against Andrew Jackson's invasion of Florida in 1817–18 and against the newly chartered Bank of the United States. By late 1827, however, he had firmly endorsed Jackson for president, only to be found among the earliest to abandon the Jackson coalition as Jackson redefined the president's role and remade the presidential office. Tyler joined with Webster, Clay, Calhoun, and others in opposing Jackson's presidency; but he never fully supported Clay's American system, the benchmark of Whig policy for almost all but the states' rights faction of the party. Nor did he completely oppose the program and policies of the Jacksonian Democrats. If anything, from his first entry into politics until his death, Tyler was not a party regular. Instead, he was a doctrinaire strict constructionist, unconditionally committed to states' rights and a weak executive. That attitude had forced him from his Senate seat in 1836, which he resigned rather than obey instructions from the Virginia legislature to vote for resolutions to expunge from the Senate journal censure of Jackson for removal of the deposits from the Second Bank of the United States.

This loyalty to principle and the Jacksonians' proscription of the Virginia senator led the states' rights faction of the Whig coalition to nominate Tyler as the vice presidential candidate on the ill-fated Hugh Lawson White divide-and-conquer ticket in the South in 1836. In 1840, Whigs united behind Harrison, and, in hopes of carrying the states' rights faction of the party in the South, added Tyler as Harrison's running mate. For the first time in the party's short history, the Whigs won the White House and anticipated legislating a program of economic recovery and prosperity following several years of a major depression.

The hoopla of the log-cabin, hard-cider campaign of 1840 soon evaporated with the death of Harrison. From the very beginning of his tenure as president, Tyler took action that alienated his supporters among congressional Whigs. As the Whigs in Congress introduced banking and tariff legislation to deal with the economic crisis, they found in Tyler a recalcitrant opponent, one who kept his own council, communicating poorly with his congressional backers on what he would approve or disapprove. The veto and states' rights became Tyler's fortresses in blocking the Whig congressional program of economic recovery. By the end of special session of Congress in the summer in 1841, Tyler lacked support in Congress and among voters. Within five months after taking office, his entire cabinet, with the exception of Daniel Webster, Secretary of State, resigned.

The special session of Congress set the tone for the remainder of Tyler's presidency. Beyond tariff revision to meet the contingency expenses of the government, the administration accomplished little with banking, tariff, and internal improvements legislation, key elements in the Whig program. In foreign policy, however, the Tyler presidency achieved great success, settling the northeastern boundary controversy that had long plagued British-American relations, establishing ties and protection for the Hawaiian Islands, and making initial efforts to trade with China and Japan. But the question of Texas annexation, which Tyler adopted as the issue to win election to the presidency in his own right in 1844, drove off the architect of his very successful foreign policy, Webster, and alienated others of his potential backers. As a campaign platform,

Texas annexation failed to serve Tyler, and in 1845, he retired to his home in Virginia to spend the next fifteen years largely in seclusion with his family. In 1860–61, as the threat of disunion loomed, Tyler reemerged as a public figure, calling for efforts to resolve the issues between North and South through compromise. But compromise failed, and, in 1861, Tyler shifted his allegiance to the Confederacy, the only president in the history of the republic to endorse the breakup of the very Union he had sworn to protect and defend.

Tyler and his presidency have not received the extensive scholarly study accorded many other presidents, and much of what has been written has been highly opinionated. The single major printed collection of his papers, edited by his son, Lyon G. Tyler, appeared in three volumes between 1884 and 1896 and is largely filiopietistic. The Library of Congress microfilm edition, published in 1961, supplemented the published series and constitutes the fullest single microfilm collection of Tyler's papers. Only two twentieth-century full-length scholarly biographies have been published on the tenth president. Several more-focused studies have appeared covering various aspects of Tyler's presidency, his accession to office, his relations with Congress, and his attitudes toward various issues, such as the bank and tariff. But, as the bibliography reveals, there are abundant materials, many of which have been largely unused, for fuller studies of Tyler and his presidency, and particularly his relations with his cabinet, his use of patronage, and his foreign and domestic policy.

This bibliography has been prepared following the general format of the other volumes of the *Bibliographies of the Presidents of the United States* series. It seeks to present in usable format most of the materials by and dealing directly with Tyler, and relevant materials of his contemporaries as well, both primary sources and secondary works. An effort has been made to detail some of the major works dealing with the period during which Tyler lived and served as a public officer. It is not, however, a comprehensive bibliography of the literature of the times of Tyler— it is merely an introduction to that.

In preparing this bibliography I have incurred many debts. The project could not have been completed without the continuous assistance of the staffs of the John C. Hodges Library and of Special Collections, Hoskins Library, the University of Tennessee. I owe a tremendous debt as well to the staff of the Virginia Historical Society for their support of my work through an Andrew W. Mellon Research Fellowship. Two of my students, Bob Haas and Clint Clifft, the latter now assistant editor with the Papers of Andrew Jackson, carried out much of the legwork for this rendering; and they did so with meticulous attention. My daughter, Beth, assisted with the input of the data, checked much of the citations, and for better or for worse, seems to have developed an interest in history despite that tedium. My wife, Carolyn, spent many hours bringing her editorial and computer expertise to the task and even remained calm and pleasant when I became irritable because I did not understand certain instructions. To each and all I am deeply indebted.

Mary Ellen McElligott, my editor, has given generously of her time in reading and critiquing the bibliography. She has saved me from many errors, and I am grateful for that. If errors remain, they are mine alone.

And finally, I want to thank my parents for teaching me to enjoy learning, always encouraging me to question, and providing me with an environment in which that was acceptable. The dedication of this volume to them reflects but a small token of my deep appreciation.

Chronology

1790

March 29

Born at Greenway, Charles City County, Virginia, to John Tyler and Mary Armistead Tyler

1797

April

Mary Armistead Tyler, John Tyler's mother, died at the age of 37

1802

Entered preparatory division of the College of William and Mary

1804?

Entered College of William and Mary; delivered address on female education at graduation

1807

July

Graduated from College of William and Mary; began study of law under Edmund Randolph

1808

December 1

Father began his first term as governor of Virginia

1809-1810?

Admitted to bar in Virginia

1811

January

Father's term as governor expired; began law practice in Charles City County; father appointed judge of the District Court of the United States for Virginia by President James Madison

December	Elected member of Virginia House of Delegates at age of 21

1812

January 14	Introduced resolution censuring Virginia senators William B. Giles and Richard Brent for ignoring instructions of the Virginia House of Delegates on renewal of the charter of the Bank of the United States

1813

January 6	Father died
March 29	Married Letitia Christian, daughter of Robert Christian of Cedar Grove, New Kent County
Summer	Headed a Charles City County company for the defense of Richmond and the James River region; won him the title "Captain"
Fall	Reelected to Virginia legislature

1815

	Elected member of Virginia Executive Council; resigned seat in House of Delegates
April 15	Daughter, Mary, born

1816

Summer	Elected to House of Representatives
September 9	Son, Robert, born
December 17	Took seat in U.S. House of Representatives, having defeated Andrew Stevenson in the election; served until 1821

1817

January 18	Made first speech in Congress in opposition to increase of salary for members of Congress
Summer	Reelected to Congress

1818

November 30	Appointed to House committee to investigate activities of the Second Bank of the United States

1819

February 1	Denounced Andrew Jackson's invasion of Florida and the executions of Alexander Arbuthnot and Robert Christie Ambrister
February 20	Delivered speech before the House of Representatives on the unconstitutionality of the Second Bank of the United States
April 20	Son, John, Jr., born
Summer	Reelected to House of Representatives

1820

February 17	Opposed restrictions on the admission of Missouri

1821

January 15	Resigned seat in the House of Representatives because of failing health
May 11	Daughter, Letitia, born
	Purchased Greenway

1822

June	Horsewhipped John Mason over alleged insult in court

1823

April	Again elected to Virginia House of Delegates; took seat in December
July 11	Daughter, Elizabeth, born

1824

	First appointed to Board of Visitors for College of William and Mary; served until his death
	Nominated for U.S. Senate but defeated by Littleton W. Tazewell
Fall	Favored William H. Crawford in presidential election

1825

February 5	Voted in House of Delegates against a bill to take the voice of the people as to whether a convention should be called to revise the state constitution
April	Daughter, Anne Contesse, born
July	Daughter, Anne Contessee, died
December 10	Elected governor of Virginia for a one-year term by the state legislature; reelected to a second term

1826

July 11
Delivered eulogy on the death of Thomas Jefferson in Richmond

December 4
Advocated internal improvements and educational reorganization in his message to the legislature

December 10
Reelected governor

1827

January 13
Elected to U.S. Senate before completing his second term as governor, replacing John Randolph; served until February 1836

March 27
Daughter, Alice, born

December 3
Took seat as U.S. senator from Virginia

1828

February 4
Delivered first speech in U.S. Senate; opposed federal internal improvements

May 13
Voted against tariff of 1828

1829

October 5
Took seat as member of the Second Constitutional Convention of Virginia; served on committee on legislative branch of government
Moved to Gloucester Place, Gloucester County

1830

January 15
Virginia constitutional convention adjourned

December 6
Son, Tazewell, born

1832

February 9-10
Delivered speech in the U.S. Senate in opposition to the tariff bill

June 9
Voted against rechartering the Bank of the United States

1833

February 6
Delivered speech in the U.S. Senate against Andrew Jackson's Force Bill

February 15
Nominated for second term as senator from Virginia

February 20
Cast the single vote in the U.S. Senate against the Force Bill

March 1
Voted for compromise tariff

March 4
Reelected to U.S. Senate by the Virginia legislature

December 26   Henry Clay introduced resolutions censuring Jackson and Roger B. Taney for their action in the removal of the government deposits

1834

February 24   Delivered speech in U.S. Senate in opposition to removal of deposits

March 28   Voted for resolution of censure of Andrew Jackson

June 24   Voted against confirmation of Roger B. Taney as Secretary of the Treasury

June 30   Served as chairman of Senate Finance Committee to investigate activities of the Bank of the United States after Daniel Webster, chair, declined to serve during the recess of Congress

December 18   Reported on the Bank of the United States

1835

August 26   Delivered speech at Gloucester Courthouse against abolitionists and their pamphlet propaganda

December 14   Resolutions introduced in Virginia legislature instructing its senators to vote for Thomas Hart Benton's expunging resolutions

December   Nominated as presidential running mate with William Henry Harrison by Maryland Whig convention and as running mate with Hugh Lawson White by Virginia, Tennessee, North Carolina, and Georgia Whigs; Francis Granger nominated for vice presidency by Pennsylvania and Indiana Whigs and Anti-Masons

1836

February 10   Virginia legislature passed resolutions instructing Virginia senators to vote for expunging resolutions of censure of Jackson; nominated for vice presidency as running mate with Hugh Lawson White by convention of states' rights Whigs at Richmond

February 22   William Henry Harrison nominated for presidency in Ohio Whig convention

February 29   Resigned Senate seat rather than vote to expunge resolutions of censure; decision stamped Tyler as a true Whig

December 7   Received 47 electoral votes for vice president, as compared to Richard M. Johnson's 147, Francis Granger's 77, and William Smith's 23

1837

January 16	Expunging resolutions passed Senate
Fall	Purchased a residence in Williamsburg and sold farm in Gloucester

1838

January 10	Delivered address before the Virginia branch of the African Colonization Society on his election as president; speech published in *African Repository*, April 1838.
April 26	Reelected to Virginia House of Delegates as a Whig
June 19	Delivered address before the two literary societies of Randolph-Macon College

1839

January 17	Delivered report in the Virginia House of Delegates in favor of distribution among the states of the proceeds of the sale of public lands
September 12	Son, Robert, and Priscilla Cooper married
September	Whig state convention at Staunton expressed a preference for Nathaniel P. Tallmadge for Whig vice presidential ticket
December 4	Nominated for vice president by the Whig convention meeting at Harrisburg, Pennsylvania, without the support of the Virginia delegation

1840

May 5	Democratic convention in Baltimore renominated Martin Van Buren for the presidency
July 4	Van Buren signed into law the subtreasury bill
September/October	Made campaign swing into western Virginia, Ohio, and Pennsylvania
September 10	Made campaign speech in Pittsburgh
September 25	Addressed convention of Conservative Democrats at Columbus, Ohio
October 6	Addressed Whig convention in Pittsburgh
December 2	Received 234 electoral votes for vice president

1841

February 9	Arrived in Washington for inauguration as vice president
February 22	Daniel Webster resigned his Senate seat
March 4	Tyler took oath of office as vice president of the United States; William Henry Harrison inaugurated president

March 17	President William Henry Harrison called for special session of Congress to deal with the financial crisis
April 4	William Henry Harrison died
April 5	Fletcher Webster informed Tyler, then in Williamsburg, of the death of Harrison
April 6	Tyler reached Washington and took oath of office as president of the United States following the death of William Henry Harrison
April 8	Washington Whigs met and adopted resolutions praising Tyler
April 9	Tyler issued "inaugural address"
April 14	Tyler and family moved into White House
April 24	Tyler met diplomatic corps in the White House
May 8	Secretary of the Treasury Thomas Ewing notified Henry Clay that Tyler wished to avoid the issue concerning reorganization of the bank
May 31	Special session of the 27th Congress convened in Washington, having been called by Harrison
June 1	Tyler sent message to special session of Congress
June 3	Secretary of the Treasury Thomas Ewing presented report to the House of Representatives calling for repeal of the subtreasury (Independent Treasury Act of 1840) and the creation of a fiscal agent of the United States
June 4	Henry Clay introduced in the Senate a bill to repeal the subtreasury
June 7	Henry Clay outlined for Whig majority in Congress a plan for action during the special session: repeal of the subtreasury, incorporation of a bank, increase in tariff, authorization of a treasury loan, distribution of the proceeds from the sale of public lands, division of labor between the two houses so as to facilitate passage
June 8	Resolution passed Senate requesting the Secretary of the Treasury Thomas Ewing to draft a plan for a national bank; Senate passed bill repealing the Independent Treasury Act
June 9	Senator John Henderson of Mississippi introduced a bill to establish a uniform system of bankruptcy
June 12	Secretary of the Treasury Thomas Ewing reported a plan for a bank in compliance with the Senate resolution; i.e., a national bank in the District of Columbia with branch banks in those states assenting
June 21	Henry Clay presented report in the Senate on the expediency and constitutionality of a national bank

June 27	Henry Clay's bank bill passed Senate
August 6	Henry Clay's bank bill passed House of Representatives, having earlier passed the Senate, and was sent to Tyler for consideration
August 13	Subtreasury repealed
August 16	Tyler returned bank bill to Congress with reasons for refusal to sign; John Minor Botts published his Richmond Coffee House letter denouncing Tyler
August 17	Tyler burnt in effigy for veto of bank bill
August 19	Senate tried to override presidential veto of bank bill but failed; Tyler signed bill establishing a uniform system of bankruptcy
August 20	Congress passed and Tyler signed bill for the repeal of the subtreasury
August 23	House of Representatives passed the fiscal corporation bill
September 1	Congress passed distribution bill, tying it to tariff duties and declaring that the act should cease if duties were raised above the twenty percent level
September 3	Senate passed the fiscal corporation bill
September 4	Tyler signed into law the distribution act
September 9	Tyler vetoed a second bank, the fiscal corporation bill
September 11	Cabinet members Secretary of War John Bell, Secretary of the Navy George E. Badger, Attorney General John J. Crittenden, and Secretary of the Treasury Thomas Ewing resigned
September 12/13	Replaced cabinet members who had resigned
September 13	Postmaster General Francis Granger of the cabinet resigned, leaving Secretary of State Daniel Webster as the only carryover from the Harrison administration; Whig congressional caucus repudiated Tyler and expelled him from the Whig party; Congress adjourned
September 14	Tyler completed the appointment of his new cabinet
October 11	Tyler first suggested annexation of Texas to Secretary of State Daniel Webster
October 30	*Niles' Register* touted Winfield Scott as a Whig presidential candidate for the 1844 election
November 2	Tyler disclosed his own bank plan to a longtime friend and adviser, Littleton Waller Tazewell
December 7	Tyler recommended exchequer plan in his first annual message to Congress
December 21	Tyler sent his bank plan, the exchequer, to Congress for consideration

1842

January 31	Tyler's daughter Elizabeth married in White House; Letitia Christian Tyler made her first and only appearance on the first floor of the White House
March 8	Tyler sent special message to Congress on the growing treasury deficit
March 25	Tyler sent special message to Congress recommending upward revision of tariff to meet treasury deficit
March 30	Henry Clay resigned his Senate seat
April 4	Samuel Ward King, Governor of Rhode Island, requested protection against domestic violence in the state: Lord Ashburton arrived in the United States to enter into discussions regarding the northeastern boundary between Canada and the United States
June 10	House of Representatives took under consideration Tyler's recommendation of 8 March
June 17	Daniel Webster and Lord Ashburton began negotiations in Washington on the northeastern boundary question
June 25	Congress passed provisional tariff act; Tyler signed into law the congressional apportionment act
June 29	Tyler vetoed the "little tariff" bill
July 4	Tyler outlined his views on the extent and nature of the veto power of the president to friends in Philadelphia
July 10	John Minor Botts introduced resolution to inquire into the conduct of the president with a view toward recommending impeachment
August 5	Congress passed second tariff and distribution bill and sent it to the president for approval
August 9	Treaty of Washington signed
August 10	Tyler signed into law the Tariff Act of 1842
August 29	Treaty of Nanking signed
August 11	Tyler submitted Treaty of Washington to Senate for ratification
August 31	Twenty-seventh Congress, referred to as the "Long Parliament," adjourned, having been in session 269 days and passing 290 bills
September 10	Letitia Christian Tyler, Tyler's wife, died
Fall 1842	Congressional elections resulted in the replacement of a Whig majority of 25 by a Democratic majority of 60
October 13	Ratifications of Treaty of Washington exchanged in London
December 6	Sent second annual message to Congress

December 30	Tyler sent to Congress message prepared by Secretary of State Daniel Webster extending the Monroe Doctrine to the Hawaiian Islands

1843

January 1843	Exchequer plan defeated in Congress
January 9	James Buchanan endorsed as presidential candidate by Democrats at Harrisburg, Pennsylvania
January 10	John Minor Botts introduced resolution for establishment of a committee to prepare charges of impeachment against Tyler
February 15	Tyler signed bill repealing bankruptcy law
February 27	Tyler nominated Henry A. Wise minister to France
March 2	Tyler nominated Caleb Cushing Secretary of the Treasury, replacing John C. Spencer; Senate refused confirmation
March 3	Senate refused confirmation of Henry A. Wise
March 4	Congress adjourned; John C. Calhoun retired from the Senate
March 15	Group of supporters in New York nominated Tyler for the presidency
May 8	Daniel Webster resigned as Secretary of State; Caleb Cushing accepted appointment as commissioner to China
June 8	Tyler left Washington for Boston to attend ceremonies dedicating the Bunker Hill Monument
June 17	Attended dedication of Bunker Hill Monument
June 20	Hugh Swinton Legaré, Daniel Webster's successor as Secretary of State, died in Boston
June 28	Appointed John Nelson of Maryland Attorney General
August 31	National Liberty party convention met in Buffalo, New York, naming James G. Birney for president and Thomas Morris for vice president
December 4	Congress reconvened
December 5	Tyler sent third annual message to Congress

1844

February 15	Tyler nominated Thomas W. Gilmer and William Wilkins secretaries of Navy and War, respectively
February 28	Explosion on board the *Princeton* killed Secretary of State Abel Parker Upshur and Secretary of the Navy Thomas W. Gilmer and ten others
April 9	Tyler laid before Senate treaty for the annexation of Texas
April 22	Tyler sent treaty for the annexation of Texas to the Senate for ratification

April 27	Martin Van Buren's and Henry Clay's Texas letters printed in Washington, both opposing annexation of Texas
May 1	National Whig convention met in Baltimore nominating Henry Clay for president and Theodore Frelinghuysen for vice president
May 10	Congress voted down repeal of the tariff
May 27	Democratic national convention met in Baltimore nominating James K. Polk for president and George M. Dallas for vice president; Tyler convention also met in Baltimore
May 30	Tyler nominated for president by Democrat-Republican convention in Baltimore
June 8	Senate rejected treaty for the annexation of Texas
June 17	Senate confirmed Tyler's nominee Caleb Cushing for mission to China
June 26	At age 54, John Tyler married Julia Gardiner, 24, in New York at the Episcopal Church of the Ascension
July 1	Henry Clay wrote his first Alabama letter
July 3	Treaty of Wanghai with China concluded
August 20	Tyler withdrew from presidential race
December 3	In fourth annual message to Congress, Tyler urged immediate annexation of Texas

1845

January 16	Senate ratified Treaty of Wanghai with China
March 1	Senate ratified annexation of Texas by joint resolution
March 5	Tyler retired from the presidency; left Washington for farm, Sherwood Forest, in Virginia; James Knox Polk inaugurated president

1846

February 9	Charles Jared Ingersoll, in the House of Representatives, charges Tyler's Secretary of State Daniel Webster with misconduct in connection with the negotiations of the northeastern boundary treaty
May	Tyler appeared as witness on Daniel Webster's behalf before the House Foreign Affairs Committee investigating Webster's use of secret service funds as Tyler's Secretary of State
June 9	House of Representatives exonerated Webster of wrongdoing in connection with his duties as Tyler's secretary of state
July 12	Son, David Gardiner Tyler, born

1847

February 24   Denied John C. Calhoun's claim to the authorship of Texas
                     annexation

1848

April 7   Son, John Alexander Tyler, born

1849

December 25   Daughter, Julia Gardiner Tyler, born

1851

December 2   Son, Lachlan Tyler, born

1853

August 24   Son, Lyon Gardiner Tyler, born

1855

March 20   Delivered address in Baltimore before the Maryland
                     Institute for the Promotion of Mechanic Arts

1859

                     Elected Chancellor of the College of William and Mary

1860

June 20   Daughter, Pearl Tyler, born
December 14   Proposed conference of border states to promote peace in
                     the sectional crisis

1861

January 17   Virginia legislature called peace convention of all the states
                     of the Union
February 5   Elected president of the Washington Peace Conference
March 1   Elected member of the Virginia Secession Convention
April 17   Elected delegate to Provisional Congress of the Confederate
                     states
July 20   Took seat as delegate to Confederate Provisional Congress

1862

January 18   Died at Richmond, Virginia
January 20   Buried in Hollywood Cemetery, Richmond

I

Manuscript and Archival Sources

A. UNPUBLISHED PERSONAL AND ADMINISTRATIVE PAPERS OF JOHN TYLER

1. American Statesman Collection of Edward Carleton Stone. Boston University Library, Boston. Collection of about 200 items, mainly letters of the presidents of the United States.

2. Cooper Family Papers. University of Alabama Library, University. Collection of family papers of President John Tyler's daughter-in-law, Priscilla; contains numerous references to Tyler and to life in the White House during his administration.

3. Curry, Jabez Lamar Monroe, Papers. Manuscript Division, Library of Congress, Washington. Collection includes autographs of nineteenth-century presidents.

4. Gardiner-Tyler Family Papers. Yale University Library, New Haven. A major collection of the papers of the family of Tyler's second wife; covers courtship and marriage of Tyler and Julia Gardiner and social and political life in New York, Washington, and Virginia.

5. General Records of the Department of State, Record Group 59. Letters to Presidents Requesting Authorization of Disbursements, Bureau of Accounts. National Archives, Washington. Useful in understanding the use of the secret service fund in the Tyler administration.

6. Meares, Adelaide Savage, Papers. Perkins Library, Duke University, Durham. Includes a letter of introduction for Frederick C. Hill, 1841, to John Tyler.

7. Miscellaneous Manuscripts. Manuscripts and Special Collections, New York State Library, Albany. Letter from Tyler, 1849.

8. Miscellaneous Manuscripts. Special Collections, University of Iowa Libraries, Iowa City. Includes letter, Tyler to Henry A. Wise, December 26, 1838, discussing Wise's prospects for reelection to Congress.

9. O'Geran Autograph Collection. Arents Research Library, Syracuse University, Syracuse, N.Y. Presidential items.

10. Papers of Presidents and Vice Presidents of the United States, 1766-1924. Albany Institute of History and Art, Albany, N.Y. Several Tyler items.

11. Parker, Daniel, Papers. Historical Society of Pennsylvania, Philadelphia. Collection of the adjutant and inspector general, War Department, 1810-1845, contains Tyler letters relating to official duties.

12. Personal Papers Collection. Archives Branch, Virginia State Library and Archives, Richmond. Includes about eight Tyler items, 1835-1860, dealing with slaves; letters regarding correspondence of John Tyler, Sr., and Patrick Henry; documents relating to the Webster-Ashburton Treaty, Texas annexation, and Tyler's will, and one letter relating to the 1835 congressional campaign.

13. Presidential Autographs, 1794-1954. Special Collections, Stanford University Libraries, Stanford.

14. Records of the Boundary and Claims Commissions and Arbitrations and Miscellaneous Documents Relating to the Northeast Boundary, 1827-1842, Record Group 76. National Archives, Washington. An important collection for background on the Treaty of Washington.

15. Records of the Executive Branch. Auditor of Public Accounts, Record Group 48. Archives Branch, Virginia State Library and Archives, Richmond. Contains general records, records of congressional delegations, daybooks, attendance books and payrolls, and pay vouchers for the general assembly, as well as land and personal property tax records.

16. Records of the Executive Branch. Office of the Governor of Virginia, Letters Received, Record Group 3. Archives Branch, Virginia State Library and Archives, Richmond. Letters and papers received during Tyler's tenure as governor of Virginia, 1825-1827.

17. Records of the Executive Branch. Office of the Governor of Virginia, Letterbooks, 1780-1860, Record Group 3. Archives Branch, Virginia State Library and Archives, Richmond. Contains the outgoing letters of the years of Tyler's governorship.

18. Records of the Executive Branch. Secretary of the Commonwealth, Election Records, 1776-1946, Record Group 13. Archives Branch, Virginia State Library and Archives, Richmond. Contains records relating to Tyler's election to the House of Representatives and the presidential elections of 1836, 1840, and 1844.

19. Records of the Legislative Branch. Senate of Virginia, Record Group 80. Archives Branch, Virginia State Library and Archives, Richmond. Contains journals and minutes covering years of Tyler's service.

20. Records of the Legislative Branch. Virginia Constitutional Convention of 1829-1830, Record Group 91. Archives Branch, Virginia State Library and Archives, Richmond. Important for understanding Tyler's role in the convention.

21. Records of the Legislative Branch. Virginia General Assembly, Record Group 78. Archives Branch, Virginia State Library and Archives, Richmond. Contains documents revealing Tyler's service in the Virginia Assembly; includes enrolled bills and legislative petitions.

22. Records of the Legislative Branch. Virginia House of Delegates, Record Group 79. Archives Branch, Virginia State Library and Archives, Richmond. Materials covering Tyler's service in the House of Delegates, including attendance books, bills, minutes, and joint resolutions.

23. Ryland, Charles H., Collection. Archives Branch, Virginia State Library and Archives, Richmond. Collection of fifty-nine items includes some Tyler correspondence.

24. Statesmen Autograph Collection. New Jersey Historical Society, Newark. Collection includes Tyler letters.

25. Strauss, Lewis Lichtenstein, Collection. Virginia Historical Society, Richmond. Tyler letter, 1853, concerning James Campbell and Henry E. Orr.

26. Tyler Family Papers. Manuscripts and Rare Books Department, Swem Library, College of William and Mary, Williamsburg. Several different collections, one of twenty-two boxes contains some correspondence of John Tyler on politics, presidential election of 1840, land purchases in western Virginia, Kentucky, and Illinois, and the management of his farm at Sherwood Forest.

27. Tyler, John, Letters. Special Collections, Northwestern University Library, Evanston. Four letters, n.d, and 1843-1844.

28. Tyler, John, Papers. Boston Public Library, Boston. Collection of about thirteen items.

29. Tyler, John, Papers. Manuscript Department, Perkins Library, Duke University, Durham. Collection of twenty-three miscellaneous public and private papers.

30. Tyler, John, Papers. Pierpont Morgan Library, New York. Collection of about ten Tyler items.

31. Tyler, John, Papers. West Virginia and Regional History Collection, West Virginia University, Morgantown. Collection of about 200 items, mainly notes and correspondence of Oliver Perry Chitwood relating to his biography of Tyler.

32. Tyler, Julia Gardiner, Papers. Virginia Historical Society, Richmond. Includes a few Tyler letters, accounts for Sherwood Forest, 1845-1888, and a large body of correspondence with members of the Gardiner family.

33. Van Sinderen, Alfred White, Collection. Yale University Libraries, New Haven. Includes Tyler letters written while president and one following his defeat in the presidential election of 1844.

34. Virginia, Convention of 1861, Papers. Virginia Historical Society, Richmond. Contains Tyler petition, 1861, relating to doorkeeper of the Virginia House of Delegates.

35. Welsh, Samuel, Collection of Autograph Letters of the Presidents of the United States. Historical Society of Pennsylvania, Philadelphia. One Tyler letter.

B. PUBLISHED COMPILATIONS OF JOHN TYLER'S PAPERS

1. Books and Pamphlets

36. *Addresses and Messages of the Presidents of the United States, from Washington to Harrison, ... Together with a Portrait and Memoir of W. H. Harrison.* New York: E. Walker, 1841; Philadelphia: T. Cowperthwait, 1841. Contains the first printing of Tyler's early messages.

37. *America's Own Book, Containing ... the Inaugural Addresses and First Annual Messages of all the Presidents, from Washington to Pierce; ... with a Portrait and Life of Each President ....* New York: Leavitt & Allen, 1853, 1855, 1856. Also available in *Selected Americana* **[602]**.

38. Bowers, Renzo D., ed. *The Inaugural Addresses of the Presidents, ... from Washington to Hoover, with Biographical Sketches.* St. Louis.: Thomas Law Book Co., 1929.

39. Boykin, Edward, ed. *State of the Union: Highlights of American History ... as Revealed in the State-of-the-Union and War Messages of the Presidents: George Washington to John F. Kennedy.* New York: Funk & Wagnalls Co., 1963.

40. Cheney, John Vance, ed. *Inaugural Addresses of the Presidents of the United States.* 2 vols. Chicago: Donnelley & Sons, 1904-05; Chicago: Reilly & Britton, 1906.

41. *Chief Executive: Inaugural Addresses of the Presidents of the United States, from George Washington to Lyndon B. Johnson.* New York: Crown Publishers, 1965.

42. French, Jonathan, ed. *The True Republican: Containing the Inaugural Addresses, ... the First Annual Addresses and Messages of All the Presidents of the United States, from 1789 to 1845; Together with Their Farewell Addresses, and Illustrated with the Portrait of Each of the Presidents, ...* Philadelphia: G. B. Zieber, 1845; W. A. Leary, 1847; J. & J. L. Gihon, 1853; J. B. Smith & Company, 1858.

43. *Inaugural Addresses of the Presidents of the United States from George Washington, 1789, to Harry S. Truman, 1949.* Washington: Government Printing Office, 1952; ... *to John F. Kennedy* (1961); ... *to Lyndon Baines Johnson* (1965); ... *to Richard Milhous Nixon* (1969); ... *to Richard Milhous Nixon* (1974); ... *to George Bush* (1989).

44. Israel, Fred L., ed. *The State of the Union Messages of the Presidents, 1790-1966.* 3 vols. New York: Chelsea House, 1966.

45. *Letters of the Presidents of the United States of America, Reproduced from the Collection of Don Belding.* Los Angeles: Ward Ritchie Press, 1952. Has facsimile and transcription of a Tyler letter.

46. Lott, Davis Newton, ed. *The Presidents Speak: The Inaugural Addresses of the American Presidents from Washington to Kennedy.* New York: Holt, Rinehart and Winston, 1961, 1969.

47. Richardson, James Daniel, ed. *A Compilation of the Messages and Papers of the Presidents, 1789-1897.* 10 vols. Washington: Government Printing Office, 1896-99; ... *1789-1902.* 10 vols. (1903-1904); ... *1789-1905.* 11 vols. (1906); ... *1789-1908* (1909, 1911, 1912). 1896-99 edition also in *Microbook Library* [601]. One of the more useful collections.

48. Sears, M. *The American Politician, Containing ... the Inaugural and First Annual Addresses and Messages of All the Presidents ... Embellished with Portraits of the Presidents from Washington to Tyler.* Boston: B. Marsh, 1844.

49. Tyler, Lyon Gardiner. *The Letters and Times of the Tylers*. 3 vols. Richmond and Williamsburg: Whittet and Shepperson, 1884-96; New York: Da Capo Press, 1970. 1884-99 edition also in *Microbook Library* [**601**].The single most important printed collection of Tyler's personal and presidential papers; largely adulatory.

50. Williams, Edwin, and Benson J. Lossing, comps. *Statesman's Manual; Containing the Addresses and Messages of the Presidents of the United States ... from 1789 to 1858; with a Memoir of Each of the Presidents, and a History of Their Administrations: Also, Treaties between the United States and Foreign Powers ... .* 2 vols. New York: E. Walker, 1847, 1848; 4 vols. New York: E. Walker, 1858 (also several other editions with various dates). 1847-48 edition also in *Legal Treatises* [**606**].

2. Microforms

51. Congressional Information Service. *CIS Presidential Executive Orders and Proclamations, 1789-1983.* Washington: Congressional Information Service, Inc., 1986–. 5,680 fiche. Part 1, covering the period October 3, 1789 to January 15, 1921, is useful for Tyler.

52. Congressional Information Service. *CIS U.S. Senate Executive Documents and Reports.* Bethesda: Congressional Information Service, 1987. Covers Senate documents, reports, and materials not included in the U.S. Serial Set.

53. General Records of the Department of State, Record Group 59, National Archives, Washington. *Copies of Presidential Pardons, 1794-1893,* T967. 7 rolls.

54. General Records of the United States Government, Record Group 11. National Archives, Washington. *Index to Presidential Proclamations, 1789-1947,* T279. 2 rolls; *Numerical List of Presidential Proclamations, 1-2317, 1789-1838,* M1331. 1 roll; *Presidential Proclamations, 1-2160,* T1223. 11 rolls.

55. General Records of the United States Government, Record Group 11, National Archives, Washington. *Ratified Indian Treaties,* M668. 16 rolls.

56. *Smith, Lloyd W., Collection.* Morristown National Historical Park, Morristown, N.J. Contains twenty-two Tyler documents, 1830-1859.

57. *Tyler, John, Papers.* Alderman Library, University of Virginia, Charlottesville. Collection of about 378 political and personal items.

58. *Tyler, John, Papers.* Manuscript Division, Library of Congress, Washington. 3 rolls, Presidents' Papers Series. A collection of about 1,400 items, including family papers, correspondence of Julia Gardiner Tyler, correspondence with George Bancroft, etc.;

covers years 1691-1918. Some letters were published in *Letters and Times of the Tylers*. The basic and most extensive Tyler collection. For ease in searching, see Library of Congress, Manuscript Division. *Index to the John Tyler Papers*. Washington: Government Printing Office, 1961.

59. United States. *Commissioners of the City of Washington Records*. Manuscript Division, Library of Congress, Washington. Largely concerned with site designations for the District of Columbia; collection includes Tyler correspondence.

3. Articles

60. Barbee, David Rankin, ed. "A Sheaf of Old Letters." *Tyler's Quarterly Historical and Genealogical Magazine* 32 (October 1950): 77-102. Prints letter from John Tyler to Whig members of the New York legislature, March 20, 1840.

61. Barbee, David Rankin, ed. "Tyler's Intentions Become Achievements." *Tyler's Quarterly Historical and Genealogical Magazine* 31 (April 1950): 219-21. Prints Tyler letter, February 28, 1842.

62. Beard, William E. "Letters to a President of the United States." *Tennessee Historical Magazine* 9 (October 1925): 143-65. Discusses a letter from Tyler to Polk, 1845, in the Polk papers.

63. Chu Shih-chia. "Tao-Kuang to President Tyler." *Harvard Journal of Asiatic Studies* 7 (February 1943): 169-73. Discusses the response of the emperor of the Tao-kuang era to President Tyler, December 16, 1844, and the various translations of the letter by Peter Parker; illustrated by facsimile reproductions of the letters in Chinese and Manchu.

64. "Ex-President Tyler's Letter." *Tyler's Quarterly Historical and Genealogical Magazine* 32 (October 1950): 103-10. Prints Tyler letter of August 31, 1857, on the proposed reopening of the slave trade; discusses provisions of the Treaty of Washington.

65. "Letter of John Tyler to Robert Tyler, Giving an Account of the Attempted Assassination of Andrew Jackson." *Magazine of History* 16 (January 1913): 39-40. Letter dated January 31, 1835.

66. "Letter of President Tyler." *William and Mary College Quarterly* 19 (January 1911): 216. Prints letter to George Roberts, editor of the *Boston Times*, September 28, 1843, regarding the upcoming presidential election.

67. "Letters from a Tyler Collection." *Tyler's Quarterly Historical and Genealogical Magazine* 30 (October 1949): 93-114; 30 (January 1950): 184-206. Prints letters to Mrs. Tyler, November 16, 1863-August 15, 1864, August 18, 1864-August 22, 1867, from relatives and friends.

68. "Letters of John Tyler." *William and Mary College Quarterly* 18 (January 1910): 172-76. Prints several Tyler letters to Daniel Webster, 1843-1851.

69. Library of Congress. *Report of the Librarian of Congress ... for the Fiscal Year Ending June 30, 1919*. Washington: Government Printing Office, 1919. Reports on and discusses briefly the acquisition of the Tyler papers by the Library of Congress.

70. Entry number skipped.

71. Peckham, Stephen Farnum, ed. "John Tyler's Plan to Prevent the Catastrophe of the Civil War." *Journal of American History* 6 (1912): 73-86. Prints proposal to submit differences between the North and the South to arbitration by jury composed of delegates from the border states.

72. Phillips, N. Taylor. "Items Relating to the History of the Jews of New York." *Publications of the American Jewish Historical Society* 11 (1903): 149-61. Prints letter from Tyler, July 10, 1843, to Joseph Simpson discussing the constitution, government, and religious freedom in the United States.

73. Ramsdell, Charles W., ed. "The Last Hope of the Confederacy—John Tyler to the Governor and Authorities of Texas." *Texas Historical Association Quarterly* 14 (October 1910): 129-45.

74. Reed, John F. "Collector's Showcase: Presidential Letters." *Manuscripts* 23 (Winter 1971): 56-59. Prints collection of post-presidential Tyler letters seeking jobs for relatives.

75. [Tyler, Annie Baker Tucker, ed.] "John Tyler Lives Again." *Tyler's Quarterly Historical and Genealogical Magazine* 20 (January 1939): 143-54. Prints two personal letters to Tyler, 1844, and several exchanges by Lyon G. Tyler on monographs and interpretations of his father.

76. [Tyler, Annie Baker Tucker, ed.] "Letters from Tyler Trunks." *Tyler's Quarterly Historical and Genealogical Magazine* 18 (January 1937): 141-63. Prints letters between Julia and her family, 1844, discussing personal affairs and politics.

77. [Tyler, Annie Baker Tucker, ed.] "Letters From Tyler Trunks, 'Sherwood Forest,' Va." *Tyler's Quarterly Historical and Genealogical Magazine* 18 (July 1936): 8-31. Reprints a portion of Tyler's address, "The Dead of the Cabinet"; correspondence

between Julia Gardiner and family and friends, and between Tyler and the Gardiner family, 1840-1844.

78. [Tyler, Annie Baker Tucker, ed.] "Letters from Tyler Trunks." *Tyler's Quarterly Historical and Genealogical Magazine* 18 (October 1936): 88-97. Prints Gardiner and Julia Tyler correspondence, 1844, shortly after Julia's marriage to Tyler.

79. [Tyler, Lyon Gardiner, ed.?] "Correspondence of President Tyler." *William and Mary College Quarterly Historical Papers*, Series 1, 12 (January 1904): 139-41. Prints three letters: from James Iredell, December 10, 1841, commenting on Tyler's first annual message to Congress; to John Nelson, June 28, 1843; and to Waddy Thompson, August 28, 1843, on a cabinet replacement for Hugh Swinton Legaré as Attorney General and on the Texas question.

80. [Tyler, Lyon Gardiner, ed.?] "Correspondence of President Tyler." *William and Mary College Quarterly Historical Magazine*, Series 1, 13 (July 1904): 1-3. Prints Tyler letter to Simpson (see also **72**).

81. [Tyler, Lyon Gardiner, ed.?] "Letters of Tyler and Buchanan." *Tyler's Quarterly Historical and Genealogical Magazine* 11 (April 1930): 234-38. Includes letters to John B. Floyd, 1843, on the Santa Fe prisoners; to Floyd, 1860, on British policy and the question of secession; and to H. B. Grigsby, 1860, on the illness of Mrs. Tyler.

82. [Tyler, Lyon Gardiner, ed.?] "Letters to John Tyler in 1861." *William and Mary College Quarterly Historical Magazine*, Series 1, 23 (April 1915): 288-90. Prints three letters—from Robert C. Winthrop, James Buchanan, and James M. Mason—dealing with the peace convention in Washington.

83. [Tyler, Lyon Gardiner, ed.?] "Original Letters." *William and Mary College Quarterly Historical Magazine*, Series 1, 21 (July 1912): 1-11. Letters, including four from Tyler to John Floyd, 1831-33, discuss the tariff and politics during President Andrew Jackson's first term.

84. [Tyler, Lyon Gardiner, ed.?] "Original Letters." *William and Mary College Quarterly Historical Papers*, Series 1, 1 (January 1893): 172-79. Prints four letters, 1808-1809, to Thomas Newton; two letters, 1829-30, to John Rutherfoord, on politics and personal affairs.

85. Entry number skipped.

86. [Tyler, Lyon Gardiner, ed.] "The Bank Bill of 1841." *Tyler's Quarterly Historical and Genealogical Magazine* 12 (October 1930): 85-86. Prints letter to William C. Rives, May 8, 1841, on Rives's bank proposal.

87. [Tyler, Lyon Gardiner, ed.] "John Tyler and the Texas Question." *Tyler's Quarterly Historical and Genealogical Magazine* 12 (April 1931): 235-37. Prints letter to Daniel Webster, April 17, 1850.

88. [Tyler, Lyon Gardiner, ed.] "Letters." *Tyler's Quarterly Historical and Genealogical Magazine* 1 (July 1919): 46-51. Prints letter, Tyler to Hugh Blair Grigsby, January 16, 1855, discussing the Virginia Constitutional Convention of 1829-30.

89. [Tyler, Lyon Gardiner, ed.] "Letters from Tyler Trunks, 'Sherwood Forest,' Virginia: Political Letters, 1832-1834." *Tyler's Quarterly Historical and Genealogical Magazine* 17 (January 1936): 151-71. Prints letters to David Gardiner, Mrs. Tyler's father. [Tyler,

90. Lyon Gardiner, ed.] "Letters of John Tyler." *Tyler's Quarterly Historical and Genealogical Magazine* 13 (October 1931): 73-80. Prints family correspondence: Tyler to his sister, 1811; to his nephew, M. B. Seawell, 1845, 1848, 1851, 1852, 1854.

91. [Tyler, Lyon Gardiner, ed.] "Tyler Genealogy by President Tyler." *Tyler's Quarterly Historical and Genealogical Magazine* 10 (January 1929): 198-203. Prints two letters of Tyler, December 1859, discussing Tyler family genealogy.

92. [Tyler, Lyon Gardiner, ed.?] "Tyler Letters." *William and Mary College Quarterly Historical Magazine*, Series 1, 26 (July 1917): 21-26. Prints three letters, 1821, to James Monroe and an exchange, 1860, with John Henry concerning a portrait of Patrick Henry.

93. [Tyler, Lyon Gardiner, ed.?] "The Walls of the College." *William and Mary College Quarterly Historical Magazine*, Series 1, 1 (January 1903): 174-79. Prints two letters by Tyler, 1859.

94. [Tyler, Lyon Gardiner, ed.] "Webster-Tyler Letters." *Tyler's Quarterly Historical and Genealogical Magazine* 8 (July 1926): 16-29. Prints letters, 1841-1846, from the Webster papers at the New Hampshire Historical Society.

4. Printed Government Documents

95. *American State Papers: Documents, Legislative and Executive of the Congress of the United States* ... 38 vols. Washington, D.C.: Gales and Seaton, 1832-61. Prints documents relating to foreign relations, Indian affairs, finance, commerce and navigation, military affairs, naval affairs, post office department, public lands, land claims, and reparations, etc., from the First through the Twenty-fifth Congress, 1789-1838.

96. Ames, Herman V., ed. *State Documents on Federal Relations: The States and the United States.* 6 vols. Philadelphia: University of Pennsylvania, 1902-1906.

97. Benton, Thomas Hart, ed. *Abridgment of the Debates of Congress, from 1789 to 1856: From Gales and Seaton's Annals of Congress, from Their Register of Debates, and from the Official Reported Debates by John C. Rives.* 16 vols. New York: D. Appleton & Co., 1857-61.

98. Carter, Clarence Edward, and John Porter Bloom, eds. *The Territorial Papers of the United States.* 28 vols. Washington: Government Printing Office, 1934-75; New York: AMS Press, 1972. Volumes 1-27 also in *Microbook Library* **[601]**.

99. Confederate States of America. Congress. *Journal of the Congress of the Confederate States of America, 1861-1865.* 7 vols. Washington: Government Printing Office, 1904-1905. Also available in *Microbook Library* **[601]**. Provides coverage of congressional debates for Tyler's brief stint in the body.

100. *Congressional Globe, Containing the Debates and Proceedings of Congress, 1833-1873.* 46 vols. in 110. Washington: Globe Office, 1834-73. Provides coverage for Tyler's presidency and a portion of his congressional career.

101. Davids, Jules, ed. *American Diplomatic and Public Papers: The United States and China.* Series 1, 1842-60. Wilmington, Del.: Scholarly Resources, 1973. Prints documents of Caleb Cushing's mission to China.

102. *Debates and Proceedings in the Congress of the United States, with An Appendix, Containing Important State Papers and Public Documents, and All the Laws of a Public Nature ...* 42 vols. Washington: Gales and Seaton, 1834-56. Series commonly known as the *Annals of Congress* covers from the years 1789-1824.

103. *Executive Documents, 1830-1847.* Various publishers and dates. Mainly United States House of Representative documents; part of the Serial Set.

104. *House Reports.* 1819- . Various publishers and dates. Volumes in the Serial Set; covers Tyler's congressional and presidential careers.

105. Jados, Stanley S. *Documents on Russian-American Relations: Washington to Eisenhower.* Washington: Catholic University of America Press, 1965.

106. *Journal of the Executive Proceedings of the Senate of the United States, 1789-1905.* 90 vols. Washington: Various publishers, 1828-48. Useful for Senate confirmations and treaty ratifications.

107. *Journal of the House of Delegates of the Commonwealth of Virginia* ... Richmond: Various publishers and dates. Journal issued for each legislative session; important for study of Tyler as state legislator, governor, and election to Senate.

108. *Journal of the House of Representatives of the United States.* Philadelphia and Washington: Various publishers and dates. Annual volumes since 1789.

109. *Journal of the Senate of the Commonwealth of Virginia* ... Richmond: Various publishers and dates. Journal issued for each of the sessions; important for examining Tyler's career as governor and state legislator.

110. *Journal of the Senate of the United States.* Philadelphia and Washington: Various publishers and dates. Annual volumes since 1789.

111. Kappler, Charles J., ed. *Indian Affairs: Laws and Treaties.* 5 vols. Washington: Government Printing Office, 1904; New York: AMS Press, 1971. Also available in *Microbook Library* [**601**].

112. Malloy, William M., ed. *Treaties, Conventions, International Acts, Protocols and Agreements between the United States of America and Other Powers, 1776-1909.* 2 vols. Washington: Government Printing Office, 1910. Also available in *Microbook Library* [**601**].

113. Manning, William Ray, ed. *Diplomatic Correspondence of the United States, Canadian Relations, 1784-1860.* 4 vols. Washington: Carnegie Endowment for International Peace, 1940-45. Volume 3, containing Webster-Lord Ashburton notes on the *Caroline* and McLeod affairs, especially useful.

114. Manning, William Ray, ed. *Diplomatic Correspondence of the United States, Inter-American Affairs, 1831-1860.* 12 vols. Washington: Carnegie Endowment for International Peace, 1932-39. Volume 7 is particularly useful for the Tyler presidency.

115. Marraro, Howard Rosario, ed. *Diplomatic Relations between the United States and the Kingdom of the Two Sicilies: Instructions and Despatches, 1816-1861.* 2 vols. New York: S. F. Vanni, 1951-52.

116. Miller, Hunter, ed. *Treaties and Other International Acts of the United States of America.* 8 vols. Washington: Government Printing Office, 1931-48. Volume 4 covers the Tyler administration.

117. Moore, John Bassett. *A Digest of International Law as Embodied in Diplomatic Discussions, Treaties and Other International Agreements, International Awards, the*

Decisions of Municipal Courts, and the Writings of Jurists ... 8 vols. Washington: Government Printing Office, 1906.

118. Moore, John Bassett. *History and Digest of International Arbitrations* ... , *Together with Appendices Containing the Treaties Relating to Such Arbitrations, and Historical Legal Notes* ... 6 vols. Washington: Government Printing Office, 1898.

119. Moore, John Bassett. *Report on Extradition, with Returns of All Cases from August 9, 1842, to January 1, 1890.* Washington: Government Printing Office, 1890.

120. Myer, William G. *Federal Decisions: Cases Argued and Determined in the Supreme, Circuit, and District Courts of the United States* ... . 30 vols. St. Louis: Gilbert Book Company, 1884.

121. *Presidential Vetoes: List of Bills Vetoed and Action Taken Thereon by the Senate and House of Representatives, 1789-1961.* Washington: Government Printing Office, 1961; New York: Greenwood Press, 1968.

122. *Proceedings of the Senate and Documents Relative to Texas, from Which the Injunction of Secrecy Has Been Removed.* Washington: n.p., 1844. Also available in *Texas* [607]. Includes diplomatic correspondence of the Tyler administration relating to Texas annexation.

123. Prucha, Francis Paul, ed. *Documents of United States Indian Policy.* Lincoln: University of Nebraska Press, 1975, 1990.

124. *Public Documents Printed by Order of the Senate of the United States, First Session of the Twenty-Eighth Congress* ... Washington: Gales and Seaton, 1844. Also available in *Texas* [607]. Concerns the annexation of Texas.

125. *Public Documents Printed by Order of the Senate of the United States, Second Session of the Twenty-Eighth Congress, Begun and Held at the City of Washington, December 2, 1844* ... . 11 vols. Washington: Gales and Seaton, 1845. Documents cover the period 1841-45.

126. *Register of Debates, Being a Report of the Speeches Delivered in the Two Houses of Congress, Reported for the United States Telegraph.* 4 vols. Washington: Duff Green, 1834-35.

127. *Register of Debates in Congress, Comprising the Leading Debates and Incidents of the Second Session of the Eighteenth Congress* ... *[1825-1837].* 14 vols. in 29. Washington: n.p., 1825-37.

128. *Senate Documents, 1817-1849.* Various publishers and dates. Prints documents from Tyler's senatorial and presidential service.

129. *Statutes at Large of the United States of America, 1789-1873.* 17 vols. Boston: Little, Brown & Company, 1850-73.

130. Stock, Leo Francis, ed. *Consular Relations between the United States and the Papal States: Instructions and Despatches.* Washington: American Catholic Historical Association, 1945.

131. United States. Department of State. *Report from the Secretary of State, in Compliance with a Resolution of the Senate, in Relation to the Operation of the Bankrupt Law* ... [Washington: n.p., 1843]. Provides insight into efforts for enactment of bankruptcy legislation during the Tyler presidency.

132. Wharton, Francis, ed. *A Digest of the International Law of the United States, Taken from Documents Issued by Presidents and Secretaries of State, and from Decisions of Federal Courts and Opinions of Attorneys-General.* 3 vols. Washington: Government Printing Office, 1886.

C. UNPUBLISHED PERSONAL AND ADMINISTRATIVE PAPERS OF JOHN TYLER'S ASSOCIATES

1. Members of Cabinet

George Edmund Badger, Secretary of the Navy

133. Badger, George Edmund, Papers. Only small collections in Manuscript Division, Library of Congress, Washington; North Carolina Department of Archives and History, Raleigh; and in the Southern Historical Collection, University of North Carolina, Chapel Hill.

John Bell, Secretary of War

134. Bell, John, Papers. Only small collections in Tennessee Historical Society, Nashville; Manuscript Division, Library of Congress, Washington; and Southern Historical Collection, University of North Carolina, Chapel Hill.

George Mortimer Bibb, Secretary of the Treasury

135. Bibb, George Mortimer, Papers. Small collections at Boston Public Library, Boston; Kentucky Historical Society, Frankfort; Manuscript Division, Library of Congress, Washington; Pierpont Morgan Library, New York; University of Kentucky, Lexington; and Kentucky Library and Museum, Western Kentucky University, Bowling Green.

136. Bibb Family Papers. Filson Club, Louisville. Largest collection of Bibb's papers.

John Caldwell Calhoun, Secretary of State

137. Calhoun, John Caldwell, Papers. Clemson University Library, Clemson. Mainly correspondence on political and personal subjects.

138. Calhoun, John Caldwell, Papers. Small collections in Boston Public Library, Boston; Chicago Historical Society, Chicago; Pierpont Morgan Library, New York; and Rutgers University, New Brunswick.

139. Calhoun, John Caldwell, Papers. South Caroliniana Library, University of South Carolina, Columbia. Ca. 3,200 items of family, business, and political correspondence.

140. Calhoun, John Caldwell, Papers. Perkins Library, Duke University, Durham. Ca. 400 items of family, business, and political correspondence.

John Jordan Crittenden, Attorney General

141. Crittenden, John Jordan, Papers. Filson Club, Louisville. Ca. 50 letters.

142. Crittenden, John Jordan, Papers. Perkins Library, Duke University, Durham. Collection, 1786-1932, covers service as governor of Kentucky, congressman, senator, and cabinet officer; considerable discussion of Tyler's fiscal plans; some published in Coleman, *Life*.

143. Crittenden, John Jordan, Papers. University of Kentucky, Lexington. 52 items.

Thomas Ewing, Secretary of the Treasury

144. Ewing, Thomas, and Charles Ewing Family Papers. Manuscript Division, Library of Congress, Washington. 310 containers covering years 1757-1941.

145. Ewing, Thomas, Papers. Small collections in Cincinnati Historical Society, Cincinnati; Pierpont Morgan Library, New York.

146. Ewing, Thomas, Papers. Ohio Historical Society, Columbus. 1 linear foot, 1800-1866.

Hugh Swinton Legaré, Secretary of State and Attorney General

147. Legaré, Hugh Swinton, Papers. South Caroliniana Library, University of South Carolina, Columbia.

148. Legaré, Hugh Swinton, Papers. Perkins Library, Duke University, Durham. Small collection, 1837-1843, concerning politics, legal practice, and purchase of books.

149. Attorney General Letterbooks, National Archives, Washington.

John Young Mason, Secretary of the Navy

150. Mason Family Papers. Virginia Historical Society, Richmond. Considerable material regarding political, personal, and naval affairs.

Abel Parker Upshur, Secretary of State and Secretary of the Navy

151. Upshur, Abel Parker, Papers. Perkins Library, Duke University, Durham. 5 items mainly concerning cabinet posts.

152. Upshur, Abel Parker, Papers. Swem Library, College of William and Mary, Williamsburg. Extensive collection covering all aspects of his career.

William Wilkins, Secretary of War

153. Wilkins, William, Papers. Small collections of less than 21 items in Dickinson College Library, Carlisle, Pa.; Manuscript Division, Library of Congress, Washington; Pennsylvania Historical and Museum Commission, Harrisburg.

2. Members of Congress

William Segar Archer, Virginia Representative

154. Archer, William Segar, Papers. Small collections in Manuscript Division, Library of Congress, Washington; Pierpont Morgan Library, New York; Alderman Library, University of Virginia, Charlottesville; Virginia Historical Society, Richmond. Virginia senator.

James Barbour, Virginia Senator

155. Barbour Family Papers, Alderman Library, University of Virginia, Charlottesville. Mainly correspondence of James Barbour, Governor of Virginia, 1812-14, Secretary of War, 1825-28, and minister to England, 1828-29; and of Philip Pendleton Barbour; considerable discussion of state and national politics, foreign relations, tariff, and states rights.

156. Barbour, James, Papers. New York Public Library, New York. Collection of almost 300 items.

Henry Clay, Kentucky Senator

157. Clay, Henry, Papers. Alderman Library, University of Virginia, Charlottesville. Collection, ca. 500 items covering the years 1798-1851. Most either described or published in Hopkins and Hargreaves, *Papers of Henry Clay.*

158. Clay, Henry, Papers. Boston Public Library, Boston. Ca. 50 items.

159. Clay, Henry, Papers. Filson Club, Louisville, Ky. About 100 items with additional materials in other collections.

160. Clay, Henry, Papers. Historical Society of Pennsylvania, Philadelphia. About fifty letters to Josiah Stoddard Johnston, plus items in numerous other collections.

161. Clay, Henry, Papers. Indiana Historical Society, Indianapolis. About 200 typescripts, plus a few originals.

162. Clay, Henry, Papers. Lilly Library, Indiana University, Bloomington. Almost 250 items, 1812-49, plus a collection of notices of Young Men's Henry Clay Association.

163. Clay, Henry, Papers. New-York Historical Society, New York. Ca. 116 items covers years 1817-45.

164. Clay, Henry, Papers. University of Kentucky Library, Lexington. Ca. 70 letters, plus more than 200 in other manuscript collections.

165. Clay, Henry, Papers. Perkins Library, Duke University, Durham. Collection of about 137 items, 1802-52, of personal and political correspondence.

Caleb Cushing, Massachusetts Representative

166. Cushing, Caleb, Papers. Manuscript Division, Library of Congress, Washington. A large collection of a Massachusetts congressman and senator, sometime supporter of the Tyler administration appointed on a special mission to China in 1843.

George M. Dallas, Pennsylvania Senator

167. Dallas, George Mifflin, Papers. Historical Society of Pennsylvania, Philadelphia. Collection of ca. 1,400 items, 1791-1880, dealing mainly with politics.

168. Dallas, George Mifflin, Papers. Pennsylvania Historical and Museum Commission, Harrisburg. Collection of 47 items, dealing mainly with politics and patronage.

169. Dallas, George Mifflin, Papers. Rare Books and Manuscript Division, Temple University, Philadelphia. Collection of ca. 200 items.

James Dellet, Alabama Representative

170. Dellet, James, Papers. Alabama Department of Archives and History, Montgomery. Papers cover years 1839-1845; important for Whig politics in Alabama.

John Fairfield, Maine Representative and Senator

171. Fairfield, John, Papers. Maine Historical Society, Portland. About 8 boxes of legal and political correspondence; important for Maine politics and for acceptance in the state of the Treaty of Washington.

172. Fairfield, John, Papers. Manuscript Division, Library of Congress, Washington. Collection of seven boxes covering years 1828-67.

John Floyd, Virginia Representative

173. Floyd, John, Papers. Manuscript Division, Library of Congress, Washington. About thirty items; includes letters from Tyler relating to national and state politics, 1823-32.

William Fitzhugh Gordon, Virginia Representative

174. Gordon Family Papers. Alderman Library, University of Virginia, Charlottesville. Collection includes Calhoun and Tyler letters discussing opposition to Martin Van Buren and a strong executive.

Edmund Wilcox Hubard, Virginia Representative

175. Hubard Family Papers. Southern Historical Collection, University of North Carolina, Chapel Hill. Large collection of papers discussing Virginia and national politics.

Robert M. T. Hunter, Virginia Representative and Senator

176. Hunter Family Papers. Virginia Historical Society, Richmond. Important for background on the Calhoun movement in Virginia and the South.

177. Hunter, Robert Mercer Taliaferro, Papers. Archives Branch, Virginia State Library and Archives, Richmond. Ca. 875 items covering years 1820-76.

James Iredell, North Carolina Senator

178. Iredell, James, Jr. and Sr., Papers. Perkins Library, Duke University, Durham. Discussion of national politics, patronage, and nullification.

Benjamin Watkins Leigh, Virginia Senator

179. Leigh, Benjamin Watkins, Papers. Alderman Library, University of Virginia, Charlottesville. Ca. 300 items, the largest collection of a delegate to the 1840 Whig presidential nominating convention.

Willie Person Mangum, North Carolina Representative and Senator

180. Mangum, Willie Person, Papers. Manuscript Division, Library of Congress, Washington. About 34 containers, covers the political career of the North Carolina senator.

181. Mangum, Willie Person, Papers. North Carolina Department of Archives and History, Raleigh. Ca. 2,000 items, in part transcripts.

182. Mangum, Willie Person, Papers. Perkins Library, Duke University, Durham. Ca. 142 items of correspondence and legal papers.

James Murray Mason, Virginia Representative and Senator

183. Mason, James Murray, Papers. Manuscript Division, Library of Congress, Washington. Covers years 1838-70.

Ebenezer Pettigrew, North Carolina Representative

184. Pettigrew Family Papers. North Carolina Department of Archives and History, Raleigh. Collection includes the papers of Ebenezer Pettigrew; some Tyler correspondence.

John Randolph, Virginia Representative and Senator

185. Randolph, John, Papers. Alderman Library, University of Virginia, Charlottesville. Ca. 1,500 items.

186. Randolph, John, Papers. Manuscript Division, Library of Congress, Washington. Six containers, covering years 1742-1835.

William C. Rives, Virginia Representative and Senator

187. Rives Family Papers. Alderman Library, University of Virginia, Charlottesville. Correspondence of William C. Rives, a Conservative Democrat-Whig and staunch supporter of the Tyler administration.

188. Rives, William Cabell, Papers. Manuscript Division, Library of Congress, Washington. A major collection for studying political and social developments, Democratic and Whig, during first half of nineteenth century.

William H. Roane, Virginia Representative and Senator

189. Roane Family Papers. Archives Branch, Virginia State Library and Archives, Richmond. Small collection, 10 items, includes Tyler correspondence.

Samuel Lewis Southard, New Jersey Senator

190. Southard, Samuel Lewis, Papers. Manuscript Division, Library of Congress, Washington, D.C. Small collection of two boxes covering period 1809-42; important for national politics and Washington journalism.

191. Southard, Samuel Lewis, Papers. Princeton University Library, Princeton, N.J. Ca. 20,000 items relating to Southard's political, social, and economic activities.

Andrew Stevenson, Virginia Representative

192. Stevenson, Papers of Andrew and John White. Manuscript Division, Library of Congress, Washington. Includes correspondence relating to affairs with Great Britain, slave trade, the *Caroline* affair, and negotiations for the settlement of the northeastern boundary.

Alexander H. H. Stuart, Virginia Representative

193. Stuart, Alexander Hugh Holmes, Papers. Alderman Library, University of Virginia, Charlottesville. Papers (about 500 items, 1791-1928) of a Virginia lawyer, congressman, and later cabinet officer.

194. Stuart Family Papers. Virginia Historical Society, Richmond. Collection, including a portion of Alexander H. H. Stuart papers, contains discussion of national and state politics.

Littleton Waller Tazewell, Virginia Representative and Senator

195. Tazewell Family Papers. Archives Branch, Virginia State Library and Archives, Richmond. Contains correspondence of Tyler with Littleton Waller Tazewell before 1843.

196. Tazewell, Littleton Waller, Papers. Alderman Library, University of Virginia, Charlottesville. Ca. 105 political and legal papers.

Robert J. Walker, Mississippi Senator

197. Walker, Robert J., Papers. Manuscript Division, Library of Congress, Washington. Important for the Texas issue during the Tyler administration.

198. Walker, Robert J., Papers. Mississippi Department of Archives and History, Jackson. Ca. 72 items of correspondence.

199. Walker, Robert J., Papers. New-York Historical Society, New York. Collection of about 65 items of correspondence.

Henry A. Wise, Virginia Representative

200. Wise Family Papers. Virginia Historical Society, Richmond. Large collection, particularly strong for the Tyler administration.

3. Supreme Court Justices

201. Story, Joseph, Papers. Manuscript Division, Library of Congress, Washington. Papers relate to judicial cases, to personal matters between Story and Webster, and to political developments.

202. Swisher, Carl Brent, Research Materials relating to Roger B. Taney. Manuscript Division, Library of Congress, Washington. Materials collected (copies and photocopies mainly) involving research for his Taney biography.

4. Journalists

203. Abell, Alexander G., Correspondence. Arents Research Library, Syracuse University, Syracuse, N.Y. Small collection of 26 items, 1843-1844, relating to Abell's canvass for subscribers for his *Life of John Tyler*, published by Harper & Brothers in 1843.

204. Bradford Family Papers. Historical Society of Pennsylvania, Philadelphia. Collection of Thomas and William Bradford, Philadelphia printers, includes Tyler correspondence.

205. Gooch Family Papers. Virginia Historical Society, Richmond. Collection includes business and political correspondence of Claiborne Watts Gooch, co-editor of the *Richmond Enquirer* with Thomas Ritchie; discussion of Tyler and of the Tyler administration.

206. Hope, James Barron, II, Papers. Swem Library, College of William and Mary, Williamsburg. Small collection of a writer and newspaper editor of Norfolk and Williamsburg includes Tyler correspondence.

207. Jones, John Beauchamp, Papers. Southern Historical Collection, University of North Carolina, Chapel Hill. Papers of an important newspaper editor contains 1844 letter from Tyler offering advice on editorial policy.

208. Ruffin, Edmund, Papers. Virginia Historical Society, Richmond. Collection of 826 items includes Tyler correspondence.

209. Walsh, Robert, Papers. Historical Society of Pennsylvania, Philadelphia. A small collection of an author and editor, includes documents signed by Tyler.

5. Others

210. Allen, Stephen. *Articles from Newspapers, Principally Referring to Mr. Webster and the Tyler Administration.* Baker Library, Dartmouth College, Hanover. Bound collection of clippings, covering mainly October 1842.

211. Aylett Family Papers. Virginia Historical Society, Richmond. Contains letters to Henry A. Wise discussing Tyler and the Texas question.

212. Barron, Samuel, Papers. Alderman Library, University of Virginia, Charlottesville. Collection of correspondence of a naval officer, includes Tyler and Wise letters.

213. Baylor Family Papers. Virginia Historical Society, Richmond. Contains a Tyler legal opinion on a land title.

214. Bennett, John, Papers. Virginia Historical Society, Richmond. Small collection of 47 items; discussion of election of 1840 in Virginia.

215. Bennett, Jonathan McCally, Papers. West Virginia University Library, Morgantown. Collection of a lawyer, banker, and political leader in western Virginia includes Tyler letters.

216. Blow Family Papers. Virginia Historical Society, Richmond. Correspondence of George Blow, 352 items, some dealing with Tyler's administration at William and Mary College and with the presidential election of 1840.

217. Bolling, William, Diary. Virginia Historical Society, Richmond. Contains several vituperative assessments of Tyler and his administration.

218. Breckinridge, James, Papers. Virginia Historical Society, Richmond. Collection of about 110 items discusses the Tyler administration.

219. Cabell, Joseph Carrington, Papers. Alderman Library, University of Virginia, Charlottesville. Collection of correspondence, diaries, and accounts includes Tyler correspondence.

220. Camp Family Papers. Manuscripts and University Archives, Olin Library, Cornell University, Ithaca, N.Y. Collection of a chief of the Quartermaster Department, Ohio legislator, and U.S. marshal includes Tyler correspondence.

221. Cheatham, Benjamin Franklin, Papers. Tennessee State Library and Archives, Nashville. Collection of a Tennessee army officer, superintendent of the state prison, and farmer, contains two letters, 1842-43, from Tyler.

222. Christian Family Papers. Archives Branch, Virginia State Library and Archives, Richmond. Small collection includes one Tyler item.

223. Corcoran, William Wilson, Autograph Album. Virginia Historical Society, Richmond. Includes Tyler autograph, 1832.

224. Curtis, Henry, Papers. Virginia Historical Society, Richmond. Contains Tyler papers relating to settlement of the estate of Anthony Tucker Dixon.

225. Davie, Preston, Papers. Virginia Historical Society, Richmond. Contains typescripts of exchange with Charles A. Wickliffe, 1848, concerning cabinet meetings during the Tyler administration and the discussion of the annexation of Texas.

226. DeCoppet, Andre, Collection. Firestone Library, Princeton University, Princeton, N.J. Includes Tyler letters.

227. Doty, James Duane, Papers. State Historical Society of Wisconsin, Madison. Small collection with discussion of Tyler administration and copy of at least one letter—Doty's resignation—to Tyler.

228. Emerson, J. Milton, Journal, 1841-1842. Manuscript Department, Perkins Library, Duke University, Durham. Describes a visit to Washington in 1842 and an audience with Tyler.

229. Ensign, Harry H., Autograph Collection. Manuscripts and Archives, Yale University, New Haven. Small collection, includes Tyler letters dealing with politics, 1840-66.

230. Ewell, Benjamin Stoddert, Papers. University Archives, Swem Library, College of William and Mary, Williamsburg. Collection of the papers of a mathematics professor and, from 1854 until 1888, the president of the College, includes Tyler correspondence relating to the college.

231. Floyd, John Buchanan, Papers. Swem Library, College of William and Mary, Williamsburg. Small collection of a governor of Virginia, Secretary of War, etc., includes Tyler letters.

232. Galloway-Maxcy-Markoe Families Papers. Manuscript Division, Library of Congress, Washington. A large collection of papers important for understanding foreign policy in the Tyler administration.

233. Gordon, Armistead Churchill, Papers. Virginia Historical Society, Richmond. Correspondence re dedication of the Tyler memorial in Richmond, 1915 and with Tyler's descendants.

234. Graham, John Lorimer, Papers. Henry E. Huntington Library, San Marino, Calif. Small collection of lawyer and postmaster in New York City, mainly relating to national and local politics; includes Tyler correspondence.

235. Granbery Family Papers. Archives Branch, Virginia State Library and Archives, Richmond. Small collection concern mainly a land claim involving Tyler.

236. Gratz, Simon, Collection. Historical Society of Pennsylvania, Philadelphia. A large collection, including autographs of many major American political figures of nineteenth-century America.

237. Greenway, Edward M., Jr., Collection. Eisenhower Library, Johns Hopkins University, Baltimore. Collection of lawyers, statesmen, and others in Tyler's administration.

238. Grigsby, Hugh Blair, Letterbook, 1854-1861. Virginia Historical Society, Richmond. Contains several Tyler letters on politics and other matters.

239. Grinnan Family Papers. Alderman Library, University of Virginia, Charlottesville. Business records and correspondence of a Fredericksburg, Virginia, family; includes Tyler materials.

240. Gwathmey (Cabell) Collection. Alderman Library, University of Virginia, Charlottesville. Consists of materials relating to or by early nineteenth-century American statesmen, including Tyler.

241. Harrison, William Henry, Papers. New-York Historical Society, New York. Small collection, but important for background on the Tyler administration.

242. Horner, Gustavus Richard Brown, Papers. Virginia Historical Society, Richmond. Contains Tyler correspondence re Horner and the U.S. Navy.

243. Hutton, Hamilton Morris, Autograph Collection. Alderman Library, University of Virginia, Charlottesville. A small collection of political figures of the mid-nineteenth century, including Tyler.

244. Johnston Family Papers. Archives Branch, Virginia State Library and Archives, Richmond. Small collection includes Tyler correspondence and diary of John Floyd.

245. Mercer Family Papers, Virginia Historical Society, Richmond. Mainly a collection of the papers of John Francis Mercer, a Virginia congressman; includes Tyler correspondence.

246. Munford-Ellis Family Papers. Perkins Library, Duke University, Durham, N.C. Large collection of a Virginia family includes materials dealing with Virginia and national politics of the Middle Period.

247. Nash Family Papers. Virginia Historical Society, Richmond. Collection has at least one Tyler letter, 1828, relating to the American Colonization Society.

248. Preston Family Papers. Virginia Historical Society, Richmond. A few Tyler business papers and letters relating to patronage; some discussion of representation in the Confederate Congress.

249. Quinby, Teackle, and Upshur Family Papers. Alderman Library, University of Virginia, Charlottesville. Includes letters of recommendation from Isaac Dashiell Jones and others to Tyler officials.

250. Rabinowitz, Louis Mayer, Collection. Manuscripts and Archives, Yale University Library, New Haven. Collection includes a few Tyler items.

251. Riggs Historical Collection. Riggs National Bank, Washington, D.C. Contains four Tyler letters, 1828, 1841, 1843, 1846.

252. Rochelle, James Henry, Papers. Perkins Library, Duke University, Durham. A relatively small collection, includes significant material on Virginia and national politics as well as letters from Tyler relating to the Rochelle family.

253. Rutherfoord, John, Papers. Perkins Library, Duke University, Durham. Papers of a lawyer, merchant, and governor of Virginia; has a few Tyler items.

254. Smith, Francis Ormand Jonathan, Papers. Maine Historical Society, Portland. Largest collection of Smith papers; important for understanding the negotiations and approval of the Treaty of Washington, 1842.

255. Smith, William Patterson, Papers. Perkins Library, Duke University, Durham. Collection of a merchant and banker of Gloucester, Va., covering politics, grain trade, social life, and customs in tidewater Virginia; includes Tyler correspondence.

256. Sparks, Jared, Papers. Harvard College Library, Cambridge. Important for understanding the map controversy in the Treaty of Washington negotiations.

257. Summers, Lewis, and George W. Summers, Papers. West Virginia University Library, Morgantown. Includes Tyler letters, 1843—discussing his hope for the country.

258. Talcott, Andrew, Diaries. Virginia Historical Society, Richmond. Records several meetings with members of the Tyler administration concerning the negotiations with Lord Ashburton and the actual survey of the boundary line.

259. Thompson, Waddy, Letters. Texas Archives, University of Texas Library, Austin. Small collection of U.S. minister to Mexico dealing with Santa Fe prisoners and political intrigues relating to Texas and California; includes Webster and Tyler correspondence.

260. Ticknor, Benajah, Papers. Manuscripts and Archives, Yale University Library, New Haven. (Photocopies in Bentley Historical Library, University of Michigan, Ann Arbor). Collection of the chief surgeon of the Boston Navy Yard includes Tyler materials.

261. Tucker-Coleman Papers. Swem Library, College of William and Mary, Williamsburg. Important collection for the Tyler presidency.

262. Tucker-Ewell Papers. Archives Branch, Virginia State Library and Archives, Richmond. Correspondence of St. George Tucker, dealing mainly with legal matters and with the College of William and Mary.

263. United States Presidents Documents, 1803-1875. Western Reserve Historical Society, Cleveland. Tyler materials consist primarily of land grants and appointments.

264. Walsh, Michael, Correspondence. New-York Historical Society, New York. Small collection covering years 1840-65, includes correspondence with Tyler and other Whig and Democratic leaders, mostly concerning politics.

265. Wellford, Beverley Randolph, Papers. Virginia Historical Society, Richmond. Contains letters, 1835, concerning Thomas Hart Benton, Andrew Jackson, and John C. Calhoun.

266. Wetmore, Robert C., Papers. Manuscripts and Special Collections, New York State Library, Albany. A collection of approximately 150 items; the letters, mainly to Wetmore, reflect on national and state Whig politics in the period from 1835-1845, when Wetmore was dismissed as Collector of Customs for the Port of New York.

267. Wickham Family Papers. Virginia Historical Society, Richmond. Includes extract of letter from Tyler to Littleton Waller Tazewell, October 24, 1842.

268. Wilson, James, Papers. New Hampshire Historical Society, Concord. Papers of a Keene, New Hampshire, businessman, U.S. congressman from New Hampshire, and a Tyler supporter; includes some correspondence with Tyler.

269. Wilson, James Southall, Papers. Alderman Library, University of Virginia, Charlottesville. Includes Tyler family materials and two letters from Tyler to Henry A. Wise relating to President Franklin Pierce, politics, and patronage.

270. Wise, Barton H., Papers. Virginia Historical Society, Richmond. Contains an 1845 letter from Henry A. Wise to Caleb Cushing discussing Texas annexation.

D. PUBLISHED PERSONAL AND ADMINISTRATIVE PAPERS OF JOHN TYLER'S ASSOCIATES

1. Printed Works

a) Members of Cabinet

John Bell, Secretary of War

271. Sioussat, St. George L., ed. "Letters of John Bell to William B. Campbell, 1839-1857." *Tennessee Historical Magazine* 3 (September 1917): 210-27. Discusses Tennessee and national politics, and the elections of 1840, 1844, 1848, and 1852.

John Caldwell Calhoun, Secretary of State

272. Boucher, Chauncey S., and Robert P. Brooks, eds. *Correspondence Addressed to John C. Calhoun*, in *Annual Report of the American Historical Association for the Year 1929*. Washington: Government Printing Office, 1930.

273. Crallé, Richard K., ed. *The Works of John C. Calhoun*. 6 vols. New York: D. Appleton and Co., 1851-1856. Also available in *Microbook Library* [601].

274. Hemphill, W. Edwin, and Clyde N. Wilson, eds. *The Papers of John C. Calhoun*. 21 vols. to date. Columbia: University of South Carolina Press, 1959–.

275. Jameson, J. Franklin, ed. *Correspondence of John C. Calhoun*. Vol. 2 of *Report of the American Historical Association for the Year 1899*. Washington: Government Printing Office, 1900.

276. Moore, Frederick W., ed. "Calhoun as Seen by His Political Friends: Letters of Duff Green, Dixon H. Lewis, Richard K. Crallé During the Period from 1831 to 1848." *Publications of the Southern History Association* 7 (1903).

John Jordan Crittenden, Attorney General

277. Coleman, Ann Mary Butler (Crittenden), ed. *The Life of John J. Crittenden, with Selections from his Correspondence and Speeches*. 2 vols. Philadelphia: J. B. Lippincott & Co., 1871; New York: Da Capo Press, 1970. Also in *Microbook Library*, [601].

278. "Letter of John Jordan Crittenden." *Collector* 24 (February 1911): 39. Dated September 11, 1841; discusses the political crisis occasioned by Tyler's second veto of the bank bill.

Thomas Ewing, Secretary of the Treasury

279. Ewing, Thomas. "Diary of Thomas Ewing, August and September, 1841." *American Historical Review* 18 (October 1912): 97-112. Also issued as offprint, [New York, 1912]. Covers cabinet meetings of the Tyler administration.

Thomas Walker Gilmer, Secretary of the Navy

280. Gilmer, Thomas Walker. *Message of the Governor of Virginia, Communicating a Correspondence Between the Governors of Virginia and New York, in Relation to Certain Fugitives from Justice.* Richmond: S. Shepherd, 1840. Correspondence with William H. Seward regarding extradition of three blacks charged with stealing a slave in Virginia.

281. Gilmer, Thomas W. *Remarks of Mr. Gilmer, of Virginia, in Committee of the Whole, March 9, 1842, on the Motion to Strike Out the Contingent Appropriations from the Bill Making Appropriations for the Civil and Diplomatic Expenses of Government* ... Washington: n.p., 1842. Also available in *Goldsmiths'* [600].

282. Gilmer, Thomas W. *Speech of Mr. Gilmer, of Virginia, on the Army Bill ... in the House of Representatives ... , May 26 and 30, 1842.* Washington: n.p., 1842. Also available in *Goldsmiths'* [600].

Hugh Swinton Legaré, Attorney General, Secretary of State

283. Bentley, Alexander J., comp. *Digest of the Official Opinions of the Attorneys-General of the United States ... Embracing the Period from 1789 to 1881.* Washington: Government Printing Office, 1885.

284. Bullen, Mary Swinton Legaré, ed. *The Writings of Hugh Swinton Legaré ... , Diary of Brussels, and Journal of the Rhine; Extracts from His Private and Diplomatic Correspondence; Orations and Speeches; and Contributions to the New-York and Southern Reviews.* 2 vols. Charleston: Burges & James, 1845-1846; New York: Da Capo Press, 1970. Also available in *Microbook Library* [601] and in *Legal Treatises* [606].

285. *Digest of the Published Opinions of the Attorneys-General, and of the Leading Decisions of the Federal Courts: with Reference to International Law, Treaties, and Kindred Subjects.* Washington: Government Printing Office, 1877. Focus is primarily on international law and foreign relations; includes Legaré opinions.

286. Hall, Benjamin F., et al., eds. *Official Opinions of the Attorneys General of the United States.* 41 vols. Washington: Government Printing Office, 1852- .

287. Law, Stephen D. *Digest of American Cases Relating to Patents for Inventions and Copyrights from 1789 to 1862, Including ... the Opinions of the Attorneys General of the United States under the Patent and Copyright Laws ...* New York: Author, 1862, 1877. Also available in *Legal Treatises* **[606]**.

288. *Opinions of Attorneys General. Message from the President of the United States, Transmitting Opinions of Attorneys General ...* 2 vols. [Washington: n.p., 1851]. Vol. 1 covers August 21, 1791-August 30, 1838; Vol. 2, September 3, 1838-February 15, 1851.

John Canfield Spencer, Secretary of War

289. Spencer, John Canfield. *Correspondence Between the Hon. John C. Spencer, and a Committee of the Friends of the General Administration, at Rochester, N.Y., October the 19th, 1842.* New York: J. Booth, 1842. Discusses policies of the Tyler administration.

290. Spencer, John Canfield. *Letter from the Secretary of War.* Providence: n.p., 1842. In a letter to Alexander Duncan, Spencer denies that Tyler wrote Governor King regarding the Dorr Rebellion.

Abel Parker Upshur, Secretary of State, Secretary of the Navy

291. [Upshur, Abel Parker]. *A Brief Enquiry Into the True Nature and Character of Our Federal Government; Being a Review of Judge Story's Commentaries on the Constitution of the United States.* Petersburg [Va.]: E. and J. C. Ruffin, 1840; Philadelphia: J. Campbell, 1863; New York: Da Capo Press, 1971. Also available in *Microbook Library* **[601]** and *Legal Treatises* **[606]**. Useful for understanding Upshur's views on federal-state relations.

Daniel Webster, Secretary of State

292. Berolzheimer, Alan R., ed. *General Index to the Papers of Daniel Webster.* Hanover: University Press of New England, 1989. Provides access to the multi-volume edition of printed papers—correspondence, speeches, legal, and diplomatic papers.

293. [Everett, Edward, ed.]. *The Diplomatic and Official Papers of Daniel Webster, While Secretary of State.* New York: Harper & Brothers, 1848. Covers the period of Webster's first term as Secretary of State under Tyler; Shewmaker edition has displaced the Everett series.

294. Everett, Edward, ed. *The Works of Daniel Webster.* 6 vols. Boston: C. C. Little and J. Brown, 1851 (also in *Legal Treatises* **[606]**); Boston: Little, Brown and Company, 1853 (7th Ed.); 1856 (9th ed.; also in *Legal Treatises* **[606]**; 1857 (10th ed.); 1860 (12th ed.); 1866 (14th ed.); 1890 (20th ed.). Contains Everett's biographical memoir and diplomatic and official papers from the Tyler administration, among other things.

295. Konefsky, Alfred S., and Andrew J. King, eds. *The Papers of Andrew Jackson: Legal Series.* 3 vols. Hanover, N.H.: University Press of New England, 1982-1989.

296. McIntyre, James W., ed. *The Writings and Speeches of Daniel Webster.* 18 vols. National Edition. Boston: Little, Brown and Company, 1903. Vols. 1-6 repeat Everett's edition; vols. 17-18, Fletcher's edition. Vol. 1, memoir and speeches on various occasions; vols. 2-4, speeches on various occasions; vol. 11, legal arguments and diplomatic papers; vol 12, diplomatic papers and miscellaneous letters; vol. 13, addresses on various occasions; vol. 14, speeches in Congress and diplomatic papers; vol. 16, letters; vols. 17-18, private correspondence.

297. Shewmaker, Kenneth E., Kenneth R. Stevens, and Anita McGurn, eds. *The Papers of Daniel Webster: Diplomatic Series.* 2 vols. Hanover, N.H.: University Press of New England, 1983– . Volume 1, covering 1841-43, is essential for studying the foreign policy of the Tyler administration.

298. Van Tyne, Claude H., ed. *The Letters of Daniel Webster, from Documents Owned Principally by the New Hampshire Historical Society.* New York: McClure, Phillips & Co., 1902; New York: Greenwood Press, 1968; New York: Haskell House, 1969; St. Clair Shores, Mich.: Scholarly Press, 1970. Some material had been previously published in Fletcher Webster's *Correspondence.*

299. Webster, Daniel. "The Ashburton Treaty." Washington *Madisonian*, December 2, 1842. Editorial.

300. Webster, Daniel. "The Boundary Maps." Washington *National Intelligencer*, February 27, 1843. Editorial.

301. Webster, Daniel. "The British Special Mission." Washington *National Intelligencer*, March 1, 1842. Editorial.

302. Webster, Daniel. "The English Mission." Washington *National Intelligencer*, July 15, 1841. Editorial.

303. Webster, Daniel. "The Exchequer." Washington *Madisonian*, December 6, 1842. Editorial.

304. Webster, Daniel. *A Memoir on the North-Eastern Boundary ... Together with a Speech on the Same Subject by ... Daniel Webster ... Delivered at a Special Meeting of the New-York Historical Society.* New York: Historical Society, 1843.

305. Webster, Daniel. "The Message." Washington *Madisonian*, December 3, 1842. Editorial.

306. Webster, Daniel. *Mr. Webster's Vindication of the Treaty of Washington of 1842, in a Speech Delivered in the Senate of the United States, on the 6th and 7th of April, 1846.* Washington: J. & G. S. Gideon, 1846. Three different editions.

307. Webster, Daniel. "The Proposed Fiscal Banks." Washington *National Intelligencer*, June 15, 16, 17, 1841. Editorials.

308. Webster, Daniel. *Reception of Mr. Webster at Boston, September 30, 1842, with His Speech Delivered in Faneuil Hall on that Occasion.* Boston: S. N. Dickinson, 1842. Discusses the Tyler administration.

309. Webster, Daniel. *Relations with England.* n.p., [c1841]. Contains exchange of letters between Henry Stephen Fox and Webster on policy issues involving the two countries.

310. Webster, Daniel. "The Suppression of the Slave Trade." Washington *National Intelligencer*, March 27, April 27, 1843. Editorials.

311. Webster, Fletcher, ed. *The Private Correspondence of Daniel Webster.* 2 vols. Boston: Little, Brown and Company, 1857, 1875. 1857 edition also in *Legal Treatises* **[606]**. Contains autobiography and personal reminiscences of Webster; includes many documents, the originals of which have not been found.

312. Wiltse, Charles M., Harold D. Moser, David G. Allen, et al., eds. *The Papers of Daniel Webster: Correspondence Series.* 7 vols. Hanover: University Press of New England, 1974-1989. Volumes 5 and 6 are particularly important for the Tyler presidency.

b) Members of Congress

John Quincy Adams, Massachusetts Representative

313. Adams, Charles Francis, ed. *Memoirs of John Quincy Adams, Comprising Portions of His Diary from 1795 to 1848.* 12 vols. Philadelphia: J. B. Lippincott and Co., 1874-1877; Freeport, N.Y.: Books for Libraries Press, [1969]; New York: AMS Press, 1970. Philadelphia publication also in *Microbook Library* **[601]**.

314. Ford, Worthington Chauncey, ed. *The Writings of John Quincy Adams.* 7 vols. New York: Macmillan Company, 1913-1917; New York: Greenwood Press, 1968. Also available in *Microbook Library* **[601]**.

Nathan Appleton, Massachusetts Representative

315. Appleton, Nathan. *Letter to the Hon. Wm. C. Rives of Virginia, on Slavery and the Union*. Boston: J. H. Eastburn's Press, 1860.

316. Appleton, Nathan. *Remarks on Currency and Banking; Having Reference to the Present Derangement of the Circulating Medium in the United States*. Boston: C. C. Little & J. Brown, 1841. Also available in *Microbook Library* [601] and in *Goldsmiths'* [600].

317. Appleton, Nathan. *Speech of Mr. Appleton, of Mass., on the Tariff and Compromise Act ... , July 5, 1842*. Washington: National Intelligencer, 1842. Also available in *Goldsmiths'* [600].

Edward Dickinson Baker, Oregon Senator

318. Baker, Edward Dickinson. *Speech of Hon. E. D. Baker of Oregon, on the Propositions of the Peace Convention*. Washington: n.p., 1861.

William Segar Archer, Virginia Senator

319. Archer, William Segar. *Speech of Mr. Archer, of Virginia, Delivered ... in Secret Session, May 1844, on the Treaty for the Annexation of Texas*. Washington: Gales and Seaton, 1844.

Daniel Dewey Barnard, New York Representative

320. Barnard, Daniel Dewey. *Speech of Mr. Barnard, of New York, on the Veto of the Provisional Tarff Bill ... , July 1, 1842*. Washington: National Intelligencer Office, 1842. Also available in *Goldsmiths'* [600]

Thomas Henry Bayly, Virginia Representative

321. Bayly, Thomas Henry. *Speech of Mr. Bayly, of Virginia, on the Annexation of Texas ... , January 7, 1845*. Washington: Globe Office, 1845. Also available in *Texas* [607].

Thomas Hart Benton, Missouri Senator

322. Benton, Thomas Hart. *Speech of Mr. Benton, of Missouri, Delivered ... May 16, 18, and 20, in Secret Session on the Treaty for the Annexation of Texas (the Injunction of Secrecy Removed)*. Washington: Globe, 1844.

323. Benton, Thomas Hart. *Thirty Years' View; Or, A History of the Working of the American Government for Thirty Years from 1820-1850* ...   2 vols. New York: D. Appleton and Company, 1854-56, 1862, 1864, 1883, 1886, 1893; Boston: F. Parker, 1854-56; New York: Greenwood Press, 1968. First edition also in *Selected Americana* [602], in *Legal Treatises* [606], and in *Microbook Library* [601]. A detailed discussion of politics and government by a major participant and observer. Title varies slightly from printing to printing.

John Macpherson Berrien, Georgia Senator

324. Berrien, John Macpherson. *Speech of John Macpherson Berrien of Georgia on the Joint Resolution to Annex Texas ... Delivered ... February 1845.* Washington: Gales and Seaton, 1845. Also available in *Texas* [607].

John Minor Botts, Virginia Representative

325. Botts, John Minor. *The Great Rebellion: Its Secret History, Rise, Progress, and Disastrous Failure.* New York: Harper & Brothers, 1866. Also available in *Selected Americana* [602] and *Microbook Library* [601]. Recounts the Whig triumph in 1840, and Tyler's "treachery"; also discusses Tyler's "little game" at the Washington Peace conference.

326. Botts, John Minor. *Speech of Mr. Botts, of Virginia, on the Objections of the President to the Bill to Establish a Fiscal Corporation ... September 10, 1841.* Washington: National Intelligencer Office, 1841. Reviews Tyler's political course, denounces veto, and discloses a private letter, August 10, 1841, he wrote to Tyler urging him to adopt Whig measures.

327. Botts, John Minor. *Speech of Mr. Botts, of Virginia, on the Bill to Incorporate the Subscribers to a Fiscal Bank of the United States, ... , August 4, 1841.* Washington: National Intelligencer Office, 1841. Also available in *Goldsmiths'* [600].

328. Botts, John Minor. *Speech of Mr. Botts, of Virginia, on the Tariff Bill ... , July 12, 1842.* Washington: National Intelligencer Office, 1842. Also available in *Goldsmiths'* [600]. Contains impeachment charges against Tyler.

Aaron Venable Brown, Tennessee Representative

329. Brown, Aaron Venable. *Speech of the Hon. Aaron V. Brown, of Tennessee, on the Correspondence of Mr. Webster with the British Minister, in Relation to the Surrender of Alexander McLeod ... , July 9 and 10, 1841.* Washington: Blair and Rives, 1841.

330. Brown, Aaron Venable. *Speeches, Congressional and Political, and Other Writings, of Ex-Governor Aaron V. Brown, of Tennessee.* Nashville: J. L. Marling and Company, 1854.

331. Brown, Aaron Venable. *Texas and Oregon: Letter and Speeches of the Hon. A.V. Brown, of Tennessee in Reply to the Hon. John Quincy Adams on the Annexation of Texas, and on the Bill for the Organization of a Territorial Government over Oregon.* Washington: Blair & Rives, 1845. Also available in *Texas* [607].

James Buchanan, Pennsylvania Senator

332. Buchanan, James. *Speech of Hon. James Buchanan, of Pennsylvania in Support of the Veto Power, and in Reply to Mr. Clay, of Kentucky ... , February 2, 1842.* n.p., 1842.

333. Moore, John Bassett, ed. *The Works of James Buchanan, Comprising His Speeches, State Papers, and Private Correspondence.* 12 vols. Philadelphia: J. B. Lippincott, 1908-1911: New York: Antiquarian Press, 1960. Also available in *Microbook Library* [601]. Contains some correspondence with Tyler.

John Campbell, South Carolina Representative

334. Stoney, Samuel G., ed. "The Poinsett-Campbell Correspondence." *South Carolina Historical Magazine* 42 (1941): 31-52, 122-36, 149-68; 43 (1942): 27-34.

Robert Looney Caruthers, Tennessee Representative

335. Caruthers, Robert Looney. *Speech of Mr. Caruthers, of Tennessee, on the Veto of the Temporary Tariff Bill ... , July 1, 1842.* Washington: National Intelligencer Office, 1842. Also available in *Goldsmiths'* [600].

Rufus Choate, Massachusetts Senator

336. Brown, Samuel Gilman, ed. *The Works of Rufus Choate, with a Memoir of his Life.* 2 vols. Boston: Little, Brown and Company, 1862; New York: AMS Press, 1972. Also available in *Microbook Library* [601] and in *Legal Treatises* [606].

337. Choate, Rufus. *Speech of Mr. Choate, of Massachusetts, on the Bill to Provide Further Remedial Justice in the Courts of the United States ... , May, 1842.* Washington: National Intelligencer Office, 1842.

Henry Clay, Kentucky Senator

338. Colton, Calvin, ed. *The Life, Correspondence, and Speeches of Henry Clay.* 6 vols. New York: A. S. Barnes, 1856-1857; New York: P. O'Shea, 1864. Volumes 1-3 print life and times of Clay, Volume 4, the private correspondence, and Volumes 5-6 the speeches.

339. Colton, Calvin, ed. *The Private Correspondence of Henry Clay.* New York: A. S. Barnes & Co., 1855, 1856; Boston: F. Frederick Parker, 1856; Freeport, N.Y.: Books for Libraries Press, 1971. The New York, 1856, edition also available in *Legal Treatises* [606]. Subsequently published as Volume 4 of the *Works of Henry Clay.*

340. Colton, Calvin, ed. *The Works of Henry Clay, Compromising His Life, Correspondence and Speeches.* 7 vols. New York: Henry Clay Publishing Company, 1897. 10 vols. New York: G. P. Putnam's Sons, 1904. Ten-volume edition also available in *Microbook Library* [601].

341. Hopkins, James F., et al. *The Papers of Henry Clay.* 11 vols. Lexington, Ky.: University of Kentucky Press, 1959-1992. The most complete, the authoritative, edition of the papers of Clay.

342. Titus, W. A. "A Bit of New York History and an Unpublished Letter of Henry Clay." *Wisconsin Magazine of History* 7 (December 1923): 214-218. Prints a letter from Clay to Nathaniel P. Tallmadge, October 30, 1841, discussing the strained relations between Tyler and the Whig party.

Thomas Lanier Clingman, North Carolina Representative

343. Clingman, Thomas Lanier. *Selections from the Speeches and Writings of Hon. Thomas L. Clingman, of North Carolina.* Raleigh: J. Nichols, 1877, 1878. Also available in *Microbook Library* [601].

344. Clingman, Thomas Lanier. *Speech of T. L. Clingman, of North Carolina, on the Late Presidential Election ... , January 6, 1845.* [Washington]: J. & G. S. Gideon, [1845].

Howell Cobb, Georgia Representative

345. Phillips, Ulrich Bonnell, ed. *The Correspondence of Robert Toombs, Alexander H. Stephens, and Howell Cobb.* Volume 2 of the *Annual Report of the American Historical Association for the Year 1911.* Washington: Government Printing Office, 1913; New York: Da Capo Press, 1970.

Caleb Cushing, Massachusetts Representative

346. Benetz, Margaret Diamond, ed. *The Cushing Reports: Ambassador Caleb Cushing's Confidential Diplomatic Reports to the United States Secretary of State, 1843-1844.* Salisbury, N.C.: Documentary Publications, 1976. Volume contains reports on Mexico, Egypt, the Barbary States, India, and Ceylon.

347. Cushing, Caleb. *Speech of Mr. Cushing, of Massachusetts, on the Post Office Bill ... , August 25, 1841.* Washington: Gales and Seaton, 1841. Discusses differences between Tyler and Whig party.

Daniel Stevens Dickinson, New York Senator

348. Dickinson, John R., ed. *Speeches, Correspondence, Etc., of the Late Daniel S. Dickinson of New York, Including Addresses on Important Public Topics, Speeches in the State and United States Senate, and in Support of the Government during the Rebellion; Correspondence, Private and Political ... .* 2 vols. New York: G. P. Putnam and Sons, 1867. Also available in *Microbook Library* [**601**].

John Adams Dix, New York Senator

349. Dix, Morgan, ed. *Memoirs of John Adams Dix.* 2 vols. New York: Harper and Brothers, 1883. Also available in *Microbook Library* [**601**].

350. Dix, John A. *Speeches and Occasional Addresses.* 2 vols. New York: D. Appleton and Company, 1864. Also available in *Microbook Library* [**601**].

Stephen Arnold Douglas, Illinois Representative

351. Johannsen, Robert W., ed. *The Letters of Stephen A. Douglas.* Urbana: University of Illinois Press, 1961. Highly selective edition of Douglas's correspondence.

George Coke Dromgoole, Virginia Representative

352. Dromgoole, George Coke. *Letter from the Hon. George C. Dromgoole, to the Editor of the Richmond Enquirer: Finances of the Federal Government ...* [Washington: n.p., 1844]. Compares expenditures, liabilities, and public debt of the Van Buren and Tyler administrations.

John Fairfield, Maine Senator

353. Staples, Arthur G., ed. *The Letters of John Fairfield: A Representative in Congress from 1835 to 1837; A Member of the Senate of the United States from 1843 to 1847, and a Governor of Maine in 1839, 1840, 1842 and a Part of 1843.* Lewiston, Maine: Lewiston Journal Company, 1922.

Millard Fillmore, New York Representative

354. Fillmore, Millard. *Speech of Mr. Fillmore, of New York, on the Tariff Bill ... , June 9,1842.* Washington: n.p., 1842. Also available in *Goldsmiths'* [600].

John Floyd, Virginia Representative

355. Ambler, Charles Henry. *The Life and Diary of John Floyd ....* Richmond: Richmond Press, 1918. Also available in *Microbook Library* [601]. Offers insights into national and state politics mainly during Tyler's senatorial career. Diary also published in *John P. Branch Historical Papers of Randolph-Macon College* 5 (June 1918).

Joshua Reed Giddings, Ohio Representative

356. Giddings, Joshua Reed. *An Exposé of the Circumstances Which Led to the Resignation by the Hon. Joshua R. Giddings, of his Office of Representative in the Congress of the United States, from the Sixteenth Congressional District of Ohio, on the 22d March, 1842.* Plainsville, Ohio: J. Leonard & Co, 1842.

William Alexander Graham, North Carolina Senator

357. Hamilton, J. G. deRoulhac, and Max R. Williams, eds. *The Papers of William Alexander Graham.* 7 vols. Raleigh: North Carolina Department of Archives and History, 1957-84.

Robert Mercer Taliaferro Hunter, Virginia Representative

358. Ambler, Charles Henry, ed. *Correspondence of Robert M. T. Hunter, 1826-1876.* Vol. 2 of *Annual Report of the American Historical Association for the Year 1916.* Washington: Government Printing Office, 1918; New York: Da Capo Press, 1971. Also available in *Microbook Library* [601].

359. Hunter, Robert Mercer Taliaferro. *Remarks of Mr. R. M. T. Hunter, of Virginia, on the Temporary Tariff Bill ... , July 4, 1842.* [Washington: n.p., 1842].

Charles Jared Ingersoll, Pennsylvania Representative

360. Ingersoll, Charles Jared. *Mr. C. J. Ingersoll's View of the Texas Question.* Washington: Blair & Rives, 1844. Also available in *Texas* [607].

John Jameson, Missouri Representative

361. Jameson, John. *Speech of Mr. Jameson, of Missouri, on the Improvement of the Western Waters.* Washington: n.p., 1844. Speech in response to Tyler's message regarding the improvement of western lakes and rivers.

Andrew Johnson, Tennessee Representative

362. Graf, Leroy P., Ralph W. Haskins, Patricia P. Clark, and Paul H. Bergeron, eds. *The Papers of Andrew Johnson.* 12 vols. to date. Knoxville: University of Tennessee Press, 1967- . Volume 1, embracing 1822-51, is most useful for the Tyler years.

Cave Johnson, Tennessee Representative

363. Sioussat, St. George L., ed. "Letters of James K. Polk to Cave Johnson, 1833-1848." *Tennessee Historical Magazine* 1 (September 1915): 209-56.

Andrew Kennedy, Indiana Representative

364. Kennedy, Andrew. *Remarks of Mr. Kennedy, of Indiana, on the Motion of Mr. Wise, to Refer So Much of the President's Message as Refers to the Improvement of the Western Rivers and Lakes to the Committee on Commerce.* Washington: Blair & Rives, 1843.

John Pendleton Kennedy, Maryland Representative

365. Kennedy, John Pendleton. *The Collected Works.* 10 vols. Hildesheim, Germany: G. Olms, 1969. First edition also available in *Microbook Library* [601].

366. Kennedy, John Pendleton. *Defence of the Whigs, by a Member of the Twenty-seventh Congress.* New York: Harper & Brothers, 1844. Campaign pamphlet reading Tyler out of the Whig party.

367. Kennedy, John Pendleton. *Letter of J. P. Kennedy to His Constituents, Citizens of the Fourth Congressional District in the State of Maryland, on the Principles and Value of the Protective System.* Baltimore: n.p., 1842.

368. Kennedy, John Pendleton. *Memoirs of the Life of William Wirt, Attorney-General of the United States.* 2 vols. Philadelphia: Lea and Blanchard, 1849, 1850, 1851, 1852,

1853, 1854, 1856; Philadelphia: J. B. Lippincott, 1860; New York: G. P. Putnam and Sons, 1872. Also available in *Selected Americana* [602] and in *Legal Treatises* [606].

369. Kennedy, John Pendleton. *Political and Official Papers.* New York: G. P. Putnam & Sons, 1872.

Thomas Butler King, Georgia Representative

370. Davis, Curtis Carroll. "Dr. Caruthers Confronts the Bureaucrats." *Georgia Historical Quarterly* 56 (Spring 1972): 101-11. Prints letters, 1841, to John Bell, and 1845-46, to Thomas Butler King seeking appointments under Tyler.

Henry Smith Lane, Indiana Representative

371. Lane, Henry Smith. *Remarks of Mr. Lane, of Indiana, on the Loan Bill ... , March 28, 1842.* Washington: National Intelligencer Office, 1842. Also available in *Goldsmiths'* [600] and in *Selected Americana* [602].

Benjamin Watkins Leigh, Virginia Senator

372. Leigh, Benjamin Watkins. *Letter from B. W. Leigh, Esq., to the General Assembly of Virginia.* Washington: n.p., 1836. Discusses expunging resolution before the U.S. Senate and election of senator by the Virginia legislature.

Archibald Ladley Linn, New York Representative

373. Linn, Archibald Ladley. *Speech of Mr. Linn of New York, Upon the Mission to Mexico and Annexation of Texas ... , April 13, 1842.* Washington: National Intelligencer Office, 1842. Also available in *Texas* [607].

Willie Person Mangum, North Carolina Senator

374. Shanks, Henry Thomas, ed. *The Papers of Willie Person Mangum.* 5 vols. Raleigh: State Department of Archives and History, 1950-56. Provide insight into the Tyler administration through the eyes of a southern Clay Whig.

Thomas Francis Marshall, Kentucky Representative

375. Barre, W. L., ed. *Speeches and Writings of Hon. Thomas F. Marshall.* Cincinnati: Applegate & Company, 1858.

Samson Mason, Ohio Representative

376. Mason, Samson. *Speech of Mr. S. Mason, of Ohio, on the Objections of the President to the Bill to Establish a Fiscal Corporation ... , Sept. 10, 1841.* Washington: National Intelligencer Office, 1841. Also available in *Goldsmiths'* [600].

Willoughby Newton, Virginia Representative

377. Newton, Willoughby. *Letter of Willoughby Newton, of Virginia, Addressed to his Constituents, Chiefly in Explanation and Defense of the Joint Resolutions, Passed by the House of Representatives, for the Admission of Texas into the Union.* Washington: J. and G. S. Gideon, 1845.

John Strother Pendleton, Virginia Representative

378. Pendleton, John Strother. *Speech of Mr. Pendleton of Rappahannock, on the Election of a United States Senator, Delivered in the H. of Delegates, on the 15th February, 1839.* Richmond: Bailie and Gallaher, 1839. Announces his determination to vote for William C. Rives, a Conservative Democrat, for U.S. senator in the Virginia legislature.

William Campbell Preston, South Carolina Senator

379. Yarborough, Minnie Clare, ed. *The Reminiscences of William C. Preston.* Chapel Hill: University of North Carolina Press, 1933.

George H. Proffit, Indiana Representative

380. Proffit, George H. *Speech of Mr. Proffit, of Indiana, on the Objections of the President to the Bill to Establish a Fiscal Corporation, and in Reply to Mr. Botts, of Virginia ... , September 10, 1841.* Washington: n.p., 1841. Also available in *Goldsmiths'* [600].

John Reynolds, Illinois Representative

381. Reynolds, John. *My Own Times, Embracing Also the History of My Life.* Chicago, 1879. A colorful autobiography by a congressman, 1834-1837, 1839-1843.

William Cabell Rives, Virginia Senator

382. Peyton, William Madison. *Letter from Wm. M. Peyton to Wm. C. Rives, on 'the present crisis.'"* n.p., 1861. Discusses secession and the efforts to resolve differences between North and South peaceably.

383. Rives, William C. *Proceedings at a Public Dinner in Albemarle County, Virginia, Given to Mr. William C. Rives, Late a Senator of the United States from that State.* n.p., [1834]. Involves contest between Rives and Tyler for election to the United States Senate.

384. Rives, William Cabell. *History of the Life and Times of James Madison.* 3 vols. Boston: Little, Brown and Company, 1859-68, 1870-78; Freeport, N.Y.: Books for Libraries Press, 1970. Also available in *Microbook Library* [601].

385. Rives, William Cabell. *Letter from the Hon. William C. Rives to a Friend, on the Important Questions of the Day.* Richmond: Whig Book and Job Office, 1860. Rives's remarks are dated January 27, 1860, and deal with sectional differences and the upcoming presidential campaign.

386. Rives, William Cabell. *Remarks of William C. Rives, of Virginia, on Resigning His Seat in the Senate of the United States.* [Washington?]: n.p., 1834. Also available in *Goldsmiths'* [600]. Speech of February 22, 1834, involves contest with Tyler.

387. Rives, William Cabell. *Remarks of the Hon. William C. Rives, of Virginia, on the Provisional Tariff Bill ... , June 24, 1842.* Washington: Madisonian Office, 1842.

388. Rives, William Cabell. *Speech of Hon. William C. Rives, on the Proceedings of the Peace Conference and the State of the Union, Delivered in Richmond, Virginia, March 8, 1861.* Richmond: Whig Book and Job Office, 1861.

389. Rives, William Cabell. *Speech of Mr. Rives, of Virginia, in Support of Mr. Benton's Expunging Resolutions ... , March 18, 1836.* Washington: Blair & Rives, 1836. Involved in senatorial contest between Rives and Tyler.

390. Rives, William Cabell. *Speech of Mr. Rives, of Virginia, in Vindication of the Freedom of Elections Against the Interference of Federal Executive Officers ... , February 12, 1839.* Washington: Gales and Seaton, 1839.

391. Rives, William Cabell. *Speech of Mr. Rives, of Virginia, in Favor of His Amendment to the Bank Bill ... , July 1, 1841.* n.p.: [1841?].

392. Rives, William Cabell. *Speech of Mr. Rives of Virginia on the Texas Treaty ... , June 6, 1844.* n.p.: 1844. Also available in *Texas* [607].

393. Rives, William Cabell. *Speech of Mr. Wm. C. Rives, of Virginia, on Mr. McDuffie's Proposition to Repeal the Tariff Act of 1842 ... , May 27, 1844.* Washington: J. & G. S. Gideon, 1844. Also available in *Goldsmiths'* [600].

394. Rives, William Cabell. *Speech of the Hon. William C. Rives, of Virginia on the Resolution for the Annexation of Texas ... , February 15, 1845.* [Washington: n.p., 1845]. Also available in *Texas* [607].

395. Rives, William Cabell. *Speech of William C. Rives, of Virginia, on the Treaty with Great Britain ... , August 17 and 19, 1842.* [Washington: n.p., 1842].

396. Rives, William Cabell. *Speech of Hon. William C. Rives, on the Proceedings of the Peace Conference and the State of the Union.* Richmond: Whig Office, 1861.

397. Rives, William Cabell. *To the People of Virginia: A Vindication of His Actions as a Public Servant of the People of Virginia, Especially his Attitude towards the Van Buren Administration. Castle Hill, Albemarle Co., March 18, 1839.* n.p.: 1839.

Alexander Hugh Holmes Stuart, Virginia Representative

398. Stuart, Alexander H. H. *Remarks of Mr. A. H. H. Stuart, of Virginia, on the Veto Message of the President Returning with His Objections the Bill Extending the Laws for Laying and Collecting the Duties on Imports.* Washington: National Intelligencer Office, 1842. Also available in *Goldsmiths'* [600].

Benjamin Tappan, Ohio Senator

399. Ratcliffe, Donald J., ed. "The Autobiography of Benjamin Tappan." *Ohio History* 85 (Spring 1976): 109-57.

Richard Wigginton Thompson, Indiana Representative

400. Thompson, Richard W. *Recollections of Sixteen Presidents From Washington to Lincoln.* 2 vols. Indianapolis: Bowen-Merrill Company, 1894. Discusses the Tyler administration and relates anecdotes of the times.

401. Thompson, Richard W. *Speech of Mr. R. W. Thompson, of Indiana, on the Tariff Bills: Reported by the Committee of Ways and Means and the Committee on Manufactures ... , June 20, 1842.* Washington: National Intelligencer Office, 1842. Also in *Goldsmiths'* [600].

Joseph Leonard Tillinghast, Rhode Island Representative

402. Tillinghast, Joseph Leonard. *Speech of the Hon. Joseph L. Tillinghast, of Rhode Island, on the Message of the President, Returning the Provisional Bill with His Objections ... , June 30, 1842.* Washington: National Intelligencer Office, 1842. Also in *Goldsmiths'* [600].

Robert J. Walker, Mississippi Senator

403. Walker, Robert J. *Abstract of Mr. Walker's Texas Speech ... , May 20, 1844.* [Washington: J. Heart, 1844?]. Also in *Texas* [607].

404. Walker, Robert J. *Argument of Robert J. Walker, Esq.* Philadelphia: J. C. Clark, 1841. Argument before Supreme Court in a Mississippi case involving slavery and slave trade.

405. Walker, Robert J. *Letter of Mr. Walker, of Mississippi, Relative to the Annexation of Texas, in Reply to the Call of the People of Carroll County, Kentucky, to Communicate His Views on that Subject.* Washington: Globe Office, 1844; St. Louis: Missourian Office, 1844. Also in *Texas* [607] and *Microbook Library* [601].

406. Walker, Robert J. *The South in Danger.* Washington: n.p., 1841.

407. Walker, Robert J. *Speech of Mr. Walker of Mississippi ... , May 20 and 21, in Secret Session on the Treaty for the Reannexation of Texas, the Injunction of Secrecy Removed.* Washington: Globe Office, 1844.

John Wentworth, Illinois Representative

408. Wentworth, John. *Congressional Reminiscences: Adams, Benton, Calhoun, Clay and Webster ...* Chicago: Fergus Printing Company, 1882. Also in *Microbook Library* [601]. Reminiscences of an Illinois representative who first took his seat in Congress in 1843.

Joseph Livingston White, Indiana Representative

409. White, Joseph Livingston. *Speech of Mr. White, of Indiana, on the Message of the President Returning with His Objections the Bill "to Extend for a Limited Period the Present Laws for Collecting Duties on Imports."* Washington: National Intelligencer Office, 1842. Also in *Goldsmiths'* [600].

Henry Alexander Wise, Virginia Representative

410. Boyett, Gene W., ed. "A Letter from Archibald Yell to Henry A. Wise, July 12, 1841." *Arkansas Historical Quarterly* 32 (Winter 1973): 337-41. Expresses the hope that Tyler will, in his presidency, adhere to his longheld positions and views and not be bullied into acceptance of a Clay program.

411. Wise, Henry A. *Seven Decades of the Union* .... Philadelphia: J. B. Lippincott, 1872, 1876; Freeport, N.Y.: Books for Libraries Press, 1971. Also in *Microbook Library* [601]. A lengthy account of Tyler and his administration by an ardent admirer.

Levi Woodbury, New Hampshire Senator

412. Capen, Nahum, ed. *Writings of Levi Woodbury, LL.D.: Political, Judicial and Literary: Now First Selected and Arranged.* 3 vols. Boston: Little, Brown, and Co., 1852. Also in *Microbook Library*, [601] and in *Legal Treatises* [606]. Volume 1 covers Woodbury's political career, Volume 2 his judicial, and Volume 3, his literary.

413. Woodbury, Charles Levi. *Memoir of Hon. Levi Woodbury, LL.D.* Cambridge, Mass.: J. Wilson, 1881; Boston: D. Clapp & Son, 1894. Also in *Legal Treatises* [606].

William Lowndes Yancey, Alabama Representative

414. Yancey, William Lowndes. *Remarks of Mr. Yancey, of Alabama, on Mr. C. J. Ingersoll's Resolutions of Inquiry into the Conduct of Daniel Webster, in Expending the Contingent Fund While Secretary of State ... , April 9 and 10, 1846.* Washington: J. T. Towers, 1846.

415. Yancey, William Lowndes. *Speech of Hon. Wm. Lowndes Yancey of Alabama on the Annexation of Texas ... , Jan. 7, 1845.* Washington: Harris & Heart, 1845. Also in *Texas* [607].

c) Supreme Court Justices

Henry Baldwin

416. Baldwin, Henry. *A General View of the Origin and Nature of the Constitution and Government of the United States ... .* Philadelphia: J. C. Clark, 1837; New York: Da Capo Press, 1970. Also in *Legal Treatises* [606].

Joseph Story

417. Story, William W., ed. *Life and Letters of Joseph Story, Associate Justice of the Supreme Court of the United States and Dane Professor of Law at Harvard University.* 2 vols. London: J. Chapman, 1851; Boston: Little and Brown, 1851; Freeport, N.Y.: Books for Libraries Press, 1971. Also in *Legal Treatises* [606] and in *Microbook Library* [601].

d) Journalists

Horace Greeley

418. Greeley, Horace. *Recollections of a Busy Life, Including Reminiscences of American Politics and Politicians from the Opening of the Missouri Contest to the Downfall of Slavery.* New York: J. B. Ford and Co., 1869; Miami: Mnemosyne Publishing Co., 1969. Also in *Microbook Library* [601] and in *Selected Americana* [602].

Duff Green

419. Green, Duff. "England and America: Examination of the Causes and Probable Results of a War Between These Two Countries." *Le Commerce, Journal Politique et Litteraire*, March 4-30, 1842.

420. Green, Duff. *Facts and Suggestions, Biographical, Historical, Financial, and Political Addressed to the People of the United States.* New York: Richardson, 1866; New York: Union Printing Office, 1866. Also in *Microbook Library* [601]. Very useful in assessing Green's influence with the Tyler administration.

421. Green, Duff. *The United States and England, By an American.* London: n.p., 1842. Also in *Great Western Magazine* 2 (September 1842) and in *Selected Americana* [602]. Discusses relations with Great Britain, slave trade, and right of search.

422. Sioussat, St. George L. "Duff Green's 'England and the United States': With an Introductory Study of American Opposition to the Quintuple Treaty of 1841." *Proceedings of the American Antiquarian Society* 40 (1931): 175-276. Also in *Microbook Library* [601]. Discusses Green's attitude and negotiations with Great Britain on the issues of slave trade and right of search.

George Wilkins Kendall

423. Kendall, George Wilkins. *Narrative of the Texan Santa Fe Expedition ... .* 2 vols. New York: Harper and Brothers, 1844, 1847, 1856; London: Sherwood, Gilbert, and Piper, 1845; Chicago: R. R. Donnelley & Sons, 1929; Austin: The Steck Company, 1935. Also in *Texas* [607] and in *Microbook Library* [601].

Benjamin Perley Poore

424. Poore, Benjamin Perley. *Perley's Reminiscences of Sixty Years in the National Metropolis.* 2 vols. Boston, Mass.: Hubbard, 1886; Philadelphia: Hubbard Brothers, 1886. Contains numerous references to Tyler and the Tyler administration.

Thomas Ritchie

425. Ritchie, Thomas. "Letters of Thomas Ritchie—Glimpses of the Year 1830." *John P. Branch Historical Papers of Randolph-Macon College* 1 (1902): 147-54.

Edmund Ruffin

426. Ruffin, Edmund. *The Diary of Edmund Ruffin.* Washington: Library of Congress, 1966. Seven reels; diary covers 1856-65.

427. Scarborough, William Kauffman, ed. *The Diary of Edmund Ruffin.* 3 vols. Baton Rouge: Louisiana State University Press, 1972-89.

Nathan Sargent

428. Sargent, Nathan. *Public Men and Events, from the Commencement of Mr. Monroe's Administration, in 1817, to the Close of Mr. Fillmore's Administration in 1853.* 2 vols. Philadelphia: J. B. Lippincott & Co., 1875; New York: Da Capo Press, 1970. Also in *Microbook Library* [601]. A Whig contemporary, Sargent offers insights and anecdotes of the politicians and years of Tyler's presidency.

Amos Kendall

429. Stickney, William, ed. *Autobiography of Amos Kendall.* Boston: Lee, Shepard, and Dillingham, 1872; New York: P. Smith, 1949. Account of a former Jacksonian government appointee and, during the Tyler presidency, a newspaper editor.

Thurlow Weed

430. Weed, Harriet A., and Thurlow Weed Barnes, eds. *Life of Thurlow Weed, Including His Autobiography and Memoir.* 2 vols. Boston: Houghton Mifflin, 1883-84. *Autobiography* edited by Weed's daughter; *Memoir*, by Weed's grandson. Also in *Microbook Library* [601].

e) Others

431. Abel, Annie Heloise, and Frank J. Klingberg, eds. *A Side-Light on Anglo-American Relations, 1839-1858, Furnished by the Correspondence of Lewis Tappan and Others with the British and Foreign Anti-Slavery Society.* New York: A. M. Kelley, 1970.

432. Adams, Ephraim Douglass, ed. *British Diplomatic Correspondence Concerning the Republic of Texas, 1838-1846.* Austin: Texas State Historical Association, 1918. Also

in *Microbook Library* [601]. Mainly prints letters and reports to the British government by Charles Elliot and William Kennedy.

433. Adams, Ephraim Douglass, ed. "Correspondence from the British Archives Concerning Texas, 1837-1846." *Quarterly of the Texas State Historical Association* 15 (January 1912): 201-355.

434. Adams, George Jones. *A Letter to His Excellency John Tyler, Touching on the Signs of the Times and the Political Destiny of the World.* New York: C. A. Calhoun, 1844; Independence, Mo.: Joseph Smith, Jr.'s Rare Reprints, 1990.

435. Adams, Henry, ed. *The Writings of Albert Gallatin.* 3 vols. Philadelphia: J. B. Lippincott, 1879; New York: Antiquarian Press, 1960. Volume 2 contains letters covering the Tyler period; and Volume 3, a speech regarding banks, currency, and specie payments (1841).

436. Adams, Herbert Baxter. *The Life and Writings of Jared Sparks, Comprising Selections from His Journals and Correspondence.* 2 vols. Boston: Houghton, Mifflin, and Company 1893; Freeport, N.Y.: Books for Libraries Press, [1970]. 1893 edition also in *Microbook Library* [601]. Contains discussion of the Treaty of Washington, 1842, and some correspondence with Webster relating to the Webster-Ashburton treaty negotiations.

437. Aderman, Ralph M., ed. *The Letters of James Kirke Paulding.* Madison: University of Wisconsin Press, 1962. The most complete published collection of Paulding's papers.

438. Aderman, Ralph M., Herbert L. Kleinfield, and Jenifer S. Banks, eds. *The Letters of Washington Irving.* 4 vols. Boston: Twayne Publishers, 1978-1982. Volume 3, covering 1839-45, contains letters to secretaries of state while Irving served as Tyler's minister to Spain.

439. *Address to the People of Virginia, by the Democratic Party, in the General Assembly of 1834-35.* n.p., n.d. Deals with the election of senator, 1834-1835.

440. Alexander, John Rufus. *Adventures of a Mier Prisoner, Being the Thrilling Experiences of John Rufus Alexander, Who Was with the Ill-Fated Expedition Which Invaded Mexico.* Bandera, Texas: Frontier Times, [1912].

441. Allen, George. *The Complaint of Mexico, and Conspiracy against Liberty.* Boston: J. W. Alden, 1843. Also in *Texas* [607]. On the annexation of Texas; contains letter on the subject from Webster to Waddy Thompson.

442. *Annexation of Texas: Proceedings of a Meeting of Citizens of Petersburg, Va., in Favor of the Re-Annexation of Texas to the United States.* Washington: Blair & Rives, 1844.

443. Ashley, Evelyn. *The Life and Correspondence of Henry John Temple, Viscount Palmerston.* 2 vols. London: Richard Bentley & Son, 1879.

444. Baker, George E., ed. *The Life of William H. Seward with Selections from His Works.* New York: Redfield, 1855, 1860. Also in *Selected Americana* [602].

445. Baker, George E., ed. *The Works of William H. Seward.* 5 vols. New York: Redfield, 1853-1884: New York: Houghton, Mifflin and Company, 1884. Also in *Microbook Library* [601]. Useful in tracing the relationship between the New York governor, Webster, and the Tyler administration.

446. Barker, Nancy Nichols, ed. *The French Legation in Texas.* 2 vols. Austin: Texas State Historical Association, 1971-73.

447. Basler, Roy P., Marion Dolores Pratt, and Lloyd A. Dunlap, eds. *The Collected Works of Abraham Lincoln.* 9 vols. New Brunswick, N.J.: Rutgers University Press, 1953-1955. The most comprehensive printed edition of Lincoln's works; Volume 1 covers the Tyler administration.

448. Basler, Roy P., ed. *The Collected Works of Abraham Lincoln, 1832-1865.* Supplement. Westport, Conn.: Greenwood Press, 1974.

449. Basler, Roy P., and Christian O. Basler, eds. *The Collected Works of Abraham Lincoln, 1848-1865.* Second Supplement. New Brunswick, N.J.: Rutgers University Press, 1990.

450. Bass, Feris A., Jr., and B. R. Brunson, eds. *Fragile Empires: The Texas Correspondence of Samuel Swartwout and James Morgan, 1836-1856.* Austin: Shoal Creek Publishers, Inc., 1978. Contains numerous references to the Tyler administration's posture on Texas.

451. Bassett, John S., and J. Franklin Jameson, eds. *The Correspondence of Andrew Jackson.* 7 vols. Washington: Carnegie Institution of Washington, 1926-35; New York: Kraus Reprint, 1969. An older collection of Jackson's papers but still useful; will be supplanted by printed edition currently under way at the University of Tennessee.

452. Beardsley, Levi. *Reminiscences; Personal and Other Incidents; Early Settlement of Otsego County; Notices and Anecdotes of Public Men; Judicial, Legal and Legislative Matters; Field Sports; Dissertations and Discussions.* New York: C. Vinten, 1852.

Reminiscences of an important local New York politician and capitalist; useful for understanding several of Webster's decisions as Secretary of State under Tyler.

453. Bell, Thomas W. *A Narrative of the Capture and Subsequent Sufferings of the Prisoners in Mexico, Captured in the Cause of Texas, Dec. 26th, 1842, and Liberated Sept. 16th, 1844.* n.p.: R. Morris & Co., 1845; Waco: Texian Press, 1964. 1845 edition also in *Texas* **[607]**. Discussion of the Mier expedition by one of the Americans captured.

454. Benham, Priscilla. "Diplomatic Correspondence of the United States Chargé d'Affaires to the Republic of Texas, 1837-1843." *Red River Valley Historical Review* 5 (Winter 1980): 37-55.

455. Benson, Arthur C., and Viscount Esher, eds. *The Letters of Queen Victoria: A Selection from Her Majesty's Correspondence between the Years 1837 and 1861.* 3 vols. London: J. Murray, 1907.

456. Binkley, William C., ed. *Official Correspondence of the Texan Revolution, 1835-1836.* 2 vols. New York: D. Appleton-Century Company, 1936. Also in *Microbook Library* **[601]**.

457. Bourne, Kenneth, ed. *British Documents on Foreign Affairs: Reports and Papers from the Foreign Office Confidential Prints.* Part 1, Series C; North America, 1838-1914. 4 vols. Frederick, Md.: University Publications of America, 1986.

458. *British and Foreign State Papers.* 170 vols. London: HMSO, 1812-1968. Vols. 32, 33, and 34 are important for the Tyler years.

459. Bungay, George W[ashington]. *Crayon Sketches and Off-Hand Takings of Distinguished American Statesmen, Orators, Divines, Essayists, Editors, Poets, and Philanthropists.* Boston: Stacy and Richardson, 1852. Also in *Selected Americana* **[602]** and in *Legal Treatises* **[606]**. Contains brief biographical sketches of several of Tyler's senatorial colleagues and two of his cabinet members, Webster and Calhoun.

460. Butler, Clement Moore. *Address Delivered by Rev. Clement M. Butler, at the President's Mansion, on the Occasion of the Funeral of Abel P. Upshur, T. W. Gilmer, and Others, Who Lost Their Lives by the Explosion on Board the* Princeton, *February 28, 1844.* Washington: J. and G. S. Gideon, 1844.

461. Butler, William Allen. *A Retrospect of Forty Years, 1825-1865.* New York: C. Scribner's Sons, 1911. Also in *Microbook Library* **[601]**.

462. Cass, Lewis. *Examen de la question aujourd'hui pendante entre le gouvernement des Etats-Unis et celui de la Grande-Bretagne; concernment le droit de visite.* Paris: H. Fournier, 1842.

463. Cass, Lewis. *An Examination of the Question Now in Discussion Between the American & British Governments, Concerning the Right of Search.* Paris: H. Fournier, 1842.

464. Cass, Lewis. *The Right of Search: An Examination of the Question, Now in Discussion, between the American and British Governments, Concerning the Right of Search By an American.* Baltimore: N. Hickman, 1842; Paris: H. Fournier, 1842. Also in *Microbook Library* [601]. Denounced British search and warned of a resurgence of impressment; to some extent a campaign pamphlet in behalf of Cass specifically and of the Conservative Democratic faction generally in 1844.

465. Channing, William. *The Duty of the Free States, or Remarks Suggested by the Case of the Creole: A Review of the Late Instructions of the Secretary of State to the American Minister at the Court of St. James's.* Boston: W. Crosby & Company, 1842. Also in *Microbook Library* [601].

466. Cheves, Langdon. *Letter of the Hon. Langdon Cheves to the Editors of the Charleston Mercury, Sept. 11, 1844.* [Charleston: Walker & Burke, 1844]. Also in *Texas* [607]. Discusses annexation of Texas.

467. Chittenden, Lucius Eugene. *Report of the Debates and Proceedings in the Secret Sessions of the Conference Convention for Proposing Amendments to the Constitution of the United States, Held at Washington, D.C., in February, A.D. 1861.* New York: D. Appleton & Company, 1864, 1900, 1983; New York: Da Capo Press, 1971. Also in *Legal Treatises* [606] and in *Microbook Library* [601].

468. Clark, John Chamberlain. *To the Electors of Chenango County, N.Y.* n.p.: [1841?]. Discusses the Tyler administration and Thomas Ewing's relationship to it.

469. Clark, Raymond B., Jr., ed. "Observations on Washington Society: Mrs. W. C. Rives-Miss Maria L. Gordon Letters, 1842." *Papers of the Albemarle County Historical Society* 11 (1950-1951): 53-61. Comments on the social activities of Washington, a ball in honor of the Russian Czar, and the visit of Charles Dickens.

470. Cole, Donald B., and John J. McDonough, eds. *Witness to the Young Republic: A Yankee's Journal, 1828-1870.* Hanover: University Press of New England, 1989. Diary of Benjamin Brown French; detailed comments and discussion of Washington society and politics.

471. Commons, John R., et al. *A Documentary History of American Industrial Society.* 11 vols. Cleveland: A. H. Clark Company, 1910-1911. Also in *Microbook Library* [601]. An older but still useful collection of materials relating to labor and the laboring classes.

472. Confederate States of America. Congress. *Proceedings of the First Confederate Congress, End of Second Session, Third Session in Part.* Wilmington, N.C.: Broadfoot Publishing Company, 1930. Covers Tyler's activities as a delegate.

473. Confederate States of America. *Laws of the Provisional Congress of the Confederate States in Relation to the War Department, 1861.* Richmond: Tyler, Wise & Allegre, 1861. Covers legislation passed while Tyler sat as delegate.

474. *Correspondence Relative to the Negotiation of the Question of Disputed Right to the Oregon Territory, on the North-west Coast of America, Subsequent to the Treaty of Washington of August 9, 1842, Presented to Both Houses of Parliament by Command of Her Majesty, 1846.* London: T. R. Harrison, 1846. Covers, in part, negotiations of the Tyler administration with Sir Richard Pakenham.

475. Cumming, Hiram. *Secret History of the Perfidies, Intrigues, and Corruptions of the Tyler Dynasty, with the Mysteries of Washington City, Connected with that Vile Administration, in a Series of Letters to the Ex-Acting President.* Washington: Author, 1845. The first of eight projected numbers, the author offers a vituperative attack on the Tyler administration and its policy toward Texas.

476. Cutler, Julia Perkins. *Life of Ephraim Cutler, Prepared from His Journals and Correspondence.* Cincinnati: R. Clarke & Co., 1890; New York: Arno Press, 1971. Gives day-by-day account of the proceedings of the Whig convention at Harrisburg, Pennsylvania, in 1839, when Harrison and Tyler were nominated for presidency and vice presidency.

477. *A Defence of the President, Against the Attacks of Mr. Botts and the Clay Party ...* [Washington: Madisonian Office, 1843?].

478. *Desultory Observations on the Abuses of the Banking System.* Petersburg, Va.: n.p., 1841.

479. *Documents of the Assembly of the State of New York.* Vol. 7. 64th Sess, 1841, No. 292. Contains materials relating to the McLeod affair.

480. *Documents Relating to the Affairs of Rhode Island.* [n.p.: Rhode Island?, 1842?].

481. Donald, David, et al., eds. *Diary of Charles Francis Adams.* 8 vols. Cambridge, Mass.: Harvard University Press, 1964-86. Covers up to 1840.

482. [Dorsey, John Larkin]. *Observations on the Political Character and Service of President Tyler, and His Cabinet By a Native of Maryland.* Washington: Peter Force, 1841. Offers a brief review of the Tyler administration, a lengthy discussion of Webster (pp. 10-106 out of a total of 127 pages), and short accounts of Thomas Ewing, John Bell, George E. Badger, Francis Granger, and John J. Crittenden in the Tyler cabinet; publication smacks of a defense of Webster's decision to remain in the Tyler cabinet following the resignations of September 1841.

483. Dumond, Dwight Lowell, ed. *Letters of James Gillespie Birney, 1831-1857.* 2 vols. New York: D. Appleton-Century Company, 1938; Gloucester, Mass.: P. Smith, 1966. Correspondence of the Liberty party candidate for the presidency in 1844.

484. Ellet, E. F. *The Court Circles of the Republic; or, The Beauties and Celebrities of the Nation ... from Washington to Grant.* Hartford, Conn.: Hartford Publishing Company, 1869, 1899; New York: Arno Press, 1975. Also in *Selected Americana* [602]. Discussion of social life and people of Washington.

485. Elliott, Richard Smith. *Notes Taken in Sixty Years.* St. Louis: R. P. Studley & Co., 1883; Boston: Cupples, Upham, 1884. Some discussion of Tyler and succession.

486. Ellis, George W. *A Poem on the Awful Catastrophe on Board the U.S. Steam Frigate* Princeton. *Together with a Full Description of the Terrible Calamity, the Proceedings at Washington, and the Funeral Obsequies.* Boston: A. J. Wright, 1844. In addition to the poem, contains newspaper accounts of the explosion, Tyler's proclamation re mourning, and other accounts of the events in Washington.

487. Emerson, Everett H., and Katherine T. Emerson. "Some Letters of Washington Irving, 1833-1843." *American Literature* 35 (May 1963): 156-172. Covers, in part, years while Irving was minister to Spain.

488. Esarey, Logan, ed. *The Messages and Letters of William Henry Harrison.* 2 vols. Indianapolis: Indiana Historical Commission, 1922; New York: Arno Press, 1975. Also in *Microbook Library* [601]. Includes papers while governor of Indiana Territory.

489. Falconer, Thomas. *Notes of a Journey through Texas and New Mexico in the Years 1841 and 1842.* [n.p.: 1844?]. Also in *Texas* [607]. Discussion of the Texan Santa Fe expedition, 1841.

490. Featherstonhaugh, George William. *Observations upon the Treaty of Washington, Signed August 9, 1842; with the Treaty Annexed, Together with a Map, to Illustrate the*

Boundary Line as Established by the Treaty between Her Majesty's Colonies of New Brunswick and Canada and the United States of America. London: J. W. Parker, 1843.

491. Field, Maunsell Bradhurst. *Memories of Many Men and of Some Women: Being Personal Recollections of Emperors, Kings, Queens, Princes, Presidents, Statesmen, Authors, and Artists, at Home and Abroad, During the Last Thirty Years.* New York: Harper & Brothers, 1874. Recounts the events surrounding Webster's speech at Niblo's Saloon, Tyler's Irish coachman, and other politicians of the 1840s; served as secretary of legation under John Young Mason.

492. Fitzpatrick, John C., ed. *The Autobiography of Martin Van Buren.* Washington: United States Government Printing Office, 1920; New York: A. M. Kelley, 1969. Also in *Microbook Library* [601].

493. Folsom, George. *Mexico in 1842: A Description of the Country, Its Natural and Political Features, with a Sketch of Its History, Brought to the Present Year, to Which is Added an Account of the Texas Yucatan, and of the Santa Fe Expedition.* New York: C. J. Folsom, 1842. Also in *Texas* [607]. Provides brief discussion of the Santa Fe expedition and prisoners.

494. Frémont, Jessie Benton. *The Origin of the Frémont Explorations.* [New York: Century Publishing Co., 1891].

495. Frémont, John C. *Report of the Exploring Expedition to the Rocky Mountains in the Year 1842, and to Oregon and North California in the Years 1843-'44, 1845.* Washington: n.p..., 1845. Reprinted in Viola, Herman J., and Ralph E. Ehrenberg, eds. *The Exploring Expedition to the Rocky Mountains.* Washington: Smithsonian Institution Press, 1988. Reprint has a useful introduction on Frémont's expeditions during the Tyler administration.

496. Gallatin, Albert. *A Memoir of the North-Eastern Boundary, in Connexion with Mr. Jay's Map, Together with a Speech on the Same Subject by the Hon. Daniel Webster ... Delivered at a Special Meeting of the New-York Historical Society, April 15, 1843.* New York: New-York Historical Society, 1843. Also in *Selected Americana* [602].

497. Gallatin, Albert. *The Right of the United States to the North-Eastern Boundary Claimed by Them, Principally Extracted from the Statements Laid before the King of the Netherlands.* New York: S. Adams, 1840; Freeport, N.Y.: Books for Libraries Press, 1970. Useful for background on the 1842 Treaty of Washington.

498. Garrison, George Pierce, ed. *Diplomatic Correspondence of the Republic of Texas.* 3 vols. Washington: Government Printing Office, 1908-11. Also in *Microbook Library* [601]. Correspondence with the United States, Mexico, Yucatan, and European states.

499. Gatewood, Joanne L., ed. "Richmond During the Virginia Constitutional Convention of 1829-1830: An Extract from the Diary of Thomas Green, October 1, 1829, to January 31, 1830." *Virginia Magazine of History and Biography* 84 (July 1976): 287-332. Kept by a Richmond lawyer, the journal provides comments on weather, social activities, and delegates to the convention.

500. Green, Thomas Jefferson. *Journal of the Texian Expedition Against Mier, Subsequent Imprisonment of the Author; His Sufferings, and Final Escape from the Castle of Perote* ... New York: Harper & Brothers, 1845; Austin: Steck Company, 1935; New York: Arno Press, 1973. 1845 edition also in *Texas* [607] and *Microbook Library* [601].

501. Greene, E. B., C. W. Alvord, and Charles M. Thompson, eds. *The Governors' Letter-Books, 1818-1834, 1840-1853*, in *Collections of the Illinois State Historical Library*. Springfield: Trustees of the Illinois State Historical Library, 1909-11. Volume 1 contains the letterbooks of Edward Coles, 1822-26, of Ninian Edwards, 1826-30, and of John Reynolds, 1830-44; Volume 2 contains coverage of the administration of Thomas Ford, the letterbook of Thomas Carlin, 1840-41, of Thomas Ford, 1842-45, and of August C. French and Joel A. Matteson, 1840-53.

502. Gulick, Charles Adams, Jr., et al., eds. *The Papers of Mirabeau Buonaparte Lamar.* 6 vols. Austin: A. C. Baldwin, 1921-1927; Austin: Pemberton Press, 1968. Useful for understanding the Santa Fe expedition and the plight of the prisoners.

503. Hagner, Alexander Burton. *A Personal Narrative of the Acquaintance of My Father and Myself with Each of the Presidents of the United States.* Washington: W. F. Roberts Co, 1915. Personal account by the son of Peter Hagner, longtime clerk in the War Department.

504. Hamilton, James Alexander. *Reminiscences of James A. Hamilton; Or, Men and Events at Home and Abroad, During Three Quarters of a Century.* New York: C. Scribner & Co., 1869. Also in *Selected Americana* [602].

505. Hamilton, Stanislaus Murray, ed. *The Writings of James Monroe, Including a Collection of His Public and Private Papers and Correspondence Now for the First Time Printed.* 7 vols. New York: G. P. Putnam's Sons, 1898-1903; New York: AMS Press, 1969. Also in *Microbook Library* [601]. Volumes 6 and 7 are most useful for a study of Tyler.

506. Heilman, Grace E., and Bernard S. Levin, eds. *Calendar of the Joel R. Poinsett Papers in the Henry D. Gilpin Collection.* Philadelphia: Historical Society of Pennsylvania, 1941. An indispensable guide to the unpublished papers, offering thumbnail summaries of the documents.

507. Hill, Hamilton Andrews. *Memoir of Abbott Lawrence.* Boston: Privately printed, 1883; Boston: Little, Brown, and Company, 1884. Also in *Microbook Library* [**601**]. Offers discussion of Lawrence, a merchant, manufacturer, and philanthropist, and his role in politics and government and as a diplomat to Great Britain.

508. Hillard, George S., ed. *Life, Letters, and Journals of George Ticknor.* 2 vols. Boston: James R. Osgood, 1876, 1877; London: Sampson Low, Marston, Searle, 1876; New York: Houghton Mifflin Company, 1909; New York: Johnson Reprint Corp., 1968. Also in *Microbook Library* [**601**]. Educator, author, and close friend of Webster's.

509. Hodge, F. W., ed. *Letters and Notes on the Texan Santa Fe Expedition, 1841-1842, by Thomas Falconer.* New York: Dauber & Pine Bookshops, Inc., 1930; Chicago: Rio Grande Press, 1963.

510. *A Horrible Plot to Drench the State of Rhode Island with the Blood of Its Inhabitants!* Providence: n.p., 1842. Discusses the governor of Rhode Island and his effort to get military assistance from Tyler if needed to put down rebellion.

511. Howe, M. A. De Wolfe, ed. *The Life and Letters of George Bancroft.* 2 vols. New York: C. Scribner's Sons, 1908; New York: Da Capo Press, 1970; Port Washington, N.Y.: Kennikat Press, 1971. Also in *Microbook Library* [**601**]. Also contains bibliography of books and pamphlets by Bancroft, a historian, diplomat, and delegate to the 1844 Democratic convention.

512. Hughes, Sarah Forbes, ed. *Letters and Recollections of John Murray Forbes.* 2 vols. Boston: Houghton, Mifflin and Company, 1899. Merchant and capitalist heavily involved in the China trade.

513. Hunt, Gaillard, ed. *The First Forty Years of Washington Society Portrayed by the Family Letters of Mrs. Samuel Harrison Smith (Margaret Bayard).* New York: Scribner, 1906; London: Unwin, 1906; New York: Frederick Ungar Publishing Co., 1965. Also available in *Microbook Library* [**601**].

514. Hunt, Gaillard, ed. *The Writings of James Madison, Comprising His Public Papers and His Private Correspondence, Including Numerous Letters and Documents Now for the First Time Printed.* 9 vols. New York: G. P. Putnam's Sons, 1900-1910. Also in *Microbook Library* [**601**]. Last few volumes important for background of Tyler in Virginia and in Congress.

515. Hunter, Mrs. Thomas Lomax, ed. "Leaves from the Diary of William Saunders Brown, 1820-1898." *Northern Neck of Virginia Historical Magazine* 4 (December 1954): 310-14. Brown describes the election of 1844 in King George County, Virginia.

516. Irving, Pierre Munroe, ed. *The Life and Letters of Washington Irving.* 4 vols. New York: Putnam, 1862-64; Detroit: Gale Research Co., 1967. Also in *Microbook Library* [601]. Papers of Tyler's appointee as minister to Spain.

517. Jackson, Donald, and Mary Lee Spence, eds. *The Expeditions of John Charles Frémont.* 3 vols. Urbana: University of Illinois Press, 1977-80. The most scholarly edition on Frémont's expeditions during the Tyler administration; Volume 1 covers Frémont's 1838-44 travels.

518. Jarves, James Jackson. *History of the Hawaiian Islands or Sandwich Islands, Embracing Their Antiquities, Mythology, Legends, Discovery by Europeans in the Sixteenth Century, Re-Discovery by Cook, with Their Civil, Religious, and Political History, from the Earliest Traditionary Period to the Year 1846.* Boston: J. Munroe & Co., 1844; Honolulu: H. M. Whitney, 1872. Provides some discussion of American trade with Hawaii.

519. Jay, William. *The Creole Case, and Mr. Webster's Despatch, with the Comments of the* New-York American. New York: New-York American, 1842. Also in *Legal Treatises* [606] and *Selected Americana* [602]. A jurist actively involved in antislavery and other reform movements, discusses slavery and slave trade.

520. Jollivet, Adolphe. *Documents Americains, Annexion du Texas, Emancipation de Noirs, Politique de l'Angleterre.* Paris: De Bruneau, 1845. Also in *Texas* [607] and *Selected Americana* [602].

521. Jones, Anson. *Memoranda and Official Correspondence Relating to the Republic of Texas.* New York: n.p., 1859.

522. Julian, George W. "Political Recollections and Notes." *International Review* 12 (April 1882): 325-34. Recalls events of the presidential campaign of 1840 and discusses briefly the political views of Harrison and Tyler, the music of the campaign, and the growing influence of abolitionism during the first Whig incumbency.

523. Julian, George W. *Political Recollections, 1840 to 1872.* Chicago: Jansen, McClurg & Company, 1884; Miami, Fla.: Mnemosyne Publishing Co., 1969; New York: Negro Universities Press, 1970. Also in *Microbook Library* [601].

524. Kentucky. *Commissioners to the Peace Conference at Washington, February 1861. Report of the Kentucky Commissioners to the Late Peace Conference Held at Washington City, Made to the Legislature of Kentucky.* Frankfort: Yeoman Office, 1861.

525. Lamar, Mirabeau Buonaparte. *Address of His Excellency, Mirabeau B. Lamar, to the Citizens of Santa Fe.* Austin: Austin City Gazette Office, [1841?]. Also in *Texas*

[607]. An appeal for the union of Texas and New Mexico issued at the time of the Santa Fe expedition.

526. Lamar, Mirabeau Buonaparte. *Letter of Gen. Mirabeau B. Lamar, Ex-President of Texas, on the Subject of Annexation, Addressed to Several Citizens of Macon, Geo.* Savannah: T. Purse, 1844. Also in *Selected Americana* [602] and *Texas* [607].

527. Lawrence, William R., ed. *Extracts from the Diary and Correspondence of the Late Amos Lawrence, with a Brief Account of Some of the Incidents in His Life.* Boston: Gould and Lincoln, 1855; New York: Sheldon, Lamport & Blakeman, 1856. Offers contemporary insights into the Boston and Massachusetts scenes, as well as national political and economic development.

528. "Letter of C. W. Gooch to President Martin Van Buren, 1835." *John P. Branch Historical Papers of Randolph-Macon College* 3 (1911): 255-62.

529. *Letters and Other Writings of James Madison.* 4 vols. Philadelphia: J. B. Lippincott & Co., 1865, 1867; New York: R. Worthington, 1884. Also in *Legal Treatises* [606].

530. *Letters on the Richmond Party, Originally Published in the* Washington Republican *by A Virginian.* Washington: Republican Office, 1823. Also in *Microbook Library* [601]. Disclosed the workings of the Richmond Junto; important for understanding the political structure and basis of power in Virginia.

531. Lucey, William L., ed. "Some Correspondence of the Maine Commissioners Regarding the Webster-Ashburton Treaty." *New England Quarterly* 15 (June 1942): 332-48. Selected 1842 correspondence of Reuel Williams, Edward Kavanagh, John Fairfield, Webster, William P. Preble, John Otis, Edward Kent, D. Farnsworth, and John Anderson, relating to the settlement of the boundary question and the ratification of the treaty.

532. Lucid, Robert F., ed. *The Journals of Richard Henry Dana, Jr.* 3 vols. Cambridge, Mass.: Harvard University Press, 1968. Journal of an author, lawyer, and sailor.

533. Mansfield, Edward Deering. *Personal Memories, Social, Political, and Literary, with Sketches of Many Noted People, 1803-1843.* Cincinnati: R. Clarke & Co., 1879; New York: Arno, 1970. Also in *Microbook Library* [*601*]. Reminiscences by a Cincinnati lawyer and writer.

534. Martineau, Harriet. *Society in America.* 2 vols. New York: Saunders and Otley, 1837; 3 vols. London: Saunders and Otley, 1837, and many other editions and reprints. Also in *Microbook Library* [601] and *Goldsmiths'* [600]. Account of visit to America, 1834-1836, and her observations on Jacksonian society.

535. McCulloch, Hugh. *Addresses, Speeches, Lectures, and Letters upon Various Subjects.* Washington: W. H. Lepley, 1891. Deals mainly with economic conditions.

536. McCulloch, Hugh. *Men and Measures of Half a Century; Sketches and Comments.* New York: C. Scribner's Sons, 1888, 1889; New York: Da Capo Press, 1970.

537. McGrane, Reginald Charles, ed. *The Correspondence of Nicholas Biddle Dealing with National Affairs, 1807-1844.* Boston: Houghton Mifflin Company, 1919; Boston: J. S. Canner, 1966. Also in *Microbook Library* [601]. Excellent, short collection of letters between Tyler administration officials and Nicholas Biddle.

538. Meltzer, Milton, Patricia G. Holland, and Francine Krasno, eds. *Lydia Maria Child: Selected Letters, 1817-1880.* Amherst: University of Massachusetts Press, 1982.

539. Miller, Linus W. *Notes of an Exile to Van Diemen's Land.* Fredonia, N.Y.: W. McKinstry & Co., 1846.

540. Morrow, Josiah. *Life and Speeches of Thomas Corwin: Orator, Lawyer, and Statesman.* Cincinnati: W. H. Anderson, 1896. Also in *Microbook Library* [601].

541. Morse, Edward Lind, ed. *Samuel F. B. Morse: His Letters and Journals.* 2 vols. Boston: Houghton Mifflin Company, 1914; New York: Kraus Reprint Co., 1972; New York: Da Capo Press, 1973. Also in *Microbook Library* [601].

542. Moser, Harold D., Sharon Macpherson, David Hoth, eds. *The Papers of Andrew Jackson.* Knoxville: University of Tennessee Press, 1980–. Five volumes, of a proposed sixteen, to date.

543. Moser, Harold D., Sharon Macpherson, John H. Reinbold, Daniel Feller, eds. *The Papers of Andrew Jackson: Guide and Index to the Microfilm Editions.* Wilmington, Del.: Scholarly Resources, Inc., 1987. Provides guidance in using the Jackson Papers Microfilm Supplement.

544. Nance, Joseph Milton, ed. *Mier Expedition Diary: A Texan Prisoner's Account.* Austin: University of Texas Press, 1978. Diary of Joseph D. McCutchan.

545. Nevins, Allan, ed. *The Diary of Philip Hone, 1828-1851.* 2 vols. New York: Dodd, Mead and Company, 1927; New York: Kraus Reprint, 1969; New York: Arno Press, 1970. Provides insight into and comments on politics, social life, and customs in mid-nineteenth century New York.

546. Nevins, Allan, and Milton Halsey Thomas, eds. *The Diary of George Templeton Strong.* 4 vols. New York: Macmillan, 1952. Also in *Microbook Library* [601]. Volume

1 covers the period 1835-1849 and offers comments on politics and insights into the social life and customs of the mid-nineteenth century.

547. New York. *New York Assembly Documents*, n.p., 1842. No. 2, Document C. Contains primary documents on the McLeod case.

548. New York. Commissioners to the Peace Convention. *Majority Report of the Commissioners to the Peace Convention*. Albany: n.p., 1861.

549. Nichols, Thomas L. *Forty Years of American Life*. 2 vols. London: J. Maxwell and Company, 1864; London: Longmans, Green and Co., 1874; New York: Negro Universities Press, 1968. Also in *Microbook Library* [601]. Discusses campaign of 1840.

550. Niven, John, et al., eds. *The Salmon P. Chase Papers*. Kent: Kent State University Press, 1993. 1 vol. to date. Chase journals, 1829-1872.

551. *Official Journal of the Conference Convention Held at Washington City, February, 1861*. Washington: M'Gill & Witheros, 1861. Also in *Selected Americana* [602] and *Microbook Library* [601].

552. Palmer, Beverly Wilson. *Guide and Index to the Papers of Charles Sumner*. Alexandria, Va.: Chadwyck-Healey, Inc., 1988. Guide to the microfilm publication.

553. Parker, C. S., ed. *Sir Robert Peel, from His Private Papers*. 3 vols. London: J. Murray, 1891-99.

554. Pierce, Edward Lillie, ed. *Memoir and Letters of Charles Sumner*. 4 vols. Boston: Roberts Brothers, 1877, 1893; London: Sampson, Low, Marston, 1878; New York: Arno Press, 1969. Also in *Legal Treatises* [606].

555. *Proceedings and Debates of the Virginia State Convention of 1829-1830*. Richmond: S. Shepherd, 1830; New York: Da Capo Press, 1971.

556. *Proceedings of the Republican Convention Held in Suffolk*. n.p., 1837. Provides background to the political struggle in Virginia over the subtreasury system.

557. Quaife, Milo Milton, ed. *The Diary of James K. Polk during his Presidency, 1845 to 1849*. 4 vols. Chicago: A. C. McClurg & Co., 1910; New York: Kraus Reprint, 1970. Also in *Microbook Library* [601]. Useful for tracing the annexation of Texas and the Mexican War following Tyler's administration; has some discussion of investigation into Webster's alleged misconduct as Tyler's Secretary of State.

558. Rhode Island. *Commissioners to the Peace Conference at Washington. Report Made to the General Assembly of the State of Rhode Island, at Their January Session, 1861 ...* . Providence: Cooke & Danielson, 1861.

559. Richards, Laura E., ed. *Letters and Journals of Samuel Gridley Howe.* 2 vols. Boston: D. Estes & Company, 1909; New York: AMS Press, 1973. Papers of a Massachusetts reformer, promoter of public schools, and abolitionist.

560. Robertson, George. *Scrap Book on Law and Politics, Men and Times.* Lexington, Ky.: A. W. Elder, 1855. Also in *Microbook Library* **[601]**. Mainly a collection of speeches dealing with Kentucky and national politics.

561. Robertson, Nellie Armstrong, and Dorothy Riker, eds. *The John Tipton Papers.* 3 vols. Indianapolis: Indiana Historical Bureau, 1942. Papers of an Indiana politician of the Middle Period.

562. Rowland, Dunbar, ed. *Jefferson Davis, Constitutionalist: His Letters, Papers, and Speeches.* 10 vols. Jackson: Mississippi Department of Archives and History, 1923; New York: AMS Press, 1973. Also in *Microbook Library* **[601]**.

563. Sanderson, Charles R., ed. *The Arthur Papers, Being the Canadian Papers, Mainly Confidential, Private, and Demi-Official of Sir George Arthur.* 3 vols. Toronto: Toronto Public Library, 1943-1959.

564. Scott, Nancy N. *A Memoir of Hugh Lawson White, Judge of the Supreme Court of Tennessee, Member of the Senate of the United States, etc.*. Philadelphia: Lippincott & Co., 1856.

565. Scott, Winfield. *Memoirs of Lieut.-General Winfield Scott, LL.D., Written by Himself.* 2 vols. New York: Sheldon & Company, 1864; Freeport, N.Y.: Books for Libraries Press, 1970. Also in *Selected Americana* **[602]**.

566. Seward, Frederick W., ed. *William H. Seward: An Autobiography from 1801 to 1834, with a Memoir of His Life, and Selections from his Letters, 1831-1846.* New York: Derby & Miller, 1891. Important for understanding New York politics during the Tyler administration.

567. Sibley, Marilyn McAdams, ed. *Samuel H. Walker's Account of the Mier Expedition.* Austin: Texas State Historical Association, 1978.

568. Sioussat, St. George L., ed. "The Accident on Board the U.S.S. *Princeton,* February 28, 1844: A Contemporary News-Letter." *Pennsylvania History,* July 1937. Prints and annotates letter from George Sykes, congressman from New Jersey, to his sister Ann

Sykes, March 5-20, 1844, describing accident on ship and its aftermath; accident forced second reorganization of Tyler's cabinet.

569. Sioussat, St. George L., ed. "Letters of James K. Polk to Andrew J. Donelson, 1843-1848." *Tennessee Historical Magazine* 3 (March 1917): 51-73. Discusses Tyler's candidacy in 1844 and various efforts to secure his withdrawal from the campaign.

570. Sioussat, St. George L., ed. "Papers of Major John P. Heiss of Nashville." *Tennessee Historical Magazine* 2 (June 1916): 137-49. Includes an important 1842 letter, Robert Tyler to Heiss, October 6, written on behalf of the president, asserting that Tyler is a "pure Republican," second only to Jackson among those living in promoting "Jeffersonian principles."

571. Sioussat, St. George L., ed. "Selected Letters, 1844-1845, from the Donelson Papers." *Tennessee Historical Magazine* 3 (June 1917): 134-62. Prints letter from Andrew Jackson to John Y. Mason, August 1, 1844, praising Mason's "real republican[ism]" and suggesting that Tyler be advised to withdraw from the presidential campaign.

572. Southerner. *A Reply to the Letter of the Hon. Langdon Cheves ... .* Charleston: n.p., 1844. Also in *Texas* [607]. Discussion of Texas annexation.

573. Sparks, Jared. "The Treaty of Washington." *North American Review* 56 (April 1843): 452-96. Reviews recent publications on the treaty and negotiations.

574. Stapp, William Preston. *The Prisoners of Perote, Containing a Journal Kept by the Author, Who Was Captured by the Mexicans, at Mier, December 25, 1842, and Released from Perote, May 16, 1844.* Philadelphia: G. B. Zieber and Company, 1845; Austin: Steck Company, 1935; Austin: University of Texas Press, 1977. Also in *Microbook Library* [601] and *Texas* [607].

575. Stevens, George B., and W. Fisher Markwick, eds. *The Life, Letters, and Journals of the Rev. and Hon. Peter Parker, M.D., Missionary, Physician, Diplomatist ...* Boston: Congregational Sunday-School and Publishing Society, 1896; Wilmington, Del.: Scholarly Resources, 1972.

576. Strohm, Isaac, ed. *Speeches of Thomas Corwin, with a Sketch of His Life.* Dayton, Ohio: W. F. Comley & Co., 1859.

577. Sumner, Charles. *The Works of Charles Sumner.* 15 vols. Boston: Lee and Shepard, 1870-1873. Also in *Microbook Library* [601] and *Legal Treatises* [606].

578. Taliaferro, John. *To the Voters of the Congressional District in the State of Virginia, Composed of the Counties of Westmoreland, Richmond, Northumberland,*

Lancaster, King George, Stafford, and Prince William. n. p., 1841. Dated Washington, January 15; address discusses recent national and local elections.

579. Tallmadge, Daniel Bryant. *Review of the Opinion of Judge Cowen, of the Supreme Court of the State of New-York, in the Case of Alexander McLeod*. New York: T. Allen, 1841.

580. *Texas: Proceedings of Citizens of Prince George County, Virginia, on the Subject of Reannexing Texas to the United States*. Washington: Blair & Rives, 1844.

581. Thompson, Richard W. *Recollections of Sixteen Presidents, from Washington to Lincoln*. Indianapolis: Bowen-Merritt Company, 1894. Denounces Tyler for his strong states rights views.

582. Thompson, Waddy. *Letter of General Waddy Thompson, upon the Annexation of Texas: Addressed to the Editors of the* National Intelligencer. Washington: Gales and Seaton, 1844. Also in *Texas* [607].

583. Thompson, Waddy. *Recollections of Mexico*. New York: Wiley and Putnam, 1846, 1847. Also in *Microbook Library* [601] and *Goldsmiths'* [600]. Discusses efforts to secure release of Santa Fe prisoners after Tyler appointed him to the mission in 1842; discusses Webster's instructions to Thompson.

584. Tuckerman, Bayard, ed. *The Diary of Philip Hone, 1828-1851*. New York: Dodd, Mead, and Company, 1889, 1910. Also in *Microbook Library* [601]. Provides commentary on politics and on social life and customs in mid-nineteenth century.

585. [Tyler, Lyon Gardiner?, ed]. "Correspondence of Judge Tucker." *William and Mary College Quarterly Historical Magazine*, Ser. 1, 12 (October 1903): 84-95; 12 (January 1904): 142-44. Correspondence of Nathaniel Beverley Tucker discusses Virginia and national politics, 1833-37, and the Tyler administration, 1841-43, focusing on Webster's attitude toward the administration, cabinet discussions, and the selection of a minister to Mexico.

586. Tyler, Robert. *A Reply to the* Democratic Review. New York: n.p., 1845. Responds to a critique of his father's presidential administration.

587. U.S. Congress. House. *Select Committee Appointed to Inquire as to the Violation of "the Seal of Confidence of the State Department, and How Information was Obtained by Charles J. Ingersoll From Secret Papers and Accounts in that Department, Which the President Had Declined to Communicate to This House, in Answer to a Resolution and Request of the House." Violation of the Seal of Confidence of the State Department*. House Report No. 686, 29th Cong., 1st Sess. (Serial 490). Attempts to answer question of how Ingersoll acquired information on which he based his charges against Webster in 1846.

588. Van Buren, Martin. *Letter of Mr. Van Buren: Texas.* Columbus, Ohio: n.p.: 1844. Also in *Texas* [607].

589. Wallace, Sarah Agnes. "'Letters of the Presidentess': Julia Gardiner Tyler, 1844-1845." *Daughters of the American Revolution Magazine* 87 (May 1953): 641-46. Discusses marriage of John Tyler and Julia Gardiner, June 26, 1844, in New York.

590. Washburn, E. B., ed. *The Edwards Papers, Being a Portion of the Collection of the Letters, Papers, and Manuscripts of Ninian Edwards, Presented to the Chicago Historical Society, October 16th, 1883 ...* Chicago: Fergus Printing Co., 1884.

591. Weaver, Herbert, and Everett Wayne Cutler, eds. *Correspondence of James K. Polk.* 8 vols. to date. Nashville: Vanderbilt University Press, 1969– . Covers through the election of 1844.

592. West, Elizabeth Howard, comp. *Calendar of the Papers of Martin Van Buren, Prepared from the Original Manuscripts in the Library of Congress, Division of Manuscripts.* Washington: Government Printing Office, 1910.

593. West, Lucy Fisher, ed. *Guide to the Microfilm Edition of the James Buchanan Papers at the Historical Society of Pennsylvania.* Philadelphia: Historical Society of Pennsylvania, 1974.

594. Wheaton, Henry. *Enquiry into the Validity of the British Claim to a Right of Visitation and Search of American Vessels Suspected to be Engaged in the African Slave Trade.* London: n.p., 1842; Philadelphia: Lea & Blanchard, 1842; New York: Negro Universities Press, 1969. Also in *Microbook Library* [601].

595. Williams, Amelia W., and Eugene C. Barker, eds. *The Writings of Sam Houston.* 8 vols. Austin: University of Texas Press, 1938-1943; Austin: Jenkins Publishing Co., 1970. Also in *Microbook Library* [601]. The most complete edition of the Houston papers.

596. Winkler, Ernest William, ed. *Secret Journals of the Senate, Republic of Texas, 1836-1845.* Austin: Austin Printing Company, 1911.

597. Wise, John S. *Recollections of Thirteen Presidents.* New York: Doubleday, 1906; Freeport, N.Y.: Books for Libraries Press, 1968. Also in *Microbook Library* [601]. Reminisces about Tyler.

2. Microforms

a) General Reference Collections

598. *Amistad (Schooner) Case Collection, 1839-1868.* Amistad Research Center, Dillard University, New Orleans. Collection, six reels of microfilm, of materials scattered throughout the United States relating to the case; includes some Tyler documents and documents of other executive officers of his administration.

599. Derfler, Lisa A., and Duane R. Bogenschneider, eds. *Pamphlets in American History: A Bibliographic Guide to the Microfilm Collection.* Sanford, N.C.: Microfilming Corporation of America, 1977-84.

600. *Goldsmiths'-Kress Library of Economic Literature: A Consolidated Guide to Segments I and II of the Microfilm Collections.* 4 vols. to date. Woodbridge, Conn.: Research Publications, Inc., 1976–. Provides access to the economic and business literature in the collection.

601. Library Resources, Inc. *The Microbook Library of American Civilization.* 5 vols. Chicago: Library Resources, 1971-72. Provides access to the microfiche collection by the same name, through author catalog, title catalog, subject catalog, shelflist, and biblioguide.

602. Lost Cause Press. *Selected Americana from Sabin's Dictionary of Books Relating to America, from Its Discovery to the Present Time: A Catalogue of the Microfiche Edition to 1985.* Louisville, Ky.: Lost Cause Press, 1985. Useful for accessing the publications of the Lost Cause Press; Sabin collection sometimes referred to as *Bibliotheca Americana.*

603. Microfilming Corporation of America. *Pamphlets in American History.* [Sanford, N.C.]: Microfilming Corporation of America, [1979]. 5,193 microfiche, covering biography, Indians, revolutionary war, etc.

604. Records of the Supreme Court of the United States, Record Group 267, National Archives, Washington. M408. 20 rolls; M216. 27 rolls; M215. 41 rolls; M217. 4 rolls.

605. Records of the United States Senate, Record Group 46, National Archives, Washington. *Territorial Papers* ... , M200. 20 rolls.

606. Research Publications, Inc. *Nineteenth-Century Legal Treatises.* Woodbridge, Conn,: Research Publications, 1984–. Microfiche collection of materials.

607. *Texas as Province and Republic, 1795-1845.* Woodbridge, Conn.: Research Publications, 1979. Thirty-nine reels of microfilm of the studies included in Streeter's

Bibliography of Texas; includes material, Texas imprints, Mexican imprints, and United States and European imprints relating to Texas, many from the Tyler presidency.

608. University Microfilms International. *An Index to the Presidential Election Campaign Biographies, 1824-1972.* Ann Arbor, Mich.: University Microfilms International, 1981. Provides access to the microfiche collection.

b) Members of Cabinet

George Edmund Badger, Secretary of the Navy

609. Naval Records Collection of the Office of Naval Records and Library, Record Group 45, National Archives, Washington. *Letters Sent,* M149. M441. M472. M480. M205. M209. M124. M125. M89. M147. M148. M517. M518.

610. Records of the Bureau of Yards and Docks, Record Group 71, National Archives, Washington. *Annual Reports of the Department of the Navy, 1822-1866,* M1099.

John Bell, Secretary of War

611. *Bell, John, Papers.* Manuscript Division, Library of Congress, Washington. Small collection, one container, available on microfilm.

612. Records of the Adjutant General's Office, Record Group 94, National Archives, Washington. *Registers, Letters Sent and Received,* M711. M565. M567.

613. Records of the Bureau of Indian Affairs, Record Group 75, National Archives, Washington. *Letters Received and Sent,* M18. M21. M234. M348. M574. M856.

614. Records of the Headquarters of the Army, Record Group 108, National Archives, Washington. *Letters Sent,* M587.

615. Records of the Office of the Chief of Engineers, Record Group 77, National Archives, Washington. *Letters Sent,* M66. M505. M506. M1113.

616. Records of the Office of the Quartermaster General, Record Group 92, National Archives, Washington. *Letters,* M745.

617. Records of the Office of the Secretary of War, Record Group 107, National Archives, Washington. *Registers and Letters,* M22. M222. M6. M7. M221. M220. M127.

John Jordan Crittenden, Attorney General

618. *Crittenden, John Jordan, Papers.* Manuscript Division, Library of Congress, Washington. The largest collection of Crittenden papers, 1782-1888, fourteen reels. Access to the papers is provided by Feamster, Claudius Newman, comp. *Calendar of the Papers of John Jordan Crittenden.* Washington: Government Printing Office, 1913.

619. General Records of the Department of Justice, Record Group 60, National Archives, Washington. *Letters Sent,* M699.

620. General Records of the Department of Justice, Record Group 60, National Archives, Washington. *U.S. Marshals,* T577. Useful in identifying officials and in studying patronage during Tyler's brief presidency.

John Caldwell Calhoun, Secretary of War

621. *Calhoun, John Caldwell, Papers.* Manuscript Division, Library of Congress, Washington. Collection covering years 1819-1850, plus six reels of microfilm of Calhoun manuscripts from other Library of Congress collections.

Thomas Ewing, Secretary of the Treasury

622. *Ewing, Thomas, Sr., Papers.* University of Notre Dame, South Bend. Collection of 121 boxes; six reels. Research is eased by *Guide to the Microfilm Edition of the Thomas Ewing, Sr., Papers, University of Notre Dame Archives.* Notre Dame, 1967.

623. General Records of the Department of the Treasury, Record Group 56, National Archives, Washington. *Letters Sent and Received,* M415. M733. M174. M737. M735. M726. M175.

624. Records of the Bureau of Land Management, Record Group 49, National Archives, Washington. *Letters Sent by the General Land Office,* M25. M27.

Francis Granger, Postmaster General

625. Records of the United States Postal Service, Record Group 28, National Archives, Washington. *Appointments,* M841.

Daniel Webster, Secretary of State

626. General Records of the Department of State, Record Group 59, National Archives, Washington. *Despatches from U.S. Consuls,* T186. T373. M450. M286. T190. M101. M9. T191. T583. T192. T378. M289. T235. M308. T194. T195. T196. T197. T463. T223. T224. T415. T475. T417. T588. M459. T477. T342. T600. T420. M139. T478. T226. T1.

T344. T479. T228. T346. M462. T422. T567. T229. M76. T383. T199. T200. T566. T201. T202. T203. T204.

627. General Records of the Department of State, Record Group 59, National Archives, Washington. *Despatches from U.S. Consuls*, M161. T205. T151. T570. T64. T336. T206. T207. T276. T208. T337. T209. M284. T469. T211. T20. T212. T213. T127. M144. T31. M84. T394. T474. T214. T215. T396. M154. T180. M141. T168. T216. T169.

628. General Records of the Department of State, Record Group 59, National Archives, Washington. *Notes from ... Legations in the United States*, M47. M48. M194. T795. M49. M50. T34. M73. M51. M52. T810. M53. M58. T808. T160. M54. T953. M56. T802. M57. M39. M201. M55. M59. M60. T809. T804. T93.

629. General Records of the Department of State, Record Group 59, National Archives, Washington. *Miscellaneous Letters*, M179; *Communications from Special Agents*, M37; *U.S. Diplomatic Officers*, M586; *U.S. Consular Officers*, M587; *Letters of Application and Recommendation During the Administrations of Martin Van Buren, William Henry Harrison, and John Tyler, 1837-1845*, M687; *Domestic Letters*, M40; *Diplomatic Instructions*, M77.

630. General Records of the Department of State, Record Group 59, National Archives, Washington. *Despatches from U.S. Consuls*, M303. M465. T115. M304. T61. T690. T153. T242. T699. T148. M466. T303. T446. T447. M146. M153. M183. T243. M468. T217. T218. M455. T62. T398. T220. M281. M159. M287. T399. M296. M138. M71. T261. M485. T172. T145. T425. T231. T232. M72. T234. T233. T428. T485. M81. T431. T350. M301. T483. M199. T427. T434. T55. T56. T351. T432. M464. T238. T239. T59. T230. T443. M173. T490. M143. T45. M23. T357. T358. M100. M446. T359. T327. T181. T27. M481. T329. T362. T330. T511. T333. T121. T364. M449. T49. T366. T367. T368. T369. T262. T183. M168. T164. T184. T185. M70.

631. General Records of the Department of State, Record Group 59, National Archives, Washington. *Despatches from U.S. Ministers*, M69. T157. M193. M121. M219. M10. M92. T33. M41. M34. M44. M30. T30. M90. M97. M42. T52. M43. M35. M31. M45. T728. M46. M79.

632. *Papers of Daniel Webster, 1800-1895*. Library of Congress, Washington. Eight reels; most materials reproduced on the Dartmouth College microfilm edition.

633. Wiltse, Charles M., ed. *Microfilm Edition of the Papers of Daniel Webster*. Ann Arbor, Mich.: University Microfilms in collaboration with Dartmouth College Library, 1971. 41 reels; the most comprehensive collection of Webster's papers.

634. Wiltse, Charles M., ed. *Guide and Index to the Microfilm Edition of the Papers of Daniel Webster*. Ann Arbor: University Microfilms, 1971. Discusses briefly the history of the Webster papers, their publication history, the major Webster collections of manuscripts; provides an abbreviated Webster chronology and bibliography; brief discussions of the documents included on the microfilm, and an exhaustive name and selective subject index to the microfilm collection; collection incorporates most of the material on the Library of Congress microfilm collection.

c) Members of Congress

John Quincy Adams, Massachusetts Representative

635. *Adams Family Papers.* Massachusetts Historical Society, Boston. A major collection for any study of early nineteenth-century America.

John Macpherson Berrien, Georgia Senator

636. *Berrien, John Macpherson, Papers.* Southern Historical Collection, University of North Carolina, Chapel Hill. Collection of about 550 items, available on 3 reels of microfilm. Papers contain correspondence with most political leaders of the Tyler presidency, including Tyler and his cabinet. James Patton and Margaret Lee Neustadt, eds. *The John Macpherson Berrien Papers in the Southern Historical Collection of the University of North Carolina Library* (Chapel Hill: University of North Carolina Photographic Service, 1967) is helpful in researching the collection.

James Buchanan, Pennsylvania Senator

637. *Buchanan, James, Papers.* Historical Society of Pennsylvania, Philadelphia. The largest of the Buchanan collections, about 25,000 items. Sixty reels. Lucy Fisher West, ed. *Guide to the Microfilm Edition of the James Buchanan Papers at the Historical Society of Pennsylvania* (Philadelphia: Historical Society of Pennsylvania, 1974), is helpful in researching the collection.

Henry Clay, Kentucky Senator

638. *Clay Family Papers.* Manuscript Division, Library of Congress, Washington. The largest of the Clay collections, consists of about 20,000 items.

George Coke Dromgoole, Virginia Representative

639. *Dromgoole Family Papers.* Southern Historical Collection, University of North Carolina at Chapel Hill. Important collection of a Democratic politician, merchant, minister, and planter of Virginia, with considerable discussion of national and state politics, including the Tyler administration.

Millard Fillmore, New York Representative

640. *Fillmore, Millard, Papers.* Buffalo Historical Society, Buffalo, N.Y. Large collection of manuscripts helpful in studying mid-nineteenth-century America.

641. Severance, Frank H., ed. *Millard Fillmore Papers.* 2 vols. Buffalo, N.Y.: Buffalo Historical Society, 1907; New York: Kraus Reprint Co., 1970. Also available in *Microbook Library* **[601]**. A convenient guide to the large Buffalo Historical Society collection of Fillmore Papers.

Robert Mercer Taliaferro Hunter, Virginia Representative

642. *Hunter, Robert Mercer Taliaferro, Papers.* Alderman Library, University of Virginia, Charlottesville. One of the larger collections of Hunter papers, about 2,700 items of professional, personal, business, and political papers. Thirteen reels.

Andrew Johnson, Tennessee Representative

643. *Johnson, Andrew, Papers.* Manuscript Division, Library of Congress, Washington, D.C. The largest collection of Johnson papers, available on fifty-five rolls.

Franklin Pierce, New Hampshire Senator

644. *Pierce, Franklin, Papers.* Manuscript Division, Library of Congress, Washington. Largest collection of Pierce materials; seven reels.

Robert Barnwell Rhett, South Carolina Representative

645. *Rhett, Robert Barnwell, Papers.* South Carolina Historical Society, Charleston. Collection, 23 microfiche, consists mainly of correspondence, business and legal papers.

Nathaniel Pitcher Tallmadge, New York Senator

646. *Tallmadge, Nathaniel Pitcher, Papers.* State Historical Society of Wisconsin, Madison. A small but important collection of Tyler's appointee to the governorship of Wisconsin Territory; deals with New York, Wisconsin, and national politics, and is particularly strong for the Van Buren and Tyler presidencies; a few Tyler items.

Robert J. Walker, Mississippi Senator

647. *Walker, Robert J., Papers.* Manuscript Division, Library of Congress. Three reels.

d) Supreme Court Justices

John McLean

648. *McLean, John, Papers*. Manuscript Division, Library of Congress. Large collection of an Ohio congressman, Postmaster General under John Quincy Adams, and Supreme Court justice; important collection for background of Whig politics (available on 18 rolls).

e) Journalists

Duff Green

649. *Green, Duff, Papers*. Southern Historical Collection, University of North Carolina, Chapel Hill. Collection contains ten Tyler items, 1834-46. Papers of an important journalist, politician, and industrial promoter.

Edmund Ruffin

650. *Ruffin, Edmund, Papers*. Virginia Historical Society. Contains diary, 1843, incidents of his life, written in 1851 and 1854-55, essays and speeches, a few Tyler items.

f) Others

651. Allis, Frederick S., Jr., and Phyllis R. Girouard, eds. *Microfilm Edition of the Papers of Edward Everett*. Boston: Massachusetts Historical Society, 1972. 54 rolls of the collection at the Massachusetts Historical Society; important collection of papers of the U.S. minister to Great Britain during the Tyler administration and a leading Whig politician.

652. Boles, John B., ed. *The William Wirt Papers*. Baltimore: Maryland Historical Society, 1971. 24 reels. John B. Boles, *A Guide to the Microfilm Edition of the William Wirt Papers* (Baltimore: Maryland Historical Society, 1971), facilitates use of the collection.

653. *Campbell, David, Papers*. William R. Perkins Library, Duke University, Durham. An important collection of a Virginia Conservative Democrat and governor of the state.

654. *Harrison, William Henry, Papers*. Manuscript Division, Library of Congress, Washington. A small collection of approximately 1,000 pieces, the largest body of Harrison's papers that survived a fire in 1858, plus a few other items that have since turned up elsewhere; essential for any study of Harrison or the short Harrison administration.

655. Holland, Patricia G., and Milton Meltzer, eds. *The Collected Correspondence of Lydia Maria Child, 1817-1880*. Millwood, N.Y.: KTO Microforms, 1979. Available on 97 microfiche. Papers of a novelist and leading abolitionist.

656. *Jackson, Andrew, Papers*. Library of Congress, Washington. 78 rolls. Papers of the seventh president. Access to the collection is eased by John J. McDonough, *Index to the Andrew Jackson Papers*. Washington, D.C.: U.S. Government Printing Office, 1967.

657. *Monroe, James, Papers*. Library of Congress, Washington. Eleven reels.

658. Moser, Harold D., Sharon Macpherson, John H. Reinbold, and Daniel Feller, eds. *The Papers of Andrew Jackson: A Microfilm Supplement*. Wilmington, Del.: Scholarly Resources, Inc. 1986. Thirty-nine reels; papers not available on other microfilm publications in 1986; includes several exchanges of correspondence between Tyler and Jackson.

659. *Sumner, Charles, Papers, 1811-1874*. Alexandria, Va.: Chadwyck-Healey, 1988. 85 reels; 26,000 letters from 200 repositories.

660. *Taylor, Zachary, Papers*. Library of Congress, Washington. 2 reels.

661. *Van Buren, Martin, Papers*. Library of Congress, Washington. 35 reels. Reels 22-27 particularly useful for the Tyler administration.

E. CONTEMPORARY NEWSPAPERS

The following list is but a brief compendium of the major newspapers necessary for evaluating and discussing Tyler and the Tyler administration.

662. Abingdon, Va., *Banner*
663. Abingdon, Va., *Little Tennessean*
664. *Albany Evening Journal*
665. *Albany Argus*
666. *Baltimore Patriot*
667. Baltimore, *Sun*
668. Bangor, Me., *Bangor Whig*
669. *Boston Atlas*
670. *Boston Courier*

671. *Boston Daily Advertiser*
672. Boston, *Herald Traveler*
673. Boston, *Liberator*
674. Boston, *Semi-Weekly Advertiser*
675. Boston, *Times*
676. Boston, *Transcript*
677. Charleston, S.C., *Mercury*
678. Cincinnati, Ohio, *Enquirer*
679. *Cincinnati Republican*
680. Clarksburg, [W.] Va., *Harrison Republican*
681. Columbia, S.C., *Southern Chronicle*
682. Columbus, *Ohio People's Press*
683. Concord, *New Hampshire Courier*
684. Concord, *New Hampshire Patriot*
685. *Detroit Daily Advertiser*
686. Frankfort, Ky., *Campaign of 1844*
687. Hartford, *Connecticut Courant*
688. Helena, Ark., *Southern Shield*
689. Huntsville, Ala., *Southern Advocate*
690. Indianapolis, *Indiana Journal*
691. *Knoxville Reporter*
692. *Lexington Gazette*
693. Little Rock, *Arkansas Gazette*
694. *Louisville Journal*
695. *Milwaukee Sentinel*
696. *Mobile Daily Advertiser & Chronicle*
697. Montgomery, *Alabama Journal*
698. Nashville, *Republican Banner*
699. Nashville, *Spirit of '76*
700. Nashville *Star Spangled Banner*
701. Natchez, *Courier*
702. *New Haven Palladium*
703. New Orleans, *Bee*
704. New York, *American*
705. *New York Commercial Advertiser*
706. *New York Courier and Enquirer*
707. *New York Evening Post*
708. New York, *Herald*
709. *New York Journal of Commerce*
710. New York, *Tribune*
711. Petersburg, Va., *Bank Reformer*
712. Philadelphia, *Pennsylvania Inquirer*
713. Philadelphia, *Public Ledger*

714. *Portland Daily Advertiser*
715. *Portsmouth Journal*
716. *Providence Daily Journal*
717. *Richmond Compiler*
718. Richmond, *Crisis*
719. Richmond *Enquirer*
720. Richmond, *Yeoman*
721. *Richmond Whig*
722. St. Louis, *Commercial Bulletin*
723. Savannah, *Georgian*
724. Springfield, *Illinois Republican*
725. Tuscaloosa, *Independent Monitor*
726. *Wheeling Times*
727. Warrenton, Va., *Jeffersonian*
728. Washington *Daily Madisonian*
729. *Washington Globe*
730. Washington, *Kendall's Expositor*
731. *Washington National Intelligencer*
732. Washington, *National Journal*
733. Washington, *Republican*
734. Washington, *United States Telegraph*
735. Washington, Ark., *Washington Telegraph*
736. Wilmington, *Delaware Advertiser*
737. Wilmington, *Delaware State Gazette & American Watchman*

II

Writing and Speeches of John Tyler

A. CONTEMPORARY PUBLICATIONS

738. *An Address, Delivered Before the Literary Societies of the University of Virginia on the Anniversary of the Declaration of Independence by the State of Virginia, June 29th, 1850*. Charlottesville: J. Alexander, 1850.

739. *An Address Delivered Before the Two Literary Societies of Randolph-Macon College, June 19, 1838*. Richmond: J. C. Walker, 1838. Also published in *Southern Literary Messenger* 5 (1839): 20-25.

740. *Address Delivered by His Exc'y John Tyler and the Poem Recited by St. George Tucker, Esq., on the 166th Anniversary of the College of William and Mary in Virginia*. Williamsburg, Va.: n.p., 1859.

741. "The Dead of the Cabinet." A Lecture Delivered at Petersburg, on the 24th of April, 1856. *Southern Literary Messenger* 23 (August 1856): 81-93. Reminiscences about executive officers who served during his administration.

742. *Documents Relating to the Affairs of Rhode Island*. n.p., 1842. Contains letter from Tyler to Samuel W. King, Governor of Rhode Island.

743. *Documents Submitted to the House of Representatives, Relating to the Defence of the State of Georgia Against the Indians in Florida*. Washington, n.p., 1842. Documents relate to the Second Seminole War.

744. "Early Times of Virginia—William and Mary College." *De Bow's Review* 27 (July 1859): 136-49. Speech on history of the college.

745. *A Funeral Oration on the Death of Thomas Jefferson, Delivered at the Request of the Citizens of Richmond, on the 11th July, 1826.* Richmond: Shepherd & Pollard, 1826.

746. *Lecture Delivered Before the Maryland Institute for the Promotion of the Mechanic Arts, March 20, 1855.* Baltimore: J. Murphy & Co., 1855. Topic for the occasion was the "prominent characters and incidents of our history from 1812 to 1836."

747. *Letter of John Tyler, A Senator from the State of Virginia to the Speakers and Members of the General Assembly of Virginia.* Washington: n.p., 1836. Also in *Goldsmiths'* [600]. Responds to instruction of senators to vote to expunge the resolution from the Senate journal censuring Jackson.

748. *Message from the President of the United States, in Answer to a Resolution of the Senate of the 28th of May, 1844.* [Washington]: n.p., 1844. Deals with annexation of Texas to the United States.

749. *Message from the President of the United States Communicating Certain Information in Reply to a Resolution of the Senate of the 22d May, 1844.* [Washington]: n.p.,1844. Transmits a letter from John C. Calhoun to the President, May 30, 1844, relating to the annexation of Texas.

750. *Message from the President of the United States, Communicating ... Copies of Correspondence with the Minister of the United States at France, in Relation to the Annexation of Texas to the United States, December 23, 1844.* Washington: n.p., 1844.

751. *Message from the President of the United States, Communicating ... Information in Relation to the Abuse of the Flag of the United States in Subservience to the African Slave Trade and the Taking Away of Slaves, the Property of Portuguese Subjects, March 14, 1844.* Washington: n.p., 1844.

752. *Message from the President of the United States Communicating, in Compliance with a Resolution of the Senate, Copies of Correspondence in Relation to the Destruction of the Steamboat Caroline.* [Washington]: T. Allen, 1843. Contains the correspondence between Andrew Stevenson and Lord Palmerston, 1841, on the matter.

753. *Message from the President of the United States, Communicating, In Compliance with a Resolution of the Senate, Copies of Correspondence in Relation to the Mutiny on Board the Brig Creole, and the Liberation of Slaves who Were Passengers in the Said Vessel.* Washington: n.p., 1842. Includes transmittal letters from Tyler and Webster, correspondence with the consul, John F. Bacon, at Nassau, Bahamas.

754. *Message from the President of the United States, Communicating, In Compliance with a Resolution of the Senate, Copies of the Proceedings of the Commissioner*

Appointed to Run the Boundary Line between the United States and the Republic of Texas, 1842. Washington: Thomas Allen, 1842.

755. *Message from the President of the United States, Returning, with His Objections, the Bill "To Provide for the Better Collection, Safe-Keeping, and Disbursement of the Public Revenue, by Means of a Corporation, to be Styled the Fiscal Corporation of the United States," September 9, 1841, to the House of Representatives of the United States.* [Washington]: T. Allen, 1841.

756. *Message from the President of the United States to the Two Houses of Congress, at the Commencement of the First Session of the Twenty-Seventh Congress, June 1, 1841* ... Washington: n.p., 1841. Message to the special congress convened by President Harrison before his death to deal with the economic crisis.

757. *Message from the President of the United States to the Two Houses of Congress, December 6, 1841, at the Commencement of the Second Session of the Twenty-Seventh Congress.* Washington: T. Allen, 1841; other editions printed in Washington by Gales and Seaton and Blair and Rives, 1844.

758. *Message from the President of the United States to the Two Houses of Congress at the Commencement of the Second Session of the Twenty-Eighth Congress, December 3, 1844.* Washington: Blair & Rives, 1844. Deals mainly with the annexation of Texas.

759. *Message from the President of the United States, to the Two Houses of Congress, at the Commencement of the Third Session of the Twentieth Congress.* Washington: Blair and Rives, 1842.

760. *Message from the President of the United States, Transmitting Copies of Despatches from the American Minister at the Court of Brazil, Relative to the Slave-Trade, &c.* Washington: Blair & Rives, 1845.

761. *Message from the President of the United States Transmitting Copies of Papers Relative to Certain Fugitive Criminals from Florida.* Washington: n.p., 1844.

762. *Message from the President of the United States Transmitting Laws Passed by the Governor and Legislative Council of Florida, January 19, 1843.* [Washington: n.p., 1843].

763. *Message from the President of the United States Transmitting Report of Secretary of War Relative to Indians Remaining in Florida, January 24, 1844.* Washington: Blair & Rives, 1844.

764. *Message from the President of the United States, Transmitting a Treaty between the United States of America and the Ta Tsing Empire.* [Washington]: n.p., 1845.

765. *Message from the President of the United States, Transmitting, with His Objections, the Bill Entitled "An Act to Incorporate the Subscribers to the Fiscal Bank of the United States." August 16, 1841.* Washington, n.p., 1841.

766. "Oration Delivered at the Celebration of the 250th Anniversary of the English Settlement of Jamestown." *Southern Literary Messenger* 24 (June 1857): 435-55.

767. "Oration delivered by John Tyler, at Yorktown, October 19, 1837." *Southern Literary Messenger* 3 (December 1837): 747-52.

768. *President Tyler's Address. Rochester: Daily Advertiser, 1841.* Broadside contains text of president's speech in Rochester with newspaper comments.

769. *Proclamation [by the Governor of Rhode Island, May 11, 1842].* Newport: n.p., 1842. Broadside prints proclamation by Samuel Ward King and letter of Tyler offering aid should violence develop in Rhode Island during the Dorr Rebellion.

770. *Speech of Hon. John Tyler Delivered March 13th, 1861, in the Virginia State Convention on the Peace Conference Proposition.* n.p., 1861.

771. *Speech of Mr. Tyler, of Virginia, on the Bill to Provide Further for the Collection of Duties on Imports, Delivered in the Senate of the United States, Wednesday, February 6, 1833.* Washington: Duff Green, 1833. Also in *Goldsmiths'* **[600]**.

772. *Speech of Mr. Tyler, of Virginia, on Mr. Tazewell's Motion to Amend the General Appropriation Bill, by Striking Out So Much Thereof as Went to Provide for the Payment of Certain Commissioners Appointed by the President to Negotiate a Treaty with the Porte, In Senate, February 24, 1831.* Washington: Duff Green, 1831. Incorporates some of Tyler's views on executive power.

773. *Speech of Mr. Tyler, of Virginia, on the Subject of Mr. Clay's Resolutions Providing for a Reduction of the Duties on Imports.* Washington: Duff Green, 1832.

774. *Speech on Mr. Clay's Second Resolution on the Removal of the Deposits.* Washington: D. Green, 1834.

775. *Texas Boundaries: Message from the President of the United States, Transmitting a Report from the Secretary of State Relating to the Boundaries of Texas; and Copies of Treaties Subsisting between Texas and the Governments of France and Great Britain, &c., February 4, 1845.* Washington: Blair & Rives, 1845.

776. *Veto—Tariff of Duties, &c.: Message from the President of the United States, Returning to the House of Representatives (in which It Originated) the Bill to Provide Revenue from Imports, and to Change and Modify Existing Laws Imposing Duties on Imports, and for Other Purposes, with Objections.* Washington: n.p., 1842.

777. "Virginia Colonization Society." *African Repository and Colonial Journal*, No. 158 (April 1838): 117-23. Prints Tyler's address as president of the society.

B. EDITED PUBLICATIONS

778. "Foreign Policy of the Presidents." *Current History* 7 (November 1944): 367-73. Prints brief extracts from the inaugural addresses of Harrison (March 4, 1841) and of Tyler (April 9, 1841).

779. *A Selection of Eulogies, Pronounced in the Several States, in Honor of Those Illustrious Patriots and Statesmen, John Adams and Thomas Jefferson.* Hartford: D. F. Robinson & Co., 1826. Prints Tyler's eulogy on Jefferson.

780. Servies, James A., ed. *"Mirads of Loves and Seraphs": A Letter Written by John Tyler to His Friend, George Blow, June 7, 1807.* Williamsburg: Privately printed, 1961. Edition of single letter from the Blow Papers, College of William and Mary, limited to fifty copies.

781. "The Slave Trade, Slavery and Liberia." *Tyler's Quarterly Historical and Genealogical Magazine* 19 (July 1937): 10-29. Prints an excerpt from Tyler's speech before the colonization society in 1834 and discusses Tyler's attitude toward slave trade in the District of Columbia.

III

Biographical Publications

A. GENERAL ACCOUNTS

782. Abbott, John S. C., and Russell H. Conwell. *Lives of the Presidents of the United States of America from Washington to the Present Time ...* Portland: H. Hallett and Co., 1876, 1882; Boston: B. B. Russell, 1876. Laments Tyler's support of the Confederate cause in 1861.

783. Agar, Herbert. *The People's Choice, from Washington to Harding: A Study in Democracy.* Boston: Houghton Mifflin Co., 1933.

784. Armbruster, Maxim Ethan. *The Presidents of the United States: A New Appraisal ...* New York: Horizon Press, 1960, 1963, 1966, 1969, 1973, 1975.

785. Barringer, Paul Brandon, James Mercer Garnett, and Roswell Page. *University of Virginia: Its History, Influence, Equipment and Characteristics, with Biographical Sketches and Portraits of Founders, Benefactors, Officers and Alumni.* 2 vols. New York: Lewis Publishing Co., 1904. Volume 1 provides a brief biographical sketch of Tyler as a founder of the University.

786. Beard, Charles A. *The Presidents in American History.* New York: Julian Messner, 1935, 1946, 1956, 1957, 1961.

787. Brock, Robert Alonzo. *Virginia and Virginians, 1606-1888.* 2 vols. Richmond: H. H. Hardesty, 1888; Spartanburg, S.C.: Reprint Co., 1973. Provides brief biographical sketch and portrait.

788. Bruce, Philip Alexander. *The Virginia Plutarch.* 2 vols. Chapel Hill: University of North Carolina Press, 1929: New York: Russell & Russell, 1971.

789. Chancellor, William Estabrook. *Our Presidents and Their Office, Including Parallel Lives of the Presidents of the People of the United States and of Several Contemporaries, and a History of the Presidency.* New York: Neale Publishing Co., 1912.

790. Chandler, Julian Alvin Carroll, et al., eds. *The South in the Building of the Nation: A History of the Southern States Designed to Record the South's Part in the Making of the American Nation* ... 13 vols. Richmond: Southern Historical Publication Society, 1909-13. Volume 12 contains standard account by William Clayton-Torrence and a facsimile of a letter, February 11, 1834, from Tyler to James Bouldin.

791. Connelly, Thomas L., and Michael D. Senecal, eds. *Almanac of American Presidents, from 1789 to the Present: An Original Compendium of Facts and Anecdotes about Politics and the Presidency in the United States of America.* New York: Facts on File, 1991.

792. Cunliffe, Marcus, et al. *The American Heritage History of the Presidency.* New York: American Heritage Publishing Co., 1968.

793. Cunliffe, Marcus, et al. *American Presidents and the Presidency.* London: Eyre & Spottiswoode, 1969; New York: American Heritage Press, 1972; New York: McGraw-Hill, 1976. Mainly for the popular audience, contains many illustrations.

794. Cunningham, Auburn S., comp. *Everything You Want to Know about the Presidents* ... Chicago: A. C. McClurg & Co., 1931, 1939.

795. DeGregorio, William A. *The Complete Book of U.S. Presidents.* New York: Dembner Books, 1984, 1989; New York: Barricade Books, 1991. Includes short bibliography and synopsis of life, cabinet, and presidential term.

796. DeVries, Julian. *Lives of the Presidents.* Cleveland: World Publishing Co., 1941. Carries sketch by Virginia F. Townsend.

797. Dietz, August. *Presidents of the United States of America: Portraits and Biographies.* Richmond: Dietz Press, 1944.

798. Dunlap, Leslie W. *Our Vice-Presidents and Second Ladies.* Metuchen, N.J.: Scarecrow Press, 1988. Sees as benefits of the Tyler administration—reorganization of Navy, Webster-Ashburton treaty, and annexation of Texas.

799. Durant, John and Alice. *The Presidents of the United States.* New York: A. S. Barnes, 1964.

800. Eggleston, George Cary. "Our Twenty-One Presidents." Part 1: "The First Ten—From Washington to Tyler." *Magazine of American History* 11 (February 1884): 89-109.

801. Freidel, Frank. *Our Country's Presidents*. Washington: National Geographic Society, 1966.

802. Freidel, Frank. *The Presidents of the United States of America*. Washington: White House Historical Office, 1982.

803. Freidel, Frank. "Profiles of the Presidents." *National Geographic Magazine* 127 (January 1965): 80-121. Short coverage of Tyler on pp. 99-101.

804. Gordon, Armistead Churchill. *Virginian Portraits: Essays in Biography*. Staunton, Va.: McClure Co., 1924. Provides a short, favorable biographical sketch.

805. Graff, Henry, ed. *The Presidents: A Reference History*. New York: Charles Scribner's Sons, 1984.

806. Grosvenor, Charles H. *The Book of the Presidents*. Washington: Continental Press, 1902.

807. Kane, Joseph Nathan. *Facts About the Presidents: A Compilation of Biographical and Historical Information*. New York: Pocket Books, 1964; New York: H. W. Wilson, 1959, 1968, 1974, 1981, 1989. Provides brief coverage of Tyler.

808. Lambeth, Harry J. "Lawyers Who Became President." *American Bar Association Journal* 63 (December 1977): 1732-35. Tyler, brief discussion, pp. 1732-33.

809. Logan, Mary Simmerson Cunningham. *Thirty Years in Washington; or, Life and Scenes in Our National Capital, ... With Sketches of the Presidents and Their Wives ... from Washington's to Roosevelt's Administration*. Hartford, Conn.: A. D. Worthington & Co., 1901; Minneapolis: H. L. Baldwin Co., 1908.

810. Magill, Frank N., and John L. Loos, eds. *The American Presidents: The Office and the Men*. 3 vols. Pasadena, Calif.: Salem Press, 1986.

811. Moran, Thomas Francis. *American Presidents: Their Individualities and Their Contributions to American Progress*. New York: Thomas Y. Crowell Co., 1917, 1928, 1933; Freeport, N.Y.: Books for Libraries Press, 1974.

812. Morgan, James. *Our Presidents: Brief Biographies of Our Chief Magistrates*. New York: Macmillan Company, 1924, 1926, 1928, 1949, 1958.

813. Shea, John Dawson Gilmary. *The Story of a Great Nation; or, Our Country's Achievements, ... Our Presidents, Their Portraits and Autographs, with Biographical Sketches ...* n.p., 1886. Title tells it all.

814. Stoddard, William Osborn. *The Lives of the Presidents ...* 10 vols. New York: White, Stokes & Allen, 1886-89.

815. Stoddard, William Osborn. *William Henry Harrison, John Tyler, and James Knox Polk.* New York: F. A. Stokes & Brother, 1888. Contains a 64-page biography of Tyler.

816. Taylor, Tim. *The Book of Presidents.* New York: Arno Press, 1972. Contains biographical sketch of Tyler.

817. Townsend, Virginia F. *Our Presidents.* New York: Worthington Co., 1889. Carries brief sketch of Tyler and engraving of portrait by Hall (p. 241); Townsend's sketch became basis for one by DeVries.

818. Weaver, George Sumner. *The Lives and Graves of Our Presidents.* Chicago: National Book Concern, 1883, 1896; Chicago: Elder Publishing Co., 1884.

819. Williams, Edwin. *The Presidents of the United States ...* New York: Edward Walker, 1849. Discusses main events of the Tyler administration.

B. EXTENDED STUDIES

820. Chidsey, Donald Barr. *And Tyler Too.* Nashville: T. Nelson, 1978. Focus mainly on the presidency.

821. Chitwood, Oliver Perry. *John Tyler: Champion of the Old South.* New York: D. Appleton-Century Co., 1939; New York: Russell & Russell, 1964. The standard and best full-length study.

822. Fiske, John. "Political Career of John Tyler." In James Grant Wilson, *Presidents of the United States,* 2:49-87. 4 vols. New York: Scribner, 1914.

823. Hoyt, Edwin Palmer. *John Tyler: The Tenth President of the United States.* London: Abelard-Schuman, [1969]. Mainly for a young audience.

824. Irelan, John Robert. *The Republic, History of the Life, Administration and Times of John Tyler.* Chicago: Fairbanks and Palmer Publishing Co., 1888.

825. Seager, Robert, II. *And Tyler Too: A Biography of John & Julia Gardiner Tyler.* New York: McGraw-Hill, [1963]. The most readable and reliable of the biographies of Tyler and his second wife.

826. Shulsinger, Stephanie. "John Tyler: The President Without a Party." *Iron Worker* 41 (Spring 1977): 2-11. Explores Tyler's background, birth, education, and presidential style.

IV

Childhood and Early Development

827. Brigham, Willard Irving Tyler. *Official Report of the Fourth General Tyler Family Gathering, September 13, 1899, at Washington, D.C.* n.p., n.d. Discusses various branches of the Tyler family in the South; includes papers on Tyler's wives.

828. Brock, Robert Alonzo. "Hon. John Tyler, LL.D." in *Memorial Biographies of the New England Historic Genealogical Society*, 4:414-38. Boston: Society, 1885. Genealogy of Tyler family; brief discussion of Tyler's political rise and course; short list of Tyler's writings.

829. Coddington, John Insley, and Walter Charlton Hartridge. "Gravestones in the Waller Family Cemetery, Williamsburg, Virginia." *Virginia Genealogist* 2 (October-December 1967): 183-88. Provides birth and death dates of several of Tyler's children.

830. Culbertson, Sidney Methiot. *The Hunter Family of Virginia and Connections, Embracing Portions of Families of Alexander, Pearson, Chapman, Travers, Tyler ...* Denver: n.p., 1934. Has a section, pp. 209-18, detailing genealogy of the Tyler family.

831. Ellett, Katherine Tyler. *Young John Tyler: A True Story for Boys and Girls.* Richmond: Dietz Printing Co., 1957. Written by a Tyler descendant for children.

832. Faber, Doris. *The Mothers of the Presidents.* New York: New American Library, 1968.

833. Faber, Doris. *The Presidents' Mothers.* New York. St. Martin's Press, 1978.

834. Hardy, Sally E. Marshall. "Some Virginia Lawyers of the Past and Present." *Green Bag* 10 (January 1898): 12-25; 10 (February 1898): 57-68; 10 (March 1898): 109-21; 10

(April 1898): 149-61. Offers a brief evaluation of Judge John Tyler, Sr., President Tyler's father; brief biographical sketches of many of Tyler's contemporaries.

835. Henry, Reginald Buchanan. *Genealogies of the Families of the Presidents*. Rutland, Vt.: Tuttle Co., 1935.

836. Jackson, Ronald Vern. *John Tyler and Letitia Christian Ancestry*. Bountiful, Utah: Accelerated Indexing Systems, 1980.

837. Montgomery-Massingberd, Hugh, ed. *Burke's Presidential Families of the United States of America*. London: Burke's Peerage, 1975, 1981. Includes portrait, short sketch of the Tyler administration, chronology, and genealogy, pp. 217-33.

838. Pecquet du Bellet, Louise. *Some Prominent Virginia Families*. 4 vols. Lynchburg, Va.: J. P. Bell, 1907; Baltimore: Genealogical Publishing Co, 1976.

839. Pessen, Edward. *The Log Cabin Myth: The Social Backgrounds of the Presidents*. New Haven: Yale University Press, 1984. Traces the "patrician" origins of Tyler and offers a brief discussion of his presidency.

840. Smith, Bessie White. *The Boyhoods of the Presidents*. Boston: Lothrop, Lee & Shepard Co., 1929. Discussion of Tyler's boyhood in Williamsburg, pp. 97-104, including portrait and photograph of his birthplace.

841. United States District Court, Virginia (Eastern District). *Judge John Tyler, Sr., and His Times: Proceedings on the Presentation of His Portrait to the United States District Court for the Eastern District of Virginia*. Richmond: Richmond Press, 1927. Also in *Pamphlets* [603]. Biographical sketch of the president's father, written by Lyon G. Tyler.

842. Young, Eva. *From Cradle to the White House*. Charlotte, N.C.: Young, 1976. Homes, childhood, and youth of presidents.

V

Early Political Career, 1811–1840

A. LEGISLATIVE CAREER, 1811–1816, 1838–1840, AND GOVERNORSHIP, 1825–1827

843. Ammon, Harry. "The Republican Party in Virginia, 1798-1824." Ph.D. diss., University of Virginia, 1948.

844. Ammon, Harry. "The Richmond Junto, 1808-1824." *Virginia Magazine of History and Biography* 61 (October 1953): 395-418. An important study of political power in antebellum Virginia; some discussion of Tyler's relationship to the Junto, his position on the Missouri Compromise, and his role in Virginia politics.

845. Chandler, Julian Alvin Carroll. *The History of Suffrage in Virginia*. Baltimore: Johns Hopkins Press, 1901.

846. Chandler, Julian Alvin Carroll. *Representation in Virginia*. Baltimore: Johns Hopkins Press, 1896. Discusses slavery, representation of east and west, politics and government of Virginia in the antebellum period.

847. Conrad, Holmes. *The Old County Court System of Virginia: Its Place in History*. Richmond: Richmond Press, [1908]; also published in *Notable Virginia Bar Addresses* (Charlottesville, 1938), pp. 166-91; and in *Virginia State Bar Association Reports* 21 (1908): 322-50. Traces the origins, development, and importance of the county court system in Virginia.

848. Davis, Richard Beale. *Intellectual Life in Jefferson's Virginia, 1790-1830*. Chapel Hill: University of North Carolina Press, 1964.

849. Dodd, William Edward. "The Social Philosophy of the Old South." *American Journal of Sociology* 23 (May 1918): 735-46. Explores the development of the social philosophy of inequality, of slavery as a positive good, and of planter class leadership in the South in the late 1820s and 1830s, a reaction to the democracy of the revolution expressed best in the North by Webster and Chancellor Kent.

850. Harrison, Joseph H., Jr. "Oligarchs and Democrats: The Richmond Junto." *Virginia Magazine of History and Biography* 78 (April 1970): 184-98.

851. Hodges, Wiley E. "Pro-Governmentalism in Virginia, 1789-1836: A Pragmatic Liberal Pattern in the Political Heritage." *Journal of Politics* 25 (May 1963): 333-60.

852. Hodges, Wiley E. "The Theoretical Basis of Anti-Governmentalism in Virginia, 1789-1836." *Journal of Politics* 9 (August 1947): 325-54.

853. McDonald, Forrest. *The Presidency of Thomas Jefferson.* Lawrence: University Press of Kansas, 1976.

854. Miller, F. Thornton. "The Richmond Junto: The Secret All-Powerful Club—or Myth." *Virginia Magazine of History and Biography* 99 (July 1991): 63-80. Sees the Junto more as a myth than a political reality.

855. Pole, J. R. "Representation and Authority in Virginia from the Revolution to Reform." *Journal of Southern History* 24 (February 1958): 16-50. Discusses the evolution of constitutional changes and leadership in Virginia from the time of the revolution to 1850; provides background to understanding the political context in which Tyler grew up.

856. Risjord, Norman. *The Old Republicans: Southern Conservatism in the Age of Jefferson.* New York: Columbia University Press, 1965. A standard study of politics during the early national period.

857. Rist, Boyd Clifton. "The Jeffersonian Crisis Revived: Virginia, the Court, and the Appellate Jurisdiction Controversy." Ph.D. diss., University of Virginia, 1985. Examines the court system and the question of appellate jurisdiction in antebellum Virginia.

858. Shalhope, Robert E. "Thomas Jefferson's Republicanism and Antebellum Southern Thought." *Journal of Southern History* 42 (November 1976): 529-56. Explores southern opposition to federal aid for economic development.

859. Shepard, E. Lee. "Lawyers Look at Themselves: Professional Consciousness and the Virginia Bar, 1770-1850." *American Journal of Legal History* 25 (1981): 1-23. Analyzes the development of the state and local bar associations, the dedication to private practice in Virginia, and the influence of such men as John Tyler in the development of professional sensitivity.

860. Smith, Margaret Vowell. *Virginia 1492-1892: A Brief Review of the Discovery of the Continent of North America, With a History of the Executives of the Colony and the Commonwealth of Virginia.* Washington: W. H. Lowdermilk & Co., 1893. Contains documents relating to Virginia history and brief discussions of the governors, including Tyler and his father.

861. Staples, Waller R. "History of the Old County Court System of Virginia as it Existed Before the Late War Between the States." *Virginia State Bar Association Reports* 7 (1894): 127-56. Criticizes the county court system of Virginia.

862. Starnes, George T. *Sixty Years of Branch Banking in Virginia.* New York: Macmillan, 1931.

863. White, Leonard D. *The Federalists: A Study in Administrative History.* New York: Macmillan, 1948, 1956, 1961; Westport, Conn.: Greenwood Press, 1978. Covers the period 1789-1809.

864. White, Leonard D. *The Jeffersonians: A Study in Administrative History, 1801-1829.* New York: Macmillan, 1951, 1961, 1967.

865. White, Leonard D. *The Jacksonians: A Study in Administrative History, 1829-1861.* New York: Macmillan, 1954; New York: Free Press, 1965.

B. CONSTITUTIONAL CONVENTION OF 1829–1830 AND GREAT SLAVERY DEBATE

866. Brackett, Jeffrey R. "Democracy and Aristocracy in Virginia in 1830." *Sewanee Review* 4 (May 1896): 257-67. Discusses the struggle in Virginia for constitutional reform, which resulted in the constitutional convention.

867. Bruce, Dickson D. *The Rhetoric of Conservatism: The Virginia Constitutional Convention of 1829-30 and the Conservative Tradition in the South.* San Marino, Calif.: Huntington Library, 1982. Useful for understanding the political milieu.

868. Freehling, Alison Goodyear. *Drift Toward Dissolution: The Virginia Slavery Debate of 1831-1832.* Baton Rouge: Louisiana State University Press, 1982.

869. Grigsby, Hugh Blair. "Sketches of Members of the Constitutional Convention of 1829-1830." *Virginia Magazine of History and Biography* 61 (July 1953): 318-32. Discusses members of convention, including Tyler, then United States senator.

870. Grigsby, Hugh Blair. *The Virginia Convention of 1829-1830: A Discourse Delivered before the Virginia Historical Society, at Their Annual Meeting, Held in Richmond, December 15th, 1853.* Richmond: Macfarland & Fergusson, 1854; New York: Da Capo Press, 1969. Published also in the *Virginia Historical Reporter* 1 (1854): 15-116.

871. McConkey, Donald LeMoyne. "The Virginia State Constitutional Convention of 1829-30: A Study in Argumentation." Ph.D. diss., Ohio State University, 1971. Examines the rhetoric of the debates on representation and suffrage.

872. Moorhouse, William H. "Alexander Campbell and the Virginia Constitutional Convention of 1829-1830." *Virginia Cavalcade* 24 (Spring 1975): 184-91. General discussion of Campbell's role in the convention, with brief mention and early portrait of Tyler.

873. Pleasants, Hugh R. "Sketches of the Virginia Convention of 1829-30." *Southern Literary Messenger* 17 (March 1851): 147-54; 17 (May 1851): 297-304.

874. Polk, Lee R. "Argumentation in the Virginia General Assembly Anti-Slavery Debate of 1832." Ph.D. diss., Purdue University, 1966. Useful for understanding the rhetoric and views of many of Tyler's friends and colleagues.

875. Pulliam, David L. *The Constitutional Conventions of Virginia from the Foundation of the Commonwealth to the Present Time.* Richmond: John T. West, 1901. Brief outline sketch of life of Tyler, delegate to the Virginia Constitutional Convention, 1829-1830.

876. Robert, Joseph C. *The Road from Monticello: A Study of the Virginia Slavery Debate of 1832.* Durham: Duke University Press, 1941; New York: AMS Press, 1970.

877. Sutton, Robert Paul. *Revolution to Secession: Constitution Making in the Old Dominion.* Charlottesville: University Press of Virginia, 1989.

878. Sutton, Robert Paul. "The Virginia Constitutional Convention of 1829-30: A Profile Analysis of Late Jeffersonian Virginia." Ph.D. diss., University of Virginia, 1967. Useful for the economic, social, and intellectual life of Virginia; almost no mention of Tyler.

879. Young, Charles Henry. "Virginia Constitutional Convention of 1829." *John P. Branch Papers of Randolph-Macon College* 1 (June 1902): 100-110.

C. CONGRESSIONAL CAREER, 1816–1821, 1822–1836

880. Abernethy, Thomas Perkins. *The South in the New Nation, 1789-1822.* Baton Rouge: Louisiana State University Press, 1961, 1976.

881. Bittinger, Morris Henry. "The Attitude and Influence of Virginia in the Nullification Controversy of South Carolina, 1832-1833." M.A. thesis, University of Virginia, 1929.

882. Blight, David W. "Perceptions of Southern Intransigence and the Rise of Radical Antislavery Thought, 1816-1830." *Journal of the Early Republic* 3 (Summer 1983): 139-63.

883. Braverman, Howard. "The Economic and Political Background of the Conservative Revolt in Virginia." *Virginia Magazine of History and Biography* 60 (April 1952): 266-87.

884. Brown, Norman D. *Daniel Webster and the Politics of Availability*. Athens: University of Georgia Press, 1969. Explores Webster's pursuit of the presidency in the mid-1830s.

885. Brown, Richard H. "'Southern Planters and Plain Republicans of the North': Martin Van Buren's Formula for National Politics." Ph.D. diss., Yale University, 1955.

886. Brown, Thomas. "From Old Hickory to Sly Fox: The Routinization of Charisma in the Early Democratic Party." *Journal of the Early Republic* 11 (Fall 1991): 339-69.

887. Carroll, Eber Malcolm. *Origins of the Whig Party*. Durham: Duke University Press, 1925; Gloucester, Mass.: Peter Smith, 1964; New York: Da Capo Press, 1970. Emphasizes the opposition to a strong executive and the idea of congressional superiority over the executive as major attitudes in the ideology of the Whig party.

888. Chase, James S. *Emergence of the Presidential Nominating Convention, 1789-1832*. Urbana: University of Illinois Press, 1973. An important work on the death of congressional caucus nominations for the presidency.

889. Cole, Arthur Charles. *The Whig Party in the South*. Washington: American Historical Association, 1913; Gloucester, Mass.: P. Smith, 1962. A classic study on the Whig party; somewhat outdated by more recent scholarship.

890. Cole, Donald B. *The Presidency of Andrew Jackson*. Lawrence: University Press of Kansas, 1993. An excellent study of Jackson's presidency with brief discussion of Tyler's relationship to the administration.

891. Crenson, Matthew A. *The Federal Machine: Beginnings of Bureaucracy in Jacksonian America*. Baltimore: Johns Hopkins University Press, 1975. An important study of changes by the Jacksonians.

892. Cunliffe, Marcus. *The Nation Takes Shape: 1789-1837*. Chicago: University of Chicago Press, 1959, 1966. A brief, general account of the period.

893. Dangerfield, George. *The Awakening of American Nationalism, 1815-1828*. New York: Harper and Row, 1965. An excellent study of the period.

894. Dangerfield, George. *The Era of Good Feelings*. New York: Harcourt, Brace, and World, Inc., 1952, 1963; London: Methuen & Co., 1953; Gloucester, Mass.: P. Smith, 1973. An invaluable study of the James Monroe presidential years.

895. Dent, Lynwood Miller, Jr. "The Virginia Democratic Party, 1827-1847." Ph.D. diss., Louisiana State University, 1974.

896. Dixon, Susan Bullitt. *The True History of the Missouri Compromise and Its Repeal*. Cincinnati: Robert Clarke Co., 1899, 1903; New York: Johnson Reprint Corp., 1970. Focuses on slavery as a central factor in antebellum politics.

897. Dodd, William Edward. "The Principle of Instructing United States Senators." *South Atlantic Quarterly* 1 (October 1902): 326-32. Focuses on the Jackson-Van Buren presidencies, when the policy of instructing was accepted almost in toto by one party and partially by another.

898. Eaton, Clement. "Southern Senators and the Right of Instruction, 1789-1860." *Journal of Southern History* 18 (August 1952): 303-19. Stresses practice among Whigs, 1834-40.

899. Ellis, Richard E. *The Jeffersonian Crisis: Courts and Politics in the Young Republic*. New York: Oxford University Press, 1971; New York: Norton, 1974.

900. Ellis, Richard E. *The Union at Risk: Jacksonian Democracy, States' Rights, and the Nullification Crisis*. New York: Oxford University Press, 1987.

901. Eriksson, Erik McKinley. "The Federal Civil Service under President Jackson." *Mississippi Valley Historical Review* 13 (March 1927): 517-40. Explores Jackson's use of patronage and its impact on party development.

902. Ershkowitz, Herbert. *The Origins of the Whig and Democratic Parties: New Jersey Politics, 1820-1837*. Washington: University Press of America, 1982. Argues that there were genuine differences between the parties in ideology and on economic issues.

903. Feller, Daniel. *The Public Lands in Jacksonian Politics*. Madison: University of Wisconsin Press, 1984. Investigates public land policy and its influence on political alignments from 1815 to 1840.

904. Freehling, William W. *Prelude to Civil War: The Nullification Controversy in South Carolina, 1816-1836.* New York: Harper and Row, 1966; New York: Oxford University Press, 1992.

905. Gatell, Frank Otto, ed. *Essays on Jacksonian America.* New York: Holt, Rinehart and Winston, 1970. Brings together leading essays on the economic, political, social, and cultural aspects of the period.

906. Goldman, Perry M. "The Republic of Virtue and Other Essays on the Politics of the Early National Period." Ph.D. diss., Columbia University, 1970. Main focus is on the period previous to 1840, but study is still suggestive for understanding Tyler.

907. Goodman, Paul. "Moral Purpose and Republican Politics in Antebellum America, 1830-1860." *Maryland History* 20 (Fall-Winter 1989): 5-39.

908. Hargreaves, Mary W. M. *The Presidency of John Quincy Adams.* Lawrence: University Press of Kansas, 1985.

909. Helicher, Karl. "The Presidential Elections of 1820, 1824, 1828, and 1832, as Indicators of the Political Strength of Andrew Jackson in Pennsylvania and Montgomery County." *Bulletin of the Historical Society of Montgomery County* 25 (Fall 1985): 20-42.

910. Hoffmann, William S. *Andrew Jackson and North Carolina Politics.* Chapel Hill: University of North Carolina Press, 1958.

911. Jordan, Daniel P. *Political Leadership in Jefferson's Virginia.* Charlottesville: University Press of Virginia, 1983. Explores the decline of Virginia's influence in the councils of the nation and attributes that decline to a change in the ideal of public service and to the rise of professional politicians.

912. Jordan, Daniel P. "Virginia Congressmen, 1801-1825." Ph.D. diss., University of Virginia, 1970. Argues that there was little change in the social standing and wealth of Virginia's political leaders during period.

913. Ketcham, Ralph Louis. *Presidents Above Party: The First American Presidency, 1789-1829.* Chapel Hill: University of North Carolina Press, 1984. Contends that the first six presidents subscribed to the notion that the president should provide leadership.

914. Klamkin, Marian. *The Return of Lafayette: 1824-1825.* New York: Charles Scribner's Sons, 1975. Tyler's involvement in celebrations in Virginia and in Washington negligible.

915. Kutolowski, Kathleen Smith. "Antimasonry Reexamined: Social Bases of the Grass-Roots Party." *Journal of American History* 71 (September 1984): 269-93.

916. Latner, Richard B. *The Presidency of Andrew Jackson: White House Politics, 1829-1837.* Athens: University of Georgia Press, 1979. One of the better studies of the Jackson presidency; discusses briefly Tyler's reasons for breaking with the president.

917. Livermore, Shaw. *Early American Land Companies: Their Influence on Corporate Development.* New York: Commonwealth Fund, 1939; New York: Octagon Books, 1968. A standard study on corporate organization and development in the United States.

918. Livermore, Shaw, Jr. *The Twilight of Federalism: The Disintegration of the Federalist Party, 1815-1830.* Princeton: Princeton University Press, 1962.

919. Lynn, Alvin W. "Party Formation and Operation in the House of Representatives, 1824-1837." Ph.D. diss., Rutgers University, 1972.

920. MacDonald, William. *Jacksonian Democracy, 1829-1837.* New York: Harper & Brothers, 1906, 1968.

921. McCandless, Perry. "Benton v. Barton: The Formation of the Second-Party System in Missouri." *Missouri Historical Review* 79 (July 1985): 425-38.

922. McCormick, Richard P. *The Second American Party System: Party Formation in the Jacksonian Era.* Chapel Hill: University of North Carolina Press, 1966. Important study of party development and organization in the various states.

923. McGiffen, Steven P. "Ideology and the Failure of the Whig Party in New Hampshire, 1834-1841." *New England Quarterly* 59 (September 1986): 387-401.

924. McGrane, Reginald Charles. *The Panic of 1837: Some Financial Problems of the Jacksonian Era.* Chicago: University of Chicago Press, 1924; New York: Russell & Russell, 1965.

925. Meyers, Marvin. "The Jacksonian Persuasion." *American Quarterly* 5 (Spring 1953): 3-15.

926. Meyers, Marvin. *The Jacksonian Persuasion, Politics and Beliefs.* Stanford: Stanford University Press, 1957, 1960, 1964, 1968; New York: Vintage Books, 1960.

927. Miles, Edwin A. "The Jacksonian Era." In *Writing Southern History: Essays in Historiography in Honor of Fletcher M. Green,* pp. 125-46. Ed. Arthur S. Link and Rembert W. Patrick. Baton Rouge: Louisiana State University Press, 1965.

928. Moore, Glover. *The Missouri Controversy, 1819-1821.* Lexington: University of Kentucky Press, 1953; University Press of Kentucky, 1966; Gloucester, Mass.: P. Smith, 1967.

929. Nagel, Paul Chester. "John Tyler as Congressman and Senator." M.A. thesis, University of Minnesota, 1949. One of the few studies focusing on this aspect of Tyler's career.

930. Peck, Charles Henry. *The Jacksonian Epoch.* New York: Harper and Brothers, 1899. Surveys the political history of the United States from 1824 to 1840.

931. Perkins, Dexter. *The Monroe Doctrine, 1823-1826.* Cambridge, Mass.: Harvard University Press, 1927.

932. Pessen, Edward. *Jacksonian America: Society, Personality, and Politics.* Homewood, Ill.: Dorsey Press, 1969, 1978. A general survey of the period.

933. Pessen Edward, ed. *The Many-Faceted Jacksonian Era: New Interpretations.* Westport, Conn.: Greenwood Press, 1977. Collection of essays on various topics of the period.

934. Pessen, Edward. "Society and Politics in the Jacksonian Era." *Register of the Kentucky Historical Society* 82 (Winter 1984): 1-27.

935. Peterson, Merrill D. *Olive Branch and Sword: The Compromise of 1833.* Baton Rouge: Louisiana State University Press, 1982. Peterson's Walter Lynwood Fleming lectures delivered at Louisiana State University.

936. "The Political Crisis." *United States Magazine and Democratic Review* 2 (June 1838): 312-20. Discusses the impact of the economic crisis on political developments.

937. Remini, Robert V. *Andrew Jackson and the Bank War: A Study in the Growth of Presidential Power.* New York: Norton, 1967. One of the better studies on Jackson and the bank war; provides background for understanding the chronology of the fight against Biddle's Second Bank of the United States and the political responses to the squabble.

938. Remini, Robert V. *The Election of Andrew Jackson.* Philadelphia: J. B. Lippincott, 1963. One of the better accounts of the elections of 1824 and 1828.

939. Remini, Robert V. *The Legacy of Andrew Jackson: Essays on Democracy, Indian Removal, and Slavery.* Baton Rouge: Louisiana State University Press, 1988. Walter Lynwood Fleming Lectures in Southern History, delivered at Louisiana State University in 1984; contains brief discussion of Tyler.

940. Remini, Robert V. *Martin Van Buren and the Making of the Democratic Party.* New York: Columbia University Press, 1959. A carefully researched, and important study on the leadership behind and the formation of the Democratic party.

941. Remini, Robert V. "Martin Van Buren and the Tariff of Abominations." *American Historical Review* 63 (July 1958): 903-17.

942. Remini, Robert V. *The Revolutionary Age of Andrew Jackson.* New York: Harper and Row, 1976; New York: Harper Torchbooks, 1987.

943. Rives, Ralph Hardee. "A History of Oratory in the Commonwealth of Virginia Prior to the War Between the States." Ed.D. diss., University of Virginia, 1960.

944. Rothbard, Murray N. *The Panic of 1819: Reactions and Policies.* New York: Columbia University Press, 1962. Discusses briefly Tyler's opposition to a protective tariff.

945. Russo, David J. "The Major Political Issues of the Jacksonian Period and the Development of Party Loyalty in Congress, 1830-1840." *Transactions of the American Philosophical Society*, New Series, 62 (Part 5), Philadelphia, 1972.

946. Rutland, Robert Allen. *The Presidency of James Madison.* Lawrence: University Press of Kansas, 1990.

947. Scheiber, Harry N. "The Pet Banks in Jacksonian Politics and Finance, 1833-1841." *Journal of Economic History* 23 (June 1963): 196-214.

948. Schlesinger, Arthur M., Jr. *The Imperial Presidency.* Boston: Houghton Mifflin, 1973. Explores the evolution of the American presidency.

949. Sellers, Charles G. *The Market Revolution: Jacksonian America, 1815-1846.* New York: Oxford University Press, 1991.

950. Sellers, Charles G., Jr. "Who Were the Southern Whigs?" *American Historical Review* 59 (January 1954): 335-46.

951. Sharp, James Roger. "Andrew Jackson and the Limits of Presidential Power." *Congressional Studies* 7 (Winter 1980): 63-80. Explores background of the 1834 censure of Jackson and contends that censure is the only alternative when impeachment is politically impossible.

952. Silbey, Joel H., comp. *National Development and Sectional Crisis, 1815-1860.* New York: Random House, 1970. Volume of essays on politics, banking, economic development, ethnocultural groups, slavery, and the disruption of the Union.

953. Silbey, Joel H. *Political Ideology and Voting Behavior in the Age of Jackson.* Englewood Cliffs, N.J.: Prentice-Hall, 1973.

954. Simms, Henry Harrison. *The Rise of the Whigs in Virginia, 1824-1840.* Richmond: William Byrd Press, 1929. A classic, outdated by more recent scholarship.

955. Stampp, Kenneth M. "The Concept of a Perpetual Union." *Journal of American History* 65 (June 1978): 5-33.

956. Stenberg, Richard R. "The Jefferson Birthday Dinner, 1830." *Journal of Southern History* 4 (August 1938): 334-45. Discusses event and its meaning for party development.

957. Strickland, Haywood Louis. "The Rise of Jacksonism in Virginia, 1815-1828." M.S. thesis, University of Wisconsin-Madison, 1962.

958. Sydnor, Charles William. "The Congressional Career of John Tyler, the Tenth President." M.A. thesis, West Virginia University, 1933.

959. Turner, Frederick Jackson. *Rise of the New West, 1819-1829.* New York: Harper & Brothers, 1906; Gloucester, Mass.: Peter Smith, 1961.

960. Turner, Frederick Jackson. *The Significance of Sections in American History.* New York: Henry Holt, 1920.

961. Turner, Frederick Jackson. *The United States, 1830-1850: The Nation and Its Sections.* New York: Henry Holt, 1935. Adopts a favorable view of Tyler.

962. Tyler, Lyon Gardiner. "Anecdote of John Randolph." *Tyler's Quarterly Historical and Genealogical Magazine* 2 (October 1920): 139-40. Relates anecdote, as told by Julia Gardiner Tyler, of a meeting between Tyler and Randolph following Tyler's defeat of Randolph in the senatorial election, 1826.

963. Upton, Anthony. "The Road to Power in Virginia in the Early Nineteenth Century." *Virginia Magazine of History and Biography* 62 (July 1954): 259-80. Some discussion of Tyler's views on electioneering and qualities for success.

964. Van Deusen, Glyndon G. *The Jacksonian Era, 1828-1848.* New York: Harper and Row, 1959. General survey of the period.

965. Weaver, Richard M. "Two Orators." *Modern Age* 14 (Summer-Fall 1970): 226-41. Explores differing views of the American union as expressed in the Webster-Hayne debate.

966. Wilson, Major L. "'Liberty and Union': An Analysis of Three Concepts Involved in the Nullification Controversy." *Journal of Southern History* 33 (August 1967): 331-55.

967. Wilson, Major L. *The Presidency of Martin Van Buren.* Lawrence: University of Kansas Press, 1984. An important study of the Van Buren administration, useful for understanding the domestic and foreign policy issues inherited by the Harrison-Tyler administrations.

968. Wiltse, Charles M. *The New Nation, 1800-1845.* New York: Hill & Wang, 1961. A general survey of the period.

969. Woolsey, Ronald C. "The West Becomes a Problem: The Missouri Controversy and Slavery Expansion as the Southern Dilemma." *Missouri Historical Review* 77 (July 1983): 409-32.

970. Young, James Sterling. *The Washington Community, 1800-1828.* New York: Columbia University Press, 1966.

VI

Presidential Election of 1836

A. GENERAL ELECTION STUDIES

1. Broad Surveys

971. Bartus, Mary R. "The Presidential Election of 1836." Ph.D. diss., Fordham University, 1967.

972. Bishop, Joseph Bucklin. *Presidential Nominations and Elections: A History of American Conventions, National Campaigns, Inaugurations and Campaign Caricature.* New York: C. Scribner, 1916. Also in *Microbook Library* **[601]**.

973. Brown, William Burlie. *The People's Choice: The Presidential Image in the Campaign Biography.* Baton Rouge: Louisiana State University Press, 1960. Analyzes the function and role of the campaign biography.

974. Byrne, Gary C., and Paul Marx. *The Great American Convention: A Political History of Presidential Elections.* Palo Alto, Calif.: Pacific Books, 1976.

975. Eriksson, Erik McKinley. "Official Newspaper Organs and the Presidential Election of 1836." *Tennessee Historical Magazine* 9 (July 1925): 115-30. Discusses newspaper party affiliations and rhetoric in the campaign of 1836.

976. Hackett, Derek. "The Days of This Republic Will Be Numbered: Abolition, Slavery, and the Presidential Election of 1836." *Louisiana Studies* 15 (Summer 1976): 131-60. Assesses the importance of abolitionism in the campaign.

977. Heale, M. J. *The Presidential Quest: Candidates and Images in American Political Culture, 1787-1852*. New York: Longman, 1982. Explores the role of the candidate and his image-making in presidential elections.

978. Lorant, Stefan. *The Glorious Burden: The History of the Presidency and Presidential Elections from George Washington to James Earl Carter, Jr.* Lenox, Mass.: Authors Edition, 1976.

979. McCormick, Richard P. "Was There a 'Whig Strategy' in 1836?" *Journal of the Early Republic* 4 (Spring 1984): 47-70.

980. Melder, Keith. "The Birth of Modern Campaigning." *Campaigns & Elections* 6 (Summer 1985): 48-53. Argues that the modern political campaign emerged in the United States between 1825 and 1840.

981. Miller, T. Michael. "'If Elected ...' An Overview of How Alexandrians Voted in Presidential Elections from 1789-1984." *Fireside Sentinel* 2 (October 1988): 97-102.

982. Papale, Henry. *Banners, Buttons, and Songs: A Pictorial Review and Capsule Almanac of America's Presidential Campaigns*. Cincinnati: World Library Publications, 1968; New York: St. Martin's Press, 1984.

983. Roseboom, Eugene H. *A History of Presidential Elections*. New York: Macmillan Co., 1957.

984. Schlesinger, Arthur M., Jr., and Fred L. Israel, eds. *History of American Presidential Elections, 1789-1968*. 9 vols. New York: Chelsea House Publishers, 1971.

985. Stanwood, Edward. *A History of Presidential Elections ...* . Boston: J. R. Osgood and Co., 1884; Boston: Ticknor and Co., 1888; Boston: Houghton, Mifflin & Co., 1892.

986. Tugwell, Rexford G. *How They Became President: Thirty-Five Ways to the White House*. New York: Simon and Schuster, 1964. Sees Tyler's as one of the more interesting and important in American history.

2. Party Platforms and Voting Statistics

987. Burnham, Walter Dean. *Presidential Ballots, 1836-1892*. Baltimore: Johns Hopkins Press, 1955. Provides county and state statistics for presidential elections.

988. Chester, Edward W. *A Guide to Political Platforms*. Hamden, Conn.: Archon Books, 1977.

989. Congressional Quarterly. *Presidential Elections Since 1789*. Washington: Congressional Quarterly, 1979, 1983. Provides election statistics.

990. McKee, Thomas Hudson. *The National Conventions and Platforms of All Political Parties, 1789-1900 ...* . Washington, D.C.: Statistical Publishing Co., 1892; Baltimore: Fiedenwald Co., 1900 (also many other editions); St. Clair Shores, Mich.: Scholarly Press, 1970; New York: B. Franklin, 1971. Provides statistics for the 1836 and 1840 presidential campaigns for Tyler and Harrison.

991. *National Party Conventions, 1831-1980*. Washington: Congressional Quarterly, 1983. Deals mainly with the nomination process.

992. Porter, Kirk Harold. *National Party Platforms*. New York: Macmillan Co., 1924.

993. *Presidential Candidates from 1788 to 1964, Including Third Parties, 1832-1964, and Popular Electoral Vote: Historical Review*. Washington: Congressional Quarterly, 1964.

3. State Studies

994. Atkins, Jonathan M. "The Presidential Candidacy of Hugh Lawson White in Tennessee, 1832-1836." *Journal of Southern History* 58 (February 1992): 27-56.

995. Helbling, Mark Irving. "The Political Appeal of the Democratic Party in Virginia—1836." M.A. thesis, San Francisco State University, 1966.

996. Hoffmann, William S. "The Election of 1836 in North Carolina." *North Carolina Historical Review* 32 (January 1955): 31-51.

997. Moore, Powell. "The Revolt Against Jackson in Tennessee, 1835-1836." *Journal of Southern History* 2 (August 1936): 335-59. Studies the movement in Tennessee in favor of Hugh Lawson White's candidacy in the 1836 presidential election.

998. Petersen, Svend. *A Statistical History of the American Presidential Elections*. New York: Ungar, 1963, 1968.

999. Rogers, William Warren, Jr. "Alabama and the Presidential Election of 1836." *Alabama Review* 35 (April 1982): 111-26.

B. CAMPAIGN BIOGRAPHIES

1. Democratic

Martin Van Buren and Richard M. Johnson

1000. Crockett, David. *The Life of Martin Van Buren, Heir-Apparent to the "Government," and the Appointed Successor of General Andrew Jackson, Containing Every Authentic Particular by Which His Extraordinary Character Has Been Formed* ... Philadelphia: Robert Wright, 1835, 1836.

1001. [Emmons, William] *Biographies of Martin Van Buren and Richard M. Johnson.* New York: Childs and DeVoe, [c1835].

1002. [Emmons, William] *Biography of Martin Van Buren, Vice President of the United States.* Washington: Jacob Gideon, 1835.

1003. Grund, Franz J. *Martin Van Buren als Staatsmann und kunstiger Prasident der Vereinigten Staaten von Nord-Amerika.* [New York?]: n.p., 1835.

1004. Holland, William M. *The Life and Political Opinions of Martin Van Buren, Vice President of the United States.* Hartford, Conn.: Belknap & Hamersley, 1835.

1005. *Sketches of the Life and Public Services of Martin Van Buren, Comprehending the Principal Events in the History of His Illustrious Career.* Albany: A. J. Bready, 1836.

2. Whig

William Henry Harrison

1006. *A Biographical Sketch of the Life and Services of Gen. William Henry Harrison, Together With His Letter to Simon Bolivar* ... Montpelier, Vt.: Watchman Office, 1836.

1007. *A Brief History of the Public Services of Gen. William H. Harrison, Commander-In-Chief of the Northwestern Army in the War of 1812* ... Harrisburg: Pennsylvania Intelligencer, 1836.

1008. Hall, James. *A Memoir of the Public Services of William Henry Harrison, of Ohio.* Philadelphia: Edward C. Biddle, 1836; Philadelphia: Key & Biddle, 1836.

1009. [Jackson, Isaac Rand?] *A Brief Sketch of the Life and Public Services of William Henry Harrison, As Secretary of the North Western Territory ... Compiled from Official Documents...* New York: T. & C. Wood, 1835.

1010. [Jackson, Isaac Rand] *Narrative of the Civil and Military Services of Wm. H. Harrison, Compiled from the Most Authentic Authorities, With Engravings.* Cincinnati: Ormsby H. Donogh, 1836.

1011. [Jackson, Isaac Rand] *A Sketch of the Life and Public Services of William Henry Harrison.* Columbus: Scott & Wright, 1836.

1012. [Jackson, Isaac Rand] *A Sketch of the Life and Public Services of William Henry Harrison, Commander-In-Chief of the Northwestern Army During the War of 1812, &c.* Albany: Hoffman & White, 1836; New York: Harper & Brothers, 1836.

1013. [Jackson, Isaac Rand] *William Henry Harrison.* n.p., 1836.

1014. *Sketch of the Life of Major General William Henry Harrison, Comprising a Brief Account of His Important Civil and Military Services, Including a Description of the Victories of Tippecanoe, Fort Meiggs, and the Thames.* n.p., 1836.

Daniel Webster and Francis Granger

1015. "Mr. Webster." *New-England Magazine* 8 (March 1835): 220-28. Touts Webster's qualifications.

Hugh Lawson White and John Tyler

1016. *Richmond Compiler—Extra.* [1836]. Lists the Virginia electors on the Republican Whig Ticket.

1017. *The People, Against Official Dictation: For President, Hugh White of Tennessee, or William Henry Harrison of Ohio ... For Vice-President, that Tried Republican Statesman and Patriot, John Tyler, of Virginia ...* Richmond: n.p., 1836. Lists electors.

C. CAMPAIGN SPEECHES AND GENERAL PAMPHLETS

1018. *Address of the Anti-Van Buren Members of the General Assembly ... to the People of Virginia.* [Richmond: n.p., 1836.] Address of March 16, 1836, enlightens voters of measures of the previous assembly, which Whigs opposed.

1019. *Address of the Democratic Members of the Legislature to the People of Virginia.* Richmond: n.p., 1836.

1020. *Address of the Republican Committee of Correspondence to the People of Halifax [Virginia].* n.p., 1836.

1021. *An Address to the People of Culpeper, Urging the Importance of Electing Mr. Van Buren to the Presidency, Culpeper Court-House, October, 1836.* n.p., [1836].

1022. *Jackson Almanac, 1836.* New York: Elton [1835]. Contains a brief biography of Van Buren.

1023. *Journal of the Proceedings of the Virginia Harrison State Convention, Commenced and Held at Staunton, July 4, 1836.* n.p., 1836.

1024. *Legislative Nomination of Daniel Webster for the Presidency.* n.p., 1835.

1025. *Proceedings of a State Convention of Delegates Friendly to the Election of William Henry Harrison, for President, and Francis Granger, for Vice President, Assembled at the Capitol, Feb. 3, 1836.* Albany: Hoffman and White, 1836.

1026. *Proceedings of the Convention of the Friends of Gen. Wm. H. Harrison ...* [Indianapolis: n.p., 1835?].

1027. *Resolutions Adopted by the Antimasonic Members of the Legislature of Massachusetts, and Other Citizens of Boston and the Vicinity, Opposed to the Nomination of Martin Van Buren and Richard M. Johnson for President and Vice President of U.S. at a Meeting Held in the Chamber of the House of Representatives, March 9, 1836, with An Address to Their Antimasonic Fellow Citizens Throughout the State.* Boston: D. Hooton, 1836. In favor of Webster and Francis Granger for president and vice president.

1028. *Speech of Mr. Storer, in Defence of General William Henry Harrison, To Which Is Annexed a Short Sketch of the Principal Events of His Life.* Baltimore: Sands & Neilson, 1836.

VII

Presidential Election of 1840

A. GENERAL STUDIES

1029. Adams, John Wolcott. "The Hard Cider Campaign of 1840." *Century Magazine* 84 (September 1912): 677-80. Produces four sketches of the presidential campaign.

1030. Alexander, Thomas B. "The Presidential Campaign of 1840 in Tennessee." *Tennessee Historical Quarterly* 1 (March 1942): 21-43.

1031. Blatt, Karen Priscilla. "The Nomination of John Tyler." M.A. thesis, University of Illinois—Urbana, 1963. Explores the background of Tyler's nomination for the vice-presidency.

1032. Carwardine, Richard. "Evangelicals, Whigs, and the Election of William Henry Harrison." *Journal of American Studies* 17 (April 1983): 47-75.

1033. Chute, William J. "The New Jersey Whig Campaign of 1840." *New Jersey History* 78 (1960): 222-39.

1034. Cole, Malvaine. *Daniel Webster Spoke on Stratton Mountain: An Account of that Memorable Occasion in 1840 ... .* Jamaica, Vt.: Charter Publishers, 1965. Consists of a compilation of newspaper reports and excerpts from Webster's speech.

1035. DeFiore, Jayne Crumpler. "Come, and Bring the Ladies: Tennessee Women and the Politics of Opportunity during the Presidential Campaigns of 1840 and 1844." *Tennessee Historical Quarterly* 51 (Winter 1992): 197-212. Analyzes women's participation in the mass political gatherings.

1036. Fischer, Roger A. *Tippecanoe and Trinkets Too: The Material Culture of American Presidential Campaigns, 1828-1984*. Urbana: University of Illinois Press, 1988. Scholarly analysis of campaign memorabilia.

1037. Fitch, Agnes. "Daniel Webster in Vermont." *Vermont Historical Society Proceedings* 10 (June 1942): 104-109. Discusses the Stratton Mountain political gathering.

1038. Gilbert, Abby L. "Of Banks and Politics: The Bank Issue and the Election of 1840." *West Virginia History* 34 (October 1972): 18-45. Discusses Whig candidates' views on a national bank, which Harrison, although hedging, favored, while Tyler, selected because no other candidate identified with a bank would take the second slot on the ticket, opposed; and once in office followed conscience rather than party policy.

1039. Gunderson, Robert Gray. *The Log-Cabin Campaign*. Lexington: University of Kentucky Press, 1957; Westport, Conn.: Greenwood Press, 1977. The best book-length monograph on the election of 1840.

1040. Gunderson, Robert Gray. "Tippecanoe Belles of 1840." *American Heritage*, Fall 1952, 3-5. Discusses the "sorry campaign" of the Democrats, including the interest and participation of women in the campaign rallies.

1041. Gunderson, Robert Gray. "Webster in Linsey-Woolsey." *Quarterly Journal of Speech* 37 (February 1951): 23-30. Discusses Webster's speeches in behalf of the Whig ticket.

1042. Hannigan, James P. "Orestes Brownson and the Election of 1840." *Records of the American Catholic Historical Society of Philadelphia* 73 (March-June 1962): 45-50.

1043. "Harrison's Great Speech at the 'Log Cabin' Campaign Meeting at Ft. Meigs in 1840." *Ohio Archaeological and Historical Society Publications* 17 (April 1908): 197-207.

1044. Hart, James D. "They Were All Born in Log Cabins." *American Heritage*, August 1956, 32-34, 102-105. Discusses myths of candidates' backgrounds in presidential campaign literature.

1045. Julian, George W. "Political Recollections and Notes." *International Review* 12 (April 1882): 325-34. Discusses briefly the political views of Harrison and Tyler, the music of the campaign, and the growing influence of abolitionism during the first Whig incumbency.

1046. Minnigerode, Meade. *Presidential Years, 1787-1860*. New York: G. P. Putnam's Sons, 1928. Popular discussion of the "singing Whigs."

1047. Murray, Anne W. "Van Buren versus Harrison: The Campaign of 1840." *American Collector* 17 (October 1948): 24-25.

1048. Nicolay, John G., and John Hay. "Abraham Lincoln: A History." *Century Magazine* 33 (January 1887): 366-96; 33 (February 1887): 515-43. Discuss the campaigns of 1840 and 1844 and Tyler's move for the annexation of Texas.

1049. Norton, Anthony Banning. *The Great Revolution of 1840: Reminiscences of the Log Cabin and Hard Cider Campaign.* Mount Vernon, Ohio: A. B. Norton & Co., 1888. Also in *Microbook Library* [601]. Includes campaign songs.

1050. Norton, Anthony Banning, ed. *Tippecanoe Songs of the Log Cabin Boys and Girls of 1840.* Mount Vernon, Ohio: A. B. Norton & Co., 1888.

1051. Samson, Rebecca Middleton. "When Daniel Webster Spoke on the Mountain." *Outlook* 79 (November 30, 1921): 521-23. Recounts story of Webster's speech on Stratton Mountain.

1052. Shelden, Aure. "History in Hiding." *New-England Galaxy* 17 (1975): 39-43. Recounts the Whig political convention on Stratton Mountain in July 1840.

1053. Short, James R. "Virginia Repudiates Her Native Sons." *Virginia Cavalcade* 3 (Summer 1953): 10-11. Discusses Virginia's vote against Henry Clay, William Henry Harrison and John Tyler, Zachary Taylor, and Winfield Scott.

1054. Smith, John L. "The Virginia Election." *National Magazine and Republican Review* 2 (May 1839): 5-14. Discusses the election of William C. Rives to the United States Senate from Virginia in 1839 and its expected impact on the upcoming presidential campaign.

1055. Varon, Elizabeth R. "Tippecanoe and the Ladies, Too: White Women and Party Politics in Antebellum Virginia." *Journal of American History* 18 (September 1995): 494-521. Argues that political scholars have ignored the significance of women in antebellum politics, especially in the elections of 1840 and 1844 in Virginia.

1056. Volpe, Vernon L. "The Anti-Abolitionist Campaign of 1840." *Civil War History* 32 (December 1986): 325-39. Argues that the campaign of 1840 was more than nonsensical—that it did involve some substantive issues, namely abolition.

1057. Wentworth, W. A. "Tippecanoe and Kentucky Too." *Register of the Kentucky Historical Society* 60 (January 1962): 36-44.

1058. Wright, Martha R. "The Log Cabin Convention of 1840 Sixty Years Later: Vermonters Correct the Record." *Vermont History* 40 (1972): 237-45. Reports the recollections of E. H. and E. M. Torrey of Webster's speech on Stratton Mountain.

1059. Young, Andrew W. *The American Statesman: A Political History, Exhibiting the Origin, Nature, and Practical Operation of Constitutional Government in the United States; The Rise and Progress of Parties; and the Views of Distinguished Statesmen on Questions of Foreign and Domestic Policy* ... New York: Derby & Jackson, 1857. Contains a general discussion of politics, the presidential election of 1840, Harrison's inauguration, and the Tyler administration, drawn largely from published congressional debates.

1060. Young, Stanley Preston. *Tippecanoe and Tyler, Too!* New York: Random House, 1957. Harrison biography dealing particularly with the Battle of Tippecanoe and the presidential campaign.

1061. Yzenbaard, John H. "The Harrison Bandwagon." *American Heritage*, October 1975, 18-27.

B. CAMPAIGN BIOGRAPHIES

1. Democratic

Martin Van Buren

1062. *A Brief Account of the Life and Political Opinions of Martin Van Buren, President of the United States: From the Most Authentic Sources.* n.p., 1840.

1063. *The Claims of Martin Van Buren to the Presidency Fairly Represented, in a Sketch of the Chief Political Transactions of His Life.* n.p., 1840.

1064. Dawson, Moses. *Sketches of the Life of Martin Van Buren, President of the United States.* Cincinnati: J. W. Ely, 1840.

1065. *The Democrat's Almanac and People's Register for 1841, Containing, in Addition to the Usual Calendar Pages, a Brief Sketch of the Life of Martin Van Buren* ... Boston: E. Littlefield, 1840.

1066. *Sketch of the Life of Martin Van Buren.* Columbus: n.p., 1840.

2. Whig

Henry Clay

1067. *The Beauties of the Hon. Henry Clay, To Which is Added, a Biographical and Critical Essay* ... New York: Edward Walker, 1839.

1068. Flournoy, John James. *An Essay on the Eminent Services and Illustrious Characters of Henry Clay* ... Athens, Ga.: Whig Office, 1840.

William Henry Harrison and John Tyler

1069. *Abstract of the Public Services of William Henry Harrison.* Boston: E. Tappan and A. C. Warren, 1840.

1070. Bayard, Samuel John. *A Short History of the Life and Services of Gen. William Henry Harrison.* [Seneca Falls: Fuller & Bloomer, 1840?].

1071. Burnet, Jacob. *Notices of the Public Services of General William Henry Harrison.* n.p., [1839?].

1072. Burr, Samuel Jones. *The Life and Times of William Henry Harrison.* New York: L. W. Ransom, 1840; Philadelphia: R. W. Pomeroy, 1840.

1073. *The Civil Services of William Henry Harrison, With Extracts From His Addresses, Speeches, and Letters, and a Sketch of His Life.* [Philadelphia: C. Sherman & Co., 1840?].

1074. *A Condensed Memoir of the Public Services of William H. Harrison, From the Time of His Entering the Public Service in 1792 to the Present Time, and Showing That in Every Emergency He Has Been Ready to Peril His Life and Fortune in the Service of His Country.* n.p., [1840?].

1075. Cooke, Eleutheros. *An Address in Commemoration of the Brilliant and Glorious Defense of Fort Meigs ... in 1813: Embracing a Sketch of the Civil and Military Services of Gen. William H. Harrison* ... Perrysburg: H. T. Smith, 1840.

1076. [Cushing, Caleb]. *Brief Sketch of the Life and Public Services, Civil and Military of William Henry Harrison, of Ohio* ... Augusta, Me.: Severance and Dorr, 1840.

1077. Cushing, Caleb. *Outline of the Life and Public Services, Civil and Military, of William Henry Harrison.* Newark: Daily and Sentinel Office, 1840; Boston: Eastburn's Press, 1840; Boston: Weeks, Jordan and Co., 1840; Washington: Madisonian Office,

1840. Several other editions of this work, with only minor variations in title and content, by the same publishers.

1078. Garrard, Daniel. *Address to the Young Men of Kentucky, Comprising a Brief Review of the Military Services of General William Henry Harrison, During the Late War Between Great Britain and the United States.* Frankfort: Robinson & Adams, 1840.

1079. *General Harrison in Congress.* Washington: [National Intelligencer?], 1840.

1080. Grund, Franz J. *General Harrison's Leben und Wirken.* Philadelphia: C. J. Stollmeyer, 1840.

1081. *Hard Cider and Log Cabin Almanac for 1841: Harrison and Tyler.* Philadelphia: Turner & Fisher [1840].

1082. *The Harrison Almanac, 1841.* New York: James P. Giffing, [c1840]. Several editions by the same publisher.

1083. *Harrison and Log Cabin Song Book.* Columbus: I. N. Whiting, 1840. Lacks music.

1084. *Harrison Calender auf das Jahr, 1841.* Philadelphia: Georg W. Menz und Sohn, 1840.

1085. *Hero of Tippecanoe; or, The Story of the Life of William Henry Harrison, Related by Captain Miller to His Boys.* New York: J. P. Giffing, [c1840].

1086. Hildreth, Richard. *The Contrast; or, William Henry Harrison versus Martin Van Buren.* Boston: Weeks, Jordan & Co., 1840. Also in *Selected Americana* **[602]**. A Whig campaign pamphlet.

1087. [Hildreth, Richard]. *The People's Presidential Candidate; or, The Life of William Henry Harrison, of Ohio.* Boston: Weeks, Jordan and Co., 1839. Went through at least seven editions.

1088. *Incidents in the Life of William Henry Harrison, the People's Candidate for the Presidency.* Albany: Sun Office, 1839.

1089. [Jackson, Isaac Rand]. *A Sketch of the Life and Public Services of William Henry Harrison, With an Appendix Containing the Letters of His Aides-De-Camp John Chambers, John Speed Smith, Charles S. Todd and John O'Fallon—Extracts from Public Documents, Statistical Tables, et cetera ...* Columbus: I. N. Whiting, 1840.

1090. [Jackson, Isaac Rand]. *A Sketch of the Life and Public Services of General William Henry Harrison, Candidate of the People for President of the United States.* New Orleans: Young Men's Tippecanoe Association, 1840; Washington: Jacob Gideon, Jr., 1840; Detroit: Dawson & Bates, 1840; Hartford: J. B. Eldredge, 1840; New York: New York Express, 1839, 1840; Providence: Knowles and Vose, 1840; St. Louis: Churchill & Harris, 1840.

1091. [Jackson, Isaac Rand]. *Eine skizze des lebens und der offentlichen dienste von William H. Harrison: Nebst einem anhang enthaltend die briefe von seinen adjutanten John Chambers, John Speed Smith, Charles S. Todd und John O'Fallen.* Columbus: J. S. Wiestling, 1840.

1092. [Jackson, Isaac Rand]. *General William Henry Harrison, Candidate of the People for President of the United States.* Baltimore: Baltimore Patriot, 1840; Philadelphia: Jesper Harding, 1840. In large measure, a reissue of his 1836 work with a few new additions.

1093. [Jackson, Isaac Rand]. *Lebensgeschichte des Generals Harrison, des Candidaten des Volkes, fur die Prasidentschaft. Aus dem Englischen des I. R. Jackson.* Philadelphia: Marschall, Williams, und Butler, 1840.

1094. [Jackson, Isaac Rand]. *The Life of William Henry Harrison, the People's Candidate for the Presidency.* Philadelphia: [C. Sherman & Co.], 1840.

1095. [Jackson, Isaac Rand]. *The Life of William Henry Harrison, (of Ohio,) the People's Candidate for the Presidency. With a History of the Wars with the British and Indians on Our North-Western Frontier.* Philadelphia: W. Marshall & Co., 1840. Went through at least five editions.

1096. *Life in a Log Cabin, With Hard Cider ...* Philadelphia: M. B. Roberts, 1840.

1097. *The Life and Public Services of William Henry Harrison.* Philadelphia: Croome, Meignelle & Minot, 1840.

1098. *The Life of Major-General William Henry Harrison: Comprising a Brief Account of His Important Civil and Military Services, and an Accurate Description of the Council at Vincennes with Tecumseh, as Well as the Victories of Tippecanoe, Fort Meigs, and the Thames.* Philadelphia: Grigg & Elliot, and T. K. & P. G. Collins, 1840. Went through several editions.

1099. *The Log Cabin Song-Book: A Collection of Popular and Patriotic Songs, Respectfully Dedicated to the Friends of Harrison and Tyler.* New York: Log Cabin Office, 1840.

1100. [Mayo, Robert]. *A Word in Season; or, Review of the Political Life and Opinions of Martin Van Buren: Addressed to the Entire Democracy of the American People ... Dedicated to the Tippecanoe Clubs of the Union, by a Harrison Democrat.* Washington: W. M. Morrison, 1840. Went through at least three editions.

1101. [Montgomery, John C.]. *Montgomery's Tippecanoe Almanac, for the Year 1841. Containing a Short History of the Life and Services of General William Henry Harrison; With Testimonials of His Conduct and Character by Officers and Soldiers Who Fought Under Him and With Him, the Battles of Their Country, at Tippecanoe, Fort Meigs, and the Thames ...* Philadelphia: M'Carty & Davis; Thomas Cowperthwait & Co.; Marshall, Williams & Butler; G. W. Mentz & Son; Hogan & Thompson; Grigg & Elliot; Kay & Brother, all 1840.

1102. [Moore, Jacob Bailey]. *The Contrast: Or, Plain Reasons Why William Henry Harrison Should Be Elected President of the United States, and Why Martin Van Buren Should Not Be Reelected.* New York: J. P. Giffing, c1840.

1103. *The People's Presidential Candidate!* Worcester: Dorr, Howland & Co., [1840?].

1104. *Tip and Ty: A New Comic Whig Glee.* Boston: Parker & Ditson, [1840?]. Campaign song for unaccompanied chorus.

1105. Todd, Charles S. *Sketches of the Civil and Military Services of William Henry Harrison.* Cincinnati: U. P. James, 1840; another enlarged edition published in 1847.

1106. *The Various Charges Against General W. H. Harrison Briefly Stated and Refuted, and Some of the Objections to the Present Administration Enumerated.* Jonesborough, Tenn.: Brownlow and Garland, 1840.

1107. *The Votes and Speeches of Martin Van Buren, on the Subjects of the Right of Suffrage, the Qualifications of Coloured Persons to Vote, and the Appointment or Election of Justices of the Peace.* Albany: T. Weed, 1840. Also in *Microbook Library* [**601**].

1108. Washington, D.C., Republican Committee of Seventy-Six. *The Northern Man with Southern Principles, and the Southern Man with American Principles; Or, A View of the Comparative Claims of Gen. William H. Harrison and Martin Van Buren, Esq., Candidates for the Presidency, to the Support of the Citizens of the Southern States.* Washington: Peter Force, 1840.

1109. Wilmot, Robert. *A New Work, in Favor of the Whig Cause, and the Election of General Harrison to the Presidential Chair ...* Cincinnati: J. B. & R. P. Donogh, 1840.

1110. Workingman. *More than One Hundred Reasons Why William Henry Harrison Should and Will Have the Support of the Democracy, for President of the United States, in Preference to Martin Van Buren.* Boston: Tuttle, Dennett & Chisolm, 1840. Also in *Selected Americana* **[602]**.

C. CAMPAIGN SPEECHES AND GENERAL PAMPHLETS

1111. *Abolition! Infatuation of Federal Whig Leaders of the South.* n.p., [1840?]. Includes letter from Amos Kendall to John Minor Botts and letters from Henry A. Wise and James Lyons.

1112. *Address of the Whig Convention for the Nomination of Electors, to the People of Virginia.* Richmond: n.p., 1840.

1113. *Address of the Whig Members of the Legislature to the People of Virginia.* Richmond: Bailie and Gallaher, 1839. Enumerates reasons against holding a state convention.

1114. *Address to the People of the Slave Holding States, by the Democratic Republican Members of Congress from Those States.* Washington: n.p., 1840.

1115. Anderson, John T., et al. *Address of the Conservative Republicans of the General Assembly to the People of Virginia.* Richmond: Bailie and Gallaher, 1839. Concerns the election of senator, 1839, and the contest between William C. Rives and a subtreasury Democrat.

1116. Badger, George Edmund. *Speech Delivered at the Great Whig Meeting, in the County of Granville, on Tuesday, the Third Day of March, 1840, ... and Published at the Request of His Fellow-Citizens.* Raleigh: Raleigh Register, 1840.

1117. [Bayly, Thomas Henry]. *Speech of Mr. Bayly, of Accomack, on the Election of a United States Senator, ... , 1839.* Richmond: n.p., 1839.

1118. Bell, John. *A Looking Glass for the Federal Whig Leaders in Tennessee; or, Facts for the People.* n.p., [1839?].

1119. Burnet, Jacob. *Araeth y Barnwr Burnett, o Dalaeth Ohio. Yn Nghenhedledig Eistedelfod y Whigiaid, a Gyfarfw yn Harrisburg, Pa., yn Rhoddi byr Hanes o Fywyd y Cadg. William Henry Harrison. Agr a Gyfieuthwyd ir Iaith Gymraeg, Gan H. R. Price.* Columbus: Chas. Scott, 1840.

1120. Burnet, Jacob. *Proceedings of the Democratic Whig National Convention, Which Assembled at Harrisburg, Pennsylvania, on the Fourth of December, 1839, for the Purpose of Nominating Candidates for President and Vice President of the United States.* Harrisburg: R. S. Elliott & Co., 1839.

1121. Burnet, Jacob. *Speech of Jacob Burnet in the Whig National Convention, Giving a Brief History of the Life of Gen. William Henry Harrison.* Washington: Madisonian Office, 1839.

1122. *Campaign* ... Frankfort, Ky., April 23-October 8, 1840, May, 1841. May 1841 issue has county election statistics for each state in 1840 election, inaugural address of Harrison, funeral arrangements for Harrison, and inaugural message of Tyler.

1123. Corwin, Thomas. *Speech of Mr. Corwin, of Ohio, in Reply to General Crary's Attack on General Harrison, Delivered in the House of Representatives, February 15, 1840.* Washington: Gales & Seaton, 1840.

1124. *The Crisis, Devoted to the Support of the Democratic Principles of Jefferson.* Richmond, Va. A weekly, March 7–October 28, 1840, supporting Democratic candidates.

1125. *Daily Political Tornado* ... Columbus, Ohio. October 6–November 11, 1840. Whig periodical.

1126. Dana, Edmund P. *A Voice From Bunker-Hill, and the Fathers of the Revolutionary War, in Favor of the Hero of North Bend, Being a Few Candid Remarks and Observations on the Approaching Presidential Election, and Subjects Connected Therewith* ... Bunker-Hill: n.p., 1840.

1127. Fendall, Philip Ricard. *Proceedings of the Opponents of the Present Administration, at Public Meetings, Held in the City of Washington, February 15 and 18, 1840; with the Address of Philip R. Fendall, Esq.* n.p., [1840?].

1128. Fillmore, Millard. *Millard Fillmore Letter.* n.p., 1840. Circular decrying evils of the Van Buren administration and promoting the election of Harrison and Tyler.

1129. Garland, James. *Letter of James Garland, to His Constituents.* [Washington, 1840]. Expresses reasons for supporting Harrison and Tyler and not Van Buren.

1130. Goode, William O. *Speech of Mr. William O. Goode ... on Election of Senator to Congress, ... January 29, 1840.* n.p., 1840.

1131. Harrison, William Henry. *Gen. Harrison's Speech at the Dayton Convention, September 10, 1840*. Boston: Whig Republican Association, 1840.

1132. Harrison, William Henry. *Gen. Harrison's Speech at Fort Meigs* ... n.p., [1840?].

1133. Harrison, William Henry. "Letter from William Henry Harrison to Harmar Denny of Pittsburgh, Accepting the Nomination to the Office of the President of the United States, by the Convention of the Anti-Masonic Party, Held at Philadelphia, in the Fall of 1838." *Western Pennsylvania Historical Magazine* 1 (July 1918): 144-51.

1134. Hazard, Thomas Robinson. *Facts for the Laboring Man*. Nos. 1-12, by a Laboring Man. Newport: J. Atkinson, 1840. Also in *Goldsmiths'* [600] and *Selected Americana* [602]. An 1840 Whig campaign document originally published under the pseudonym "Narragansett" in the *Newport Herald*.

1135. Heath, James Ewell. *Whigs and Democrats: Or, Love of No Politics: A Comedy in Three Acts*. Richmond: n.p., 1839.

1136. *The Log Cabin* ... New York: May 2-November 9, 1840; December 5, 1840–November 20, 1841. Published by Horace Greeley; includes music. Whig campaign paper.

1137. *The Log Cabin & Hard Cider Melodies: A Collection of Popular and Patriotic Songs, Respectfully Dedicated to the Friends of Harrison and Tyler* ... Boston: Charles Adams, 1840. Songs lack music.

1138. *The Log Cabin Almanack for 1841*. Columbus: E. Glover, 1840.

1139. *Log Cabin Anecdotes*. New York: J. P. Giffing, 1840.

1140. McRae, A. S. *The Whig Log Cabin at the City of Richmond, in 1840: Notice of the Speech of Hon. Wm. C. Preston of South Carolina*. Richmond: Johns & Goolsby, 1881. Describes the campaign in the city of Richmond.

1141. Miller, John G. *The Great Convention: Description of the Convention of the People of Ohio, Held at Columbus, on the 21st and 22nd February, 1840*. Columbus: Cutler & Wright, 1840?

1142. *"A Mirror for the Pretended Democracy," From the* National Intelligencer *of Oct. 1, 1840, to Which is Added, a Report on Executive Patronage, Made to the Senate of the United States, May 4, 1826, by a Select Committee, Consisting of Messrs. Benton, Macon, Van Buren, White, Dickerson, Holmes, Hayne, and Johnson of Kentucky*. Washington: n.p., 1840].

1143. [Nicholas, Samuel Smith]. *Letters on the Presidency*. n.p., 1840. Contains seven letters signed "Kentucky Democrat" first addressed to Webster.

1144. Niles, William Ogden. *The Tippecanoe Text-book, Compiled from Niles' Register and Other Authentic Records ... and Respectfully Dedicated to the Young Men of the United States*. Baltimore: Duff Green, 1840; Philadelphia: Hogan & Thompson and T. K. & P. G. Collins, 1840.

1145. Ogle, Charles. *Speech ... on the Character and Services of General William H. Harrison ... in the House ... April 16, 1840*. Washington: n.p., 1840.

1146. Ogle, Charles. *Speech of Mr. Ogle, of Pennsylvania, on the Regal Splendor of the President's Palace, Delivered in the House of Representatives, April 14, 1840*. Washington: n.p., 1840?

1147. *Proceedings of a Public Dinner in Albemarle County*. n.p., 1840. Meeting of Conservative Democrats announcing their support for the Whig ticket.

1148. *Proceedings of the Democratic State Convention, Held at Charlottesville, Va., September 9 and 10, 1840*. Charlottesville: n.p., 1840. Meeting in support of Van Buren.

1149. Reser, Alva O., and J. S. Bergen, eds. "A Famous Campaign Song." *Indiana Magazine of History* 2 (December 1906): 198-99. Provides music and lyrics for "Tippecanoe and Tyler Too."

1150. Ritchie, Thomas. *Interesting Correspondence, between Thomas Ritchie and J. R. Poinsett, Secretary of War, Concerning the Reorganization of the Militia*. Richmond: n.p., 1840.

1151. [Ritchie, Thomas]. "An Address of the Democrats of Virginia, 1840, To the People of Virginia." *John P. Branch Historical Papers of Randolph-Macon College* 3 (1911): 263-70.

1152. Russell, John B. *The Log Cabin Almanac. 1841 ...* Cincinnati: Truman & Smith, [1840].

1153. *Second Address of the Central Committee of Fauquier, to the People of that County, on the Army Bill*. Washington: Madisonian Office, 1840. Whig campaign pamphlet with first address printed at end.

1154. *Spirit of '76*. Nashville. March 14–October 28, 1840, January 20, 1841. Weekly. January issue contains election statistics by county and state.

1155. Sprague, Peleg. *Remarks of Peleg Sprague at Faneuil Hall, Before the Citizens of Boston and Its Vicinity, Upon the Character and Services of Gen. William Henry Harrison, of Ohio, the Whig Candidate for the Presidency of the United States.* Boston: Whig Republican Association of Boston, 1839.

1156. Stanly, Edward. *Letter from Mr. Stanly, of N.C., to Mr. Botts, of Virginia.* Washington: n.p., 1840. Dated September 23.

1157. *To the Whigs and Conservatives of the United States* ... [Washington?: n.p., 1840]. Dated August 25.

1158. Webster, Daniel, et al. *Bunker Hill Declaration.* n.p., 1840. Also in *Selected Americana* [602]. An 1840 Whig pamphlet, drafted by Daniel Webster, William King of Maine, William Upham of Vermont, and others.

1159. Webster, Daniel. *Mr. Webster's Remarks to the Ladies of Richmond, Va., October 5, 1840.* Boston: Perkins & Marvin, 1841.

1160. Webster, Daniel. *Speech ... at the Great Mass Meeting at Saratoga, New York, on the 19th August, 1840.* Nashville: n.p., 1840.

1161. Webster, Daniel. *Speech of the Hon. Daniel Webster at the Convention at Richmond, Va., on Monday, October 5th, 1840, Reported in Full.* New York: Young & Hunt, 1840.

VIII

Vice President

A. THE WILLIAM HENRY HARRISON ADMINISTRATION

1. Inauguration

1162. Durbin, Louise. *Inaugural Cavalcade.* New York: Dodd, Mead, 1971. Describes inaugural ceremonies from George Washington to Richard Nixon.

1163. Gaines, William H., Jr. "The Last Days of a President-Elect, with Some Account of the Splendid Inauguration Accorded a Military Hero." *Virginia Cavalcade* 2 (Winter 1952): 40-42. Recounts story of Harrison's visit to his ancestral home, Berkeley, in Virginia, his trip to Washington with Tyler for the inauguration, and Webster's revision of Harrison's inaugural address.

1164. Goebel, Dorothy Burne. *Generals in the White House.* Garden City, N.Y.: Doubleday, Doran and Company, 1945, 1952; Freeport, N.Y.: Books for Libraries Press, 1971. Has short discussion of William Henry Harrison.

1165. Kittler, Glenn D. *Hail to the Chief! The Inauguration Days of Our Presidents.* Philadelphia: Chilton Books, 1965. Contains accounts of inaugurations and brief biographies.

1166. McKee, Thomas Hudson. *Presidential Inaugurations from George Washington, 1789, to Grover Cleveland, 1893, with Inaugural Addresses Complete.* Washington: Statistical Publishing Company, 1893.

1167. "Presidential Inaugurations in the House Chamber." *History in the House* 1 (January 1985): 1-4. Discusses seven inaugurations conducted in the House of Representatives chamber.

1168. "Washington Twenty Years Ago: Inauguration of President Harrison." *Leisure Hour* 10 (April 4, 1861): 215-16, 218.

2. Funeral

1169. Lewis, Edward S. "The Death and Funeral of President William Henry Harrison." *Ohio Archaeological and Historical Quarterly* 37 (October 1928): 605-12.

1170. New York (City) Common Council. *Report of the Committee of Arrangements of the Common Council of the City of New York, for the Funeral Obsequies in Memory of William H. Harrison ... .* New York: Bryant & Boggs, 1841.

1171. Peckham, Howard H. "Tears for Old Tippecanoe: Religious Interpretations of President Harrison's Death." *American Antiquarian Society Proceedings* 69 (April 1959): 17-36. Examines 138 sermons and eulogies delivered on the occasion of Harrison's death.

1172. United States War Department. *Official Arrangements for the Obsequies of the Late President, William Henry Harrison, April 7th, A. D. 1841.* Washington: n.p., 1841?.

1173. Walker, Kenneth R. "The Death of a President." *Northwest Ohio Quarterly* 28 (Summer 1956): 157-62.

3. Other

1174. "Alas, Poor Henry Clay!" *United States Magazine and Democratic Review* 7 (February 1840): 99-111.Explores status of Whig party and Clay's and Webster's places within it.

1175. Gunderson, Robert Gray. "A Search for Old Tip Himself." *Register of the Kentucky Historical Society* 86 (Autumn 1988): 330-51.

1176. Halford, E. W. "General Harrison's Attitude Toward the Presidency." *Century Magazine* 84 (June 1912): 305-10.

1177. "The Nation's Calamity." *New Yorker*, April 10, 1841, 58. Harrison's pledge to a single term placed him out of reach of the opposition, despite personal shortcomings.

1178. Shelley, Fred, ed. "The Vice President Receives Bad News in Williamsburg: A Letter of James Lyons to John Tyler." *Virginia Magazine of History and Biography* 76 (July 1968): 337-39. Letter of April 3, 1841, reveals that Tyler was aware of Harrison's serious illness even before being informed of his death by Fletcher Webster.

B. VICE PRESIDENCY

1179. Barzman, Sol. *Madmen and Geniuses: The Vice-Presidents of the United States.* Chicago: Follett, 1974. Includes thirteen-page bibliography.

1180. Bell, Christopher, ed. *Vice Presidents of the United States, 1789-1961.* Washington: Library of Congress, Legislative Reference Service, 1962.

1181. Curtis, Richard, and Maggie Wells. *Not Exactly a Crime: Our Vice Presidents from Adams to Agnew.* New York: Dial Press, 1972. Humorous account of vice presidents and the office.

1182. Harwood, Michael. *In the Shadow of Presidents: The American Vice-Presidency and Succession System.* Philadelphia: Lippincott, 1966.

1183. Hatch, Louis Clinton. *A History of the Vice-Presidency of the United States.* New York: American Historical Society, 1934; Westport, Conn.: Greenwood Press, 1970.

1184. Healy, Diana Dixon. *America's Vice-Presidents: Our First Forty-Three Vice-Presidents and How They Got to be Number Two.* New York: Atheneum, 1984.

1185. Stathis, Stephen W., and Ronald C. Moe. "America's Other Inaugurations." *Presidential Studies Quarterly* 10 (Fall 1980): 550-70. Covers vice-presidential inaugurations.

1186. Waugh, Edgar W. *Second Consul, The Vice Presidency: Our Greatest Political Problem.* Indianapolis: Bobbs-Merrill, 1956. Brief sketches of the vice presidents.

1187. Williams, Irving G. *The Rise of the Vice Presidency.* Washington: Public Affairs Press, 1956. Analysis of the evolution of the office.

1188. Young, Donald. *American Roulette: The History and Dilemma of the Vice Presidency.* New York: Holt, Rinehart and Winston, 1965, 1972.

1189. Young, Klyde, and Lamar Middleton. *Heirs Apparent: The Vice-Presidents of the United States.* New York: Prentice-Hall, 1948; Freeport, N.Y.: Books for Libraries Press, 1969.

C. SUCCESSION TO THE PRESIDENCY

1190. Binkley, Wilfred E. *The Man in the White House: His Powers and Duties.* Baltimore: Johns Hopkins Press, 1959, 1968; New York: Harper & Row, 1964. Sees Tyler's oath of office and accession to the presidency as "one of the major errors of our constitutional history"; usage determines succession of vice presidency to presidency.

1191. Brown, Everett S., and Ruth C. Silva. "Presidential Succession and Inability." *Journal of Politics* 11 (February 1949): 236-256. Explores the meaning of the succession clauses of the constitution.

1192. Burdick, Charles K. *The Law of the American Constitution: Its Origin and Development.* New York: G. P. Putnam's Sons, 1922. Unsure that the constitution provided for the succession of vice president to president but usage has made it so.

1193. Carpenter, Frank G. "A Talk with a President's Son." *Lippincott's Monthly Magazine* 41 (March 1888): 416-21. Reports an interview with Robert Tyler in which the focus of the discussion was Tyler's accession to the presidency.

1194. "Clues to Mr. Truman's Future: 6 Who Inherited the Presidency." *U.S. News and World Report,* July 16, 1948, 11-13. Discusses vice presidents who succeeded to the presidency and then sought election to office; brief discussion of the acrimonious Tyler administration includes portrait.

1195. Corwin, Edward S. *The President, Office and Powers, 1787-1948: History and Analysis of Practice and Opinion.* New York: New York University Press, 1940, 1941, 1948, 1957, 1984 (carries coverage up to year published). Argues that framers of the constitution clearly intended that "the Vice-President should remain Vice-President and assume the presidency only if elected"; i.e., Tyler was wrong in his reading of the constitution in the position he took at the time of Harrison's death.

1196. Dinnerstein, Leonard. "The Accession of John Tyler to the Presidency." M.A. thesis, Columbia University, 1960.

1197. Dinnerstein, Leonard. "The Accession of John Tyler to the Presidency." *Virginia Magazine of History and Biography* 70 (October 1962): 447-58. Discusses Daniel and Fletcher Webster's role in notifying Tyler of Harrison's death and argues that the accession question involved title more than role; contends that Tyler interpreted the constitution according to his own understanding and showed "good judgment."

1198. Hansen, Richard H. *The Year We Had No President.* Lincoln: University of Nebraska Press, 1962. Argues that usage is the determinant on presidential succession.

1199. Harper, Camille. "'And Tyler Too.'" *Northern Virginian* 14 (November-December 1984): 46-47. Discusses Tyler's role in establishing the principle of vice presidential succession and Webster's discussion with Tyler on majority rule by the cabinet.

1200. Horwill, Herbert William. *The Usages of the American Constitution*. London: Oxford University Press, 1925; Port Washington, N.Y.: Kennikat Press, 1969. Argues that usage alone transforms a vice president into president and that Tyler's decision regarding succession remains one of the most important elements in the unwritten constitution of the United States.

1201. Levin, Peter R. *Seven by Chance: The Accidental Presidents*. New York: Farrar, Straus, 1948. Discusses the political actions and doctrines of Tyler, Fillmore, Johnson, Arthur, Roosevelt, Coolidge, and Truman.

1202. "The Penny-Postman to John Tyler, Vice-President of the United States." *United States Magazine and Democratic Review* 9 (July 1841): 60-75. Discusses succession question and urges Tyler to adhere to true Democratic principles.

1203. Schlesinger, Arthur M., Jr. *The Cycles of American History*. Boston: Houghton Mifflin, 1986. Discusses briefly the matter of succession, concluding that the qualifications for the vice-presidential nominee became less significant after the development of the second American party system and the passage of the Twelfth Amendment.

1204. Siebeneck, Henry King. "John Tyler: Our First Accidental President." *Western Pennsylvania Historical Magazine* 34 (March 1951): 35-50; 34 (June 1951): 119-33. Assesses the Tyler presidency and calls Tyler "narrow and provincial, ... prejudiced and petty" for failure to submit to the majority will of the Whig party or to allow a bank bill to become law without his signature.

1205. Silva, Ruth C. *Presidential Succession*. Ann Arbor: University of Michigan Press, 1951; New York: Greenwood Press, 1968. Discusses constitutional provisions and intent on the succession question and argues that it never was "intended that the Vice President or designated officer should become President under the succession clause."

1206. Stathis, Stephen W. "John Tyler's Presidential Succession: A Reappraisal." *Prologue* 8 (Winter 1976): 223-36. Explores events and views regarding Tyler's succession to the presidency.

1207. Tyler, Lyon G. "John Tyler and the Vice-Presidency." *Tyler's Quarterly Historical and Genealogical Magazine* 9 (October 1927): 89-95. Again discusses the Tyler nomination at Harrisburg and reprints Benjamin W. Leigh letter on the matter showing that Tyler was considered a strong candidate for the post.

1208. Tyler, Lyon G. "Mr. Leigh and the Vice Presidency." *Tyler's Quarterly Historical and Genealogical Magazine* 3 (January 1922): 214-16. Denies that Tyler's nomination for the vice-presidency came after Benjamin W. Leigh declined the nomination.

1209. "The Vice Presidency—A Bridgebuilder." *Time* 63 (January 18, 1954): 25-29. Explores the traditional roles taken by several vice presidents, and briefly discusses Tyler's position and elevation to the presidency.

IX

President, 1841–1845

A. DOMESTIC ISSUES

1. Political Developments

1210. Abraham, Henry J. *Justices and Presidents: A Political History of Appointments to the Supreme Court.* New York: Oxford University Press, 1974.

1211. Adams, James Truslow. *The Epic of America.* Boston: Little, Brown and Company, 1931, 1933, 1934; New York: Triangle Books, 1941 (and several other editions).

1212. Adams, William Harrison, III. "The Louisiana Whigs." *Louisiana History* 15 (Summer 1974): 213-28.

1213. Adams, William Harrison, III. *The Whig Party in Louisiana.* Lafayette: University of Southwestern Louisiana, 1973.

1214. Alexander, Thomas B., et al. "The Basis of Alabama's Ante-Bellum Two-Party System." *Alabama Review* 19 (October 1966): 243-76.

1215. Alexander, Thomas B. *Sectional Stress and Party Strength: A Study of Roll-Call Voting Patterns in the United States House of Representatives, 1836-1860.* Nashville: Vanderbilt University Press, 1967. Explores ideological distinctions between the political parties and the strength of party loyalty through roll-call analysis.

1216. Ambler, Charles Henry. "The Cleavage between Eastern and Western Virginia." *American Historical Review* 15 (July 1910): 762-80. Examines the impact of geography on sectionalism.

1217. Ambler, Charles Henry. *Sectionalism in Virginia, 1776 to 1861*. Glendale: Arthur H. Clark, 1910; Chicago: University of Chicago Press, 1910; New York: Russell & Russell, 1964. Also in *Microbook Library* **[601]**.

1218. Ambler, Charles Henry. "Virginia and the Presidential Succession, 1840-1844." In *Essays in American History Dedicated to Frederick Jackson Turner ...* (New York: Holt, 1910), pp. 185-202. Argues that Tyler, obstinate, tried to appeal to moderates of both parties and hence signed tariff of 1842, but his effort came too late to conciliate.

1219. Ashworth, John. *"Agrarians" & "Aristocrats": Party Ideology in the United States, 1837-1846*. London: Royal Historical Society; New Jersey: Humanities Press, 1983.

1220. Ashworth, John. "The Democratic-Republicans before the Civil War: Political Ideology and Economic Change." *Journal of American Studies* 20 (December 1986): 375-90.

1221. Aull, Edward, Jr. "Calhounism in Virginia, 1830-1850." M.A. thesis, University of Alabama, 1936.

1222. Barber, Nigel Graeme. "The Corporal's Guard in Congress, 1841-1843." M.A. thesis, College of William and Mary, 1970. Explores the relationship between Tyler and his chief supporters in Congress.

1223. Barkan, Elliott R. "The Emergence of a Whig Persuasion: Conservatism, Democratism, and the New York State Whigs." *New York History* 52 (October 1971): 367-95.

1224. Bergeron, Paul H. *Antebellum Politics in Tennessee*. Lexington: University Press of Kentucky, 1982. The standard treatment of Tennessee politics in Andrew Jackson's home state.

1225. Bergeron, Paul H. *The Presidency of James K. Polk*. Lawrence: University Press of Kansas, 1987.

1226. Binkley, Wilfred E. *President and Congress*. New York: Alfred A. Knopf, 1947. One of the better discussions of the development of the office of president and of the relationship between that office and Congress.

1227. Bogue, Allan G., and Mark Paul Marlaire. "Of Mess and Men: The Boardinghouse and Congressional Voting, 1821-1842." *American Journal of Political Science* (May 1975): 207-30.

1228. Bogue, Allan G., et al. "Members of the House of Representatives and the Process of Modernization, 1789-1960." *Journal of American History* 63 (1976): 275-302.

1229. Boorstin, Daniel J. *The Americans: The National Experience*. New York: Random House, 1965. Pulitzer Prize-winning study of nineteenth-century United States.

1230. Bowers, Claude Gernade. *The Party Battles of the Jackson Period*. Boston: Houghton Mifflin Company, 1922, 1924, 1928; Chautauqua, N.Y.: Chautauqua Press, 1923.

1231. Boyett, Gene W. "Quantitative Differences Between the Arkansas Whig and Democratic Parties, 1836-1850." *Arkansas Historical Quarterly* 34 (Autumn 1975): 214-26.

1232. Brant, Irving. *Impeachment: Trials and Errors*. New York: Knopf, 1972. Examines, in part, the tensions between Tyler and Congress.

1233. Brauer, Kinley J. *Cotton versus Conscience: Massachusetts Whig Politics and Southwestern Expansion, 1843-1848*. Lexington: University of Kentucky Press, 1967. Investigates the differences among Whigs of Massachusetts on the issue of the annexation of Texas and the Mexican War.

1234. Brock, William Ranulf. *Parties and Political Conscience: American Dilemmas, 1840-1850*. Millwood, N.Y.: KTO Press, 1979.

1235. Brooks, Noah. "The Passing of the Whigs." *Scribner's Magazine* 17 (February 1895): 199-213. Discusses party origins and development from the founding of the nation to 1845.

1236. Brown, Richard H. "The Missouri Crisis, Slavery, and the Politics of Jacksonianism." *South Atlantic Quarterly* 65 (Winter 1966): 55-72. Discusses the centrality of slavery to political debate in the Jacksonian era.

1237. Brown, Stuart Gerry. *The American Presidency: Leadership, Partisanship and Popularity*. New York: Macmillan, 1966. Examines sources and uses of presidential popularity.

1238. Brown, Thomas. "Politics and Statesmanship: A Study of the American Whig Party." Ph. D. diss., Columbia University, 1981. Sees the Whig party as a political, rather than a social, identity with common ideas, beliefs, and values, which crystallized behind a general program during the economic crisis, 1837-1842, and, once Tyler was expelled from the party, Whigs sought to implement that program.

1239. Brown, Thomas. "Southern Whigs and the Politics of Statesmanship, 1833-1841." *Journal of Southern History* 46 (August 1980): 361-80. Examines sources of unity among southern Whigs; explores Tyler's relationship with the Whig party before and after his veto of the second bank bill.

1240. Brown, Thomas. "The Massachusetts Whigs and Industrialism." *Historical Journal of Massachusetts* 14 (January 1986): 25-42.

1241. Brownlow, Louis. *The President and the Presidency*. Chicago: Public Administration Service, 1949. Brief discussion of the Harrison and Tyler presidencies and of the denunciations heaped upon Tyler.

1242. Burgess, John W. *The Middle Period, 1817-1858*. New York: C. Scribner's Sons, 1897, 1901, 1924. Also in *Microbook Library* **[601]**. An older survey of nineteenth-century politics.

1243. Carlson, A. Cheree. "The Rhetoric of the Know-Nothing Party: Nativism as a Response to the Rhetorical Situation." *Southern Communication Journal* 54 (Summer 1989): 364-383.

1244. Channing, Edward. *A History of the United States*. 6 vols. New York: The Macmillan Company, 1905-1925, 1917-1940; New York: Octagon Books, 1977. Volumes 5 and 6 are important for the Tyler administration and pre-Civil War decade.

1245. Cohen, Jeffrey E. *The Politics of the U.S. Cabinet: Representation in the Executive Branch, 1789-1984*. Pittsburgh: University of Pittsburgh Press, 1988.

1246. Cole, Arthur Charles. *The Irrepressible Conflict, 1850-1865*. New York: The Macmillan Company, 1934, 1938: St. Clair Shores, Mich.: Scholarly Press, 1971. An older classic on the decade before the Civil War.

1247. Cole, Arthur Charles. *The Whig Party in the South*. Washington: American Historical Association, 1913; Gloucester, Mass.: Peter Smith, 1962. An older study of the attitude and policies of the Whig coalition in the South.

1248. Cole, Donald B. *Jacksonian Democracy in New Hampshire, 1800-1851*. Cambridge: Harvard University Press, 1970. The most thorough treatment of New Hampshire during the Jackson-Van Buren-Tyler presidencies.

1249. Coleman, Peter J. *The Transformation of Rhode Island, 1790-1860*. Providence: Brown University Press, 1963. Important for the Dorr Rebellion.

1250. Cooper, William J., Jr. *Liberty and Slavery: Southern Politics to 1860*. New York: Alfred A. Knopf, 1983. Broad history of the interaction between the concept of liberty and the reality of slavery.

1251. Cooper, William J., Jr. *The South and the Politics of Slavery, 1828-1856*. Baton Rouge: Louisiana State University Press, 1978.

1252. Corwin, Edward S. "National Power and State Interposition, 1787-1861." *Michigan Law Review* 10 (May 1912): 535-51. Discussion of several domestic issues the Tyler administration faced.

1253. Craven, Avery Odelle. *Civil War in the Making, 1815-1860.* Baton Rouge: Louisiana State University Press, 1959.

1254. Craven, Avery Odelle. *The Coming of the Civil War.* New York: C. Scribner's Sons, 1942; Chicago: University of Chicago Press, 1957, 1967.

1255. Craven, Avery Odelle. *The Growth of Southern Nationalism, 1848-1861.* Baton Rouge: Louisiana State University Press, 1953, 1962.

1256. Craven, Avery Odelle. *The Repressible Conflict, 1830-1861.* Baton Rouge: Louisiana State University Press, 1939.

1257. Crook, David Paul. *American Democracy in English Politics, 1815-1850.* Oxford, Eng.: Clarendon Press, 1965.

1258. Curtis, James C. *The Fox at Bay: Martin Van Buren and the Presidency, 1837-1841.* Lexington: University Press of Kentucky, 1970. Excellent study of the background to the political inheritance of the Whigs in 1841.

1259. Damon, Allan L. "Veto." *American Heritage,* February 1974, 12-15, 81. Examines briefly Tyler's use.

1260. Darling, Arthur B. *Political Changes in Massachusetts, 1824-1848: A Study of Liberal Movements in Politics.* New Haven: Yale University Press, 1925; Cos Cob, Conn.: J. E. Edwards, 1968. An older, but still useful, study of Massachusetts politics of the 1820s, '30s, and '40s.

1261. Degler, Carl N. *Out of Our Past: The Forces that Shaped Modern America.* New York: Harper, 1959, 1970, 1984.

1262. Dennison, George M. "The Constitutional Issues of the Dorr War: A Study in the Evolution of American Constitutionalism, 1776-1849." Ph.D. diss., University of Washington, 1967.

1263. Dennison, George M. *The Dorr War: Republicanism on Trial, 1831-1861.* Lexington: University Press of Kentucky, 1976. The standard study of the Dorr War.

1264. Dennison, George M. "The Dorr War and Political Questions." *Yearbook of the Supreme Court Historical Society* 4 (1979): 45-62.

1265. Dennison, George M. "The Dorr War and the Triumph of Institutionalism." *Social Science Journal* 15 (April 1978): 39-58.

1266. Dodd, William Edward. *Expansion and Conflict*. Boston: Houghton Mifflin Company, 1915, 1919. Explores the political consequences of continental expansion.

1267. Donovan, Herbert D. A. *The Barnburners: A Study of the Internal Movements in the Political History of New York State and of the Resulting Changes of Political Affiliation, 1830-1852.* New York: New York University Press, 1925; Philadelphia: Porcupine Press, 1974.

1268. Eaton, Clement. "Freedom of the Press in the Upper South." *Mississippi Valley Historical Review* 18 (March 1932): 479-99.

1269. Eaton, Clement. *Freedom of Thought in the Old South*. Durham, N.C.: Duke University Press, 1940; New York: P. Smith, 1951.

1270. Eaton, Clement. *The Freedom-of-Thought Struggle in the Old South*. New York: Harper & Row, 1964. General survey of the period.

1271. Eaton, Clement. *A History of the Old South*. New York: Macmillan Company, 1949, 1966, 1975. Contains a good pen portrait of Tyler.

1272. Fish, Carl Russell. *The Civil Service and the Patronage*. New York: Longmans, Green, & Company, 1905; Cambridge: Harvard University Press, 1920; New York: Russell & Russell, 1963. Also in *Microbook Library* [601]. An older, but still very useful study of patronage and political party development.

1273. Fiske, John. "Harrison, Tyler, and the Whig Coalition." In *Essays Historical and Literary*. 2 vols. New York: Macmillan, 1907.

1274. Folsom, Burton W., II. "Party Formation and Development in Jacksonian America: The Old South." *Journal of American Studies* 7 (December 1973): 217-29.

1275. Formisano, Ronald P. *The Birth of Mass Political Parties, Michigan, 1827-1861*. Princeton: Princeton University Press, 1971.

1276. Formisano, Ronald P. "Political Character, Antipartyism and the Second American Party System." *American Quarterly* 21 (Winter 1969): 683-709.

1277. Formisano, Ronald P. *The Transformation of Political Culture: Massachusetts Parties, 1790s-1840s*. New York: Oxford University Press, 1983.

1278. Fowler, Dorothy Ganfield. *The Cabinet Politician: The Postmasters General, 1829-1909.* New York: Columbia University Press, 1943; New York: AMS Press, 1967.

1279. Fraser, Hugh Russell. *Democracy in the Making: The Jackson-Tyler Era.* Indianapolis: Bobbs-Merrill Company, [1938]; New York: Kraus Reprint Company, 1969. One of the major studies of the Tyler administration; adopts a favorable view of Tyler.

1280. Freehling, William W. *The Road to Disunion.* 1 vol. to date. New York: Oxford University Press, 1990– . Study of South Carolina.

1281. Friedman, Jean E. *The Revolt of the Conservative Democrats: An Essay on American Political Culture and Political Development, 1837-1844.* Ann Arbor: UMI Research Press, 1979. Focuses mainly on independent treasury and political response.

1282. Gantz, Richard Alan. "Henry Clay and the Harvest of Bitter Fruit: The Struggle with John Tyler, 1841-1842." Ph.D. diss., Indiana University, 1986. Suggests that in his fight with Tyler over domestic policies, Clay was more concerned with the implementation of his American System than in promoting his presidential ambitions.

1283. Gatell, Frank Otto. "'Conscience and Judgment': The Bolt of the Massachusetts Conscience Whigs." *Historian* 21 (November 1958): 18-45. An important examination of factionalism within the Massachusetts Whig party.

1284. Goodman, Paul. "Moral Purpose and Republican Politics in Antebellum America, 1830-1860." *Maryland Historian* 20 (Fall-Winter 1989): 5-39.

1285. Green, Fletcher M. *Constitutional Development in the South Atlantic States, 1776-1860.* Chapel Hill: University of North Carolina Press, 1930. An important study of constitutional changes in southern state constitutions during the first half of the nineteenth century.

1286. Green, Fletcher M. "Democracy in the Old South." *Journal of Southern History* 12 (February 1946): 3-23. Explores the competition between aristocracy and democracy.

1287. Haines, Charles Grove, and Foster H. Sherwood. *The Role of the Supreme Court in American Government and Politics, 1835-1864.* Berkeley: University of California Press, 1957. Focus is on Roger B. Taney's tenure as Chief Justice of the United States.

1288. Hall, Kermit L. *The Politics of Justice: Lower Federal Judicial Selection and the Second Party System, 1829-1861.* Lincoln: University of Nebraska Press, 1979. Discusses briefly judicial patronage as used by Tyler.

1289. Harrell, Mary Ann, and Burnett Anderson. *Equal Justice under Law: The Supreme Court in American Life.* Washington: Supreme Court Historical Society, 1988. Offers discussion of the impact of court decisions on American life.

1290. Harris, Joseph P. *The Advice and Consent of the Senate: A Study of the Confirmation of Appointments by the United States Senate.* Berkeley: University of California Press, 1953; New York: Greenwood Press, 1968.

1291. Harrison, Joseph H., Jr. "Martin Van Buren and His Southern Supporters." *Journal of Southern History* 22 (November 1956): 438-57.

1292. Harrison, Lowell H. "The President Without a Party: John Tyler, Virginia Politician." *American History Illustrated* 16 (April 1981): 12-21.

1293. Hartz, Louis. *The Liberal Tradition in America: An Interpretation of American Political Thought Since the Revolution.* New York: Harcourt, Brace, 1955.

1294. Haws, Robert J. "Massachusetts Whigs, 1833-1854." Ph.D. diss., University of Nebraska, 1973.

1295. Haynes, George H. *The Senate of the United States: Its History and Practice.* New York: Houghton, Mifflin Company, 1938; New York: Russell & Russell, 1960. Treats briefly Tyler's views on sending abroad unconfirmed diplomats, his action for the annexation of Texas, his resignation from the Senate and refusal to obey Virginia legislative instructions, and the Senate's rejection of several of his cabinet nominees.

1296. Hinsdale, Mary Louise. *A History of the President's Cabinet.* Ann Arbor: G. Wahr, 1911. Also in *Microbook Library* [601].

1297. Hofstadter, Richard. *The American Political Tradition and the Men Who Made It.* New York: A. P. Knopf, 1948, 1951, 1962, 1967, 1973; New York: Vintage Books, 1954.

1298. Hofstadter, Richard. *The Idea of a Party System: The Rise of Legitimate Opposition in the United States, 1780-1840.* Berkeley: University of California Press, 1969.

1299. Holt, Edgar Allan. "Party Politics in Ohio, 1840-1850." *Ohio Archeological and Historical Publications* 37 (1928): 439-591; 38 (1929): 47-182, 260-402.

1300. Holt, Michael F. *Political Parties and American Political Development from the Age of Jackson to the Age of Lincoln.* Baton Rouge: Louisiana State University Press, 1992. Brings together many of Holt's shorter essays on American politics.

1301. Holt, Michael F. "William Henry Harrison, March-April 1841, John Tyler, 1841-1845," in C. Van Woodward, ed., *Responses of the Presidents to Charges of Misconduct*. New York: Dell Publishing Company, 1974.

1302. Hopkins, James H. *A History of Political Parties in the United States ...* . New York: G.P. Putnam's Sons, 1900.

1303. Hotchkiss, Willard E. *The Judicial Work of the Comptroller of the Treasury, As Compared with Similar Functions in the Governments of France and Germany ...* Ithaca: Cornell University Press, 1911.

1304. Howe, Daniel Walker. *The Political Culture of the American Whigs*. Chicago: University of Chicago Press, 1979. Excellent study of Whig thought and theory.

1305. Hyman, Harold M., and William M. Wiecek. *Equal Justice Under Law: Constitutional Development, 1835-1875*. New York: Harper & Row, 1982.

1306. Irelan, John Robert. *The Republic; or, A History of the United States of America in the Administrations, from the Monarchic Colonial Days to the Present Time*. Chicago: Fairbanks and Palmer Publishing Company, 1888. Volume titles vary slightly; volume 10 provides a history of the life, administration, and times of John Tyler.

1307. Jackson, Carlton. "A History of the Whig Party in Alabama, 1828-1860." Ph.D. diss., University of Alabama, 1963.

1308. Jackson, Carlton. *Presidential Vetoes, 1792-1945*. Athens: University of Georgia Press, 1967. An important account of presidential vetoes; provides chronology to Tyler's vetoes.

1309. Jacobs, Robert D. "Poe Among the Virginians." *Virginia Magazine of History and Biography* 67 (January 1959): 30-48. Recounts Edgar Allen Poe's relationship with Robert Tyler and Poe's efforts to secure an appointment from the Tyler administration.

1310. Jeffrey, Thomas E. "The Second Party System in North Carolina, 1836-1860." Ph.D. diss., Catholic University of America, 1976.

1311. Jeffrey, Thomas E. *State Parties and National Politics: North Carolina, 1815-1861*. Athens: University of Georgia Press, 1989. One of the more important studies of politics in North Carolina during the antebellum period.

1312. Johnson, Gerald White. *America's Silver Age: The Statecraft of Clay—Webster—Calhoun*. New York: Harper & Brothers, 1939. Evaluates the political roles of three of the major politicians in the age of Jackson.

1313. Johnson, Reinhard O. "The Liberty Party in Maine, 1840-1848: The Politics of Antislavery Reform." *Maine Historical Quarterly* 19 (Winter 1980): 135-76.

1314. Johnson, Reinhard O. "The Liberty Party in Massachusetts (1840-1848): Antislavery Third Party Politics in the Bay State." *Civil War History* 28 (September 1982): 237-65.

1315. Johnson, Reinhard O. "The Liberty Party in New Hampshire, 1840-1848: Antislavery Politics in the Granite State." *Historical New Hampshire* 33 (Summer 1978): 123-65.

1316. Josephy, Alvin M. *On the Hill: A History of the American Congress.* New York: Simon and Schuster, 1979. Published in 1975 under title *The American Heritage History of the Congress of the United States.*

1317. Kallenbach, Joseph Ernest. *The American Chief Executive: The Presidency and the Governorship.* New York: Harper & Row, 1966.

1318. Kaplan, Lawrence S. "The Brahmin as Diplomat in Nineteenth Century America: Everett, Bancroft, Motley, Lowell." *Civil War History* 19 (March 1973): 5-27. Discusses criteria for selection of diplomats, their attitudes and performance, and notices particularly Edward Everett, minister to England under Tyler, 1841-1845.

1319. Kesilman, Sylvan Heath. "John Tyler and the Presidency: Old School Republicanism, Partisan Realignment, and Support for His Administration." Ph.D. diss., Ohio State University, 1973.

1320. Kessler, Frank. *The Dilemmas of Presidential Leadership: Of Caretakers and Kings.* Englewood Cliffs, N.J.: Prentice-Hall, 1982.

1321. Kleber, Louis C. "John Tyler: The Tenth President of the United States, 1841-45, Who Survived a Charge of Impeachment and Acquired Texas." *History Today* 25 (October 1975): 697-703.

1322. Krueger, David W. "The Clay-Tyler Feud, 1841-1842." *Filson Club History Quarterly* 42 (April 1968): 162-77. Sees the struggle between Tyler and Clay as one between "two highly inflexible men."

1323. Kruman, Marc W. *Parties and Politics in North Carolina, 1836-1865.* Baton Rouge: Louisiana State University Press, 1983.

1324. Lambert, Oscar Doane. *Presidential Politics in the United States, 1841-1844.* Durham: Duke University Press, 1936. Offers a detailed discussion of Tyler's relationship with Congress and his cabinet and of his 1844 presidential campaign, the "fixed idea" of his administration; takes an unfavorable view of Tyler.

1325. "The Last Chief Executive." *American Review: A Whig Journal of Politics, Literature, Art and Sciences* 1 (April 1845): 331-40. Denounces the Tyler administration.

1326. "The Late Acting President." *United States Magazine and Democratic Review* 16 (March 1845): 211-14. Calls Tyler the "weakest and worst of our Presidents."

1327. Learned, Henry Barrett. *The President's Cabinet: Studies in the Origin, Formation and Structure of an American Institution.* New Haven: Yale University Press, 1912; New York: B. Franklin, [1972]. Also in *Microbook Library* [601].

1328. Leonard, Ira M. "New York City Politics, 1841-1844: Nativism and Reform." Ph.D. diss., New York University, 1965.

1329. Leonard, Ira M. "The Rise and Fall of the American Republican Party in New York City, 1843-1845." *New-York Historical Society Quarterly* 50 (April 1966): 151-92.

1330. Lerski, Jerzy Jan. *A Polish Chapter in Jacksonian America: The United States and the Polish Exiles of 1836.* Madison: University of Wisconsin Press, 1958. Mentions Tyler's approval of a bill (June 14, 1842) declaring that Polish exiles, not fulfilling the conditions of a congressional grant of land, had thereby forfeited their rights to the land.

1331. Levine, Peter D. *The Behavior of State Legislative Parties in the Jacksonian Era: New Jersey, 1829-1844.* Rutherford, N.J.: Fairleigh Dickinson University Press, 1977.

1332. Levine, Peter D. "State Legislative Parties in the Jacksonian Era: New Jersey, 1829-1844." *Journal of American History* 62 (December 1975): 591-608.

1333. Lucas, M. Philip. "'To Carry Out Great Fundamental Principles': The Antebellum Southern Political Culture." *Journal of Mississippi History* 52 (February 1990): 1-22.

1334. Lucas, M. Philip. "The Development of the Second Party System in Mississippi, 1817-1846." Ph.D. diss., Cornell University, 1983.

1335. Maness, Lonnie E., and Richard D. Chesteen. "The First Attempt at Presidential Impeachment: Partisan Politics and Intra-Party Conflict at Loose." *Presidential Studies Quarterly* 10 (Winter 1980): 51-62. Examines the efforts to impeach Tyler in 1843.

1336. Marshall, Lynn. "The Strange Stillbirth of the Whig Party." *American Historical Review* 72 (January 1967): 445-68. Emphasizes the importance of "party organization, not ideology" in the formation of the Whig party.

1337. McCardell, John M. *The Idea of a Southern Nation: Southern Nationalists and Southern Nationalism, 1830-1860.* New York: W. W. Norton & Company, 1979.

1338. McConville, Mary St. Patrick. *Political Nativism in the State of Maryland, 1830-1860.* Washington: Catholic University of America, 1928.

1339. McCormick, Richard P. "Party Formation in New Jersey in the Jacksonian Era." *New Jersey History* 83 (July 1965): 161-73.

1340. McCormick, Richard P. *The Presidential Game: The Origins of American Presidential Politics.* New York: Oxford University Press, 1982. Discusses the presidential election process through 1844.

1341. McFaul, John M. *The Politics of Jacksonian Finance.* Ithaca: Cornell University Press, 1972. Important for background on the economic issues the Whigs faced in 1841.

1342. McLaughlin, Andrew C. *A Constitutional History of the United States.* New York: Appleton-Century-Crofts, 1935. An important study of constitutional development in the United States.

1343. McMaster, John Bach. *A History of the People of the United States from the Revolution to the Civil War.* 8 vols. New York: D. Appleton and Company, 1883-1913. Volumes 5 through 8 useful for the Tyler years.

1344. McWhiney, Grady. "Were the Whigs a Class Party in Alabama?" *Journal of Southern History* 23 (November 1957): 510-22.

1345. Mering, John V. *The Whig Party in Missouri.* Columbia: University of Missouri Press, 1967.

1346. Miles, Edwin A. "The Whig Party and the Menace of Caesar." *Tennessee Historical Quarterly* 27 (Winter 1968): 361-79. Discusses ideas of Roman history and fear of militarism that influenced the rise of Whig party.

1347. Miley, Cora. "John Tyler, the President Without a Party." *Americana* 23 (October 1929): 411-20.

1348. Milton, George Fort. *The Use of Presidential Power, 1789-1943.* Boston: Little, Brown, and Company, 1944; New York: Octagon Books, 1980.

1349. Mitchell, Marjorie Dean. "Clay, Tyler and the Whig Coalition." M.A. thesis, University of Minnesota, 1933.

1350. Mohl, Raymond A. "Presidential Views of National Power, 1837-1861." *Mid-America* 52 (July 1970): 177-89.

1351. "The Moral of the Veto." *United States Magazine and Democratic Review* 9 (September 1841): 295-98. Defends Tyler's veto of the bank bill.

1352. Morgan, Robert James. "The Presidency under John Tyler: A Study in Constitutional History." Ph.D. diss., University of Virginia, 1951.

1353. Morgan, Robert James. *A Whig Embattled: The Presidency under John Tyler.* Lincoln: University of Nebraska Press, 1954; Hamden, Conn.: Archon Books, 1974. Analyzes conflict between the Tyler and Congress.

1354. Morse, Jarvis Means. *A Neglected Period of Connecticut's History, 1818-1850.* New Haven: Yale University Press, 1933; New York: Octagon Books 1978.

1355. Morse, Jarvis Means. *The Rise of Liberalism in Connecticut, 1828-1850.* New Haven: Yale University Press, 1933.

1356. Moser, Harold D. "Subtreasury Politics and the Virginia Conservative Democrats, 1835-1844." Ph.D. diss., University of Wisconsin–Madison, 1977.

1357. Mowry, Arthur May. *The Constitutional Controversy in Rhode Island in 1841.* Washington: Government Printing Office, 1895. An older study of the Dorr Rebellion.

1358. Mowry, Arthur May. *The Dorr War; or, The Constitutional Struggle in Rhode Island.* Providence: Preston & Rounds Company, 1901; New York: Johnson Reprint, 1968; New York: Chelsea House, 1970.

1359. Murray, Paul. *The Whig Party in Georgia, 1825-1853.* Chapel Hill: University of North Carolina Press, 1948.

1360. Nash, Howard P., Jr. "The 'Princeton' Explosion." *American History Illustrated* 4 (August 1969): 4-12.

1361. Norton, Clarence Clifford. *The Democratic Party in Ante-Bellum North Carolina, 1835-1861.* Chapel Hill: The University of North Carolina Press, 1930.

1362. O'Connell, Mary Jeanne Therese. "John Tyler's Attitude toward the Presidency." M.A. thesis, Loyola University–Chicago, 1900.

1363. O'Leary, Wayne M. "Who Were the Whigs and Democrats? The Economic Character of Second-Level Party Leadership in Tidewater Maine, 1843-1853." *Maine Historical Quarterly* 28 (Winter 1989): 146-69.

1364. Oakes, James. "From Republicanism to Liberalism: Ideological Change and the Crisis of the Old South." *American Quarterly* 37 (Fall 1985): 551-71.

1365. Oliver, George Brown. "A Constitutional History of Virginia, 1776-1860." Ph.D. diss., Duke University, 1959.

1366. Parks, Gordon Elliott. "Martin Van Buren and the Re-Organization of the Democratic Party, 1841-1844." Ph.D. diss., University of Wisconsin, 1965. Assesses Van Buren's role in the Democratic party during the Tyler presidency.

1367. "Passages from a Politician's Note-Book: The Adjournment: A 'President Without a Party.'" *United States Magazine and Democratic Review* 11 (October 1842): 425-30. Denounces Tyler's presidency.

1368. "Passages from a Politician's Note-Book: The Lay of the Land." *United States Magazine and Democratic Review* 13 (July 1843): 97-101. Reviews the "disgusting" political scene in Washington under Tyler— "almost enough to turn the stomach of an honest man."

1369. Paul, James C. N. *Rift in the Democracy*. Philadelphia: University of Pennsylvania Press, 1951; New York: A. S. Barnes, 1951. An important study of political developments in the early 1840s.

1370. Paullin, Charles O. *Paullin's History of Naval Administration, 1775-1911 ...* . Annapolis: United States Naval Institute Press, 1968.

1371. Peterson, Norma Lois. *The Presidencies of William Henry Harrison & John Tyler*. Lawrence: University Press of Kansas, 1989. Carefully assesses the successes and failures of the two.

1372. Phillips, Ulrich Bonnell. *The Course of the South to Secession: An Interpretation*. New York: D. Appleton-Century Company, 1939; Gloucester, Mass.: P. Smith, 1958.

1373. "Political Portraits with Pen and Pencil: John Tyler." *United States Magazine and Democratic Review* 11 (November 1842): 502-7. Praises Tyler's valuable service to the cause advocated by *Democratic Review*.

1374. Pollard, James E. *The Presidents and the Press*. New York: Macmillan Company, 1947. Brief discussion of the presidencies of Harrison and Tyler.

1375. Potter, David. *The Impending Crisis, 1848-1861*. New York: Harper and Row, 1976.

1376. Prucha, Francis Paul. *The Great Father: The United States Government and the American Indians*. 2 vols. Lincoln: University of Nebraska Press, 1984. A comprehensive history of federal Indian policy.

1377. "The Rhode Island Question." *United States Magazine and Democratic Review* 11 (July 1842): 70-83. Reviews the background of the constitutional dispute in Rhode Island.

1378. Rhodes, James Ford. *History of the United States from the Compromise of 1850*. 9 vols. New York, 1892-1928. Vols. 1-3, 1850-1862, are most useful for background of Tyler's final years.

1379. Schlesinger, Arthur M., Jr. *The Age of Jackson*. Boston: Little, Brown and Company, 1945, 1950, 1953. A classic study of the Jacksonian era.

1380. Schmidhauser, John R. "Judicial Behavior and the Sectional Crisis of 1837-1860." *Journal of Politics* 23 (November 1961): 615-40.

1381. Schmidhauser, John Richard. *The Supreme Court as Final Arbiter in Federal-State Relations, 1789-1957*. Chapel Hill: University of North Carolina Press, 1958; Westport, Conn.: Greenwood Press, 1973.

1382. Schouler James. *History of the United States of America under the Constitution*. 7 vols. New York: Dodd, Mead & Company, 1880-1913; New York: Kraus Reprint Company, 1970. Also in *Legal Treatises* [606]. Views Tyler as a prevaricator whose constitutional distinctions were flimsy and unworthy of refutation.

1383. Schroeder, John Herman. "Virginia Whig Leadership, 1834-1842." M.A. thesis, University of Virginia, 1967.

1384. Schwartz, Bernard. *From Confederation to Nation: The American Constitution, 1835-1877*. Baltimore: Johns Hopkins University Press, 1973.

1385. Shade, William G. "Pennsylvania Politics in the Jacksonian Period: A Case Study, Northampton County, 1824-1844." *Pennsylvania History* 39 (July 1972): 313-33.

1386. Shade, William G. "Politics and Parties in Jacksonian America." *Pennsylvania Magazine of History and Biography* 110 (October 1986): 483-507.

1387. Sharp, James Roger. "The Political Culture of Middle-Period United States." *Canadian Review of American Studies* 15 (Spring 1984): 49-62.

1388. Shields, Johanna Nicol. *The Line of Duty: Maverick Congressmen and the Development of American Political Culture, 1836-1860*. Westport, Conn.: Greenwood Press, 1985.

1389. Shields, Johanna Nicol. "Whigs Reform the 'Bear Garden': Representation and the Apportionment Act of 1842." *Journal of the Early Republic* 5 (Fall 1985): 355-82.

1390. Shover, Kenneth B. "Another Look at the Late Whig Party: The Perspective of the Loyal Whig." *Historian* 48 (August 1986): 539-58.

1391. Silbey, Joel H. *The American Political Nation, 1838-1893*. Stanford: Stanford University Press, 1991.

1392. Silbey, Joel H. *The Partisan Imperative: The Dynamics of American Politics before the Civil War*. New York: Oxford University Press, 1985.

1393. Silbey, Joel H. *The Shrine of Party: Congressional Voting Behavior, 1841-1852*. Pittsburgh: University of Pittsburgh Press, 1967. Investigates party strength and ideological distinctions.

1394. Simms, Henry Harrison. *Emotion at High Tide: Abolitionism as a Controversial Factor, 1830-1845*. [Baltimore?], 1960.

1395. Skeen, C. Edward. "An Uncertain 'Right': State Legislatures and the Doctrine of Instruction." *Mid-America* 71 (January 1991): 29-47.

1396. Smith, Alice E. *From Exploration to Statehood*, Vol. 1 of *History of Wisconsin*, ed. William Fletcher Thompson. Madison: State Historical Society of Wisconsin, 1973. Offers some discussion of relationship between James Duane Doty and Tyler.

1397. Smith, Theodore Clarke. *The Liberty and Free Soil Parties in the Northwest*. New York: Longmans, Green, 1897; New York: Russell & Russell, 1967. Also in *Microbook Library* [601] and *Legal Treatises* [606]. An older prize-winning essay on politics in the Midwest in the decades before the Civil War.

1398. Smith, Wilbur Wayne. "The Whig Party in Maryland, 1826-1856." Ph.D. diss., University of Maryland, 1967.

1399. Snyder, Charles McCool. *The Jacksonian Heritage: Pennsylvania Politics, 1833-1848*. Harrisburg: Pennsylvania Historical and Museum Commission, 1958.

1400. Spann, Edward K. "Gotham in Congress: New York's Representatives in the National Government, 1840-1854." *New York History* 67 (July 1986): 305-29.

1401. Sprout, Harold, and Margaret Sprout. *The Rise of American Naval Power, 1776-1918*. Princeton: Princeton University Press, 1939, 1942, 1966.

1402. Stanley, Robert H. "Party Conflict and the Secessionist Alternative: The Virginia House of Delegates as a Test Case, 1855-1861." in Corcoran Department of History, University of Virginia, *Essays in History* 24 (1980): 5-27. Attempts to test the Holt thesis as applied to interparty competition in the Virginia House of Delegates in the five years previous to secession.

1403. Stanwood, Edward. *A History of the Presidency.* 2 vols. Boston: Houghton Mifflin Company, 1898, 1904, 1906, 1916, 1924, 1928; Clifton, N.J.: A. M. Kelley, 1975.

1404. Steinberg, Alfred. *The First Ten: The Founding Presidents and Their Administrations.* Garden City, N.Y.: Doubleday & Company, Inc., 1967. Discusses at some length the Harrison and Tyler administrations.

1405. Stirton, Thomas. "Party Disruptions and the Rise of the Slavery Extension Controversy, 1840-46." Ph.D. diss., University of Chicago, 1957.

1406. Stokes, William S. "Whig Conceptions of Executive Power." *Presidential Studies Quarterly* 6 (Winter-Spring 1976): 16-35.

1407. "Political Portraits with Pen and Pencil: John Tyler." *United States Magazine and Democratic Review* 11 (November 1842): 502-7. Praises Tyler's service to the cause advocated by *Democratic Review*.

1408. "Suggestions of the Past: Administration of John Tyler." *Galaxy* 13 (February 1872): 202-11; 13 (March 1872): 347-58. Discusses Tyler's accession to the presidency and his administration.

1409. Swindler, William F. "John Tyler's Nominations: 'Robin Hood,' Congress, and the Court." *Yearbook of the Supreme Court Historical Society* (1977): 39-43. Discusses Tyler's six nominations to the Supreme Court, only one of whom, Samuel Nelson, was confirmed.

1410. Swisher, Carl Brent. *American Constitutional Development*. Boston: Houghton Mifflin Company, 1943, 1954.

1411. Swisher, Carl Brent. *The Growth of Constitutional Power in the United States.* Chicago: University of Chicago Press, 1946, 1963, 1966. Based on his lectures on constitutional history and law.

1412. Swisher, Carl Brent. *The Oliver Wendell Holmes Devise History of the Supreme Court of the United States: The Taney Period, 1836-1864.* New York: Macmillan, 1974. Excellent survey of Taney's tenure on the court.

1413. Sydnor, Charles S. *The Development of Southern Sectionalism, 1819-1848.* Baton Rouge: Louisiana State University Press, 1948, 1968.

1414. Tabachnik, Leonard. "Political Patronage and Ethnic Groups: Foreign-Born in the United States Customhouse Service, 1821-1861." *Civil War History* 17 (September 1971): 222-31.

1415. Tau. "The History of Party, and the Political Status of John Tyler." *De Bow's Review* 26 (March 1859): 300-309. Discuses reasons Tyler followed the course he did as president.

1416. Teague, William Joseph. "An Appeal to Reason: Daniel Webster, Henry Clay, and Whig Presidential Politics, 1836-1848." Ph.D. diss., North Texas State University, 1977.

1417. Thornton, J. Mills, III. *Politics and Power in a Slave Society: Alabama, 1800-1860.* Baton Rouge: Louisiana State University Press, 1978.

1418. Tregle, Joseph G., Jr. "Political Corruption in the Early Republic: Louisiana as a Case Study." *Louisiana History* 31 (Spring 1990): 125-39.

1419. Tucker, Spencer C. "U.S. Navy Steam Sloop *Princeton*." *American Neptune* 49 (Spring 1989): 96-113.

1420. "The Twenty-Eighth Congress." *American Review, A Whig Journal of Politics, Literature, Art and Science* 1 (March 1845): 221-31. Discusses Tyler's defection from the Whig party and its injury to the Whig cause.

1421. Tyler, Lyon Gardiner. "John Tyler and His Presidency." *Eclectic Magazine* 148 (May 1907): 387-403. Praises Tyler's contributions to constitutional government.

1422. Tyler, Lyon Gardiner. *Parties and Patronage in the United States.* New York: G. P. Putnam's Sons, 1891. Defends Tyler's usage of spoils.

1423. Van Deusen, Glyndon G. "Some Aspects of Whig Thought and Theory in the Jacksonian Period." *American Historical Review* 63 (January 1958): 305-22.

1424. Vaughn, William Preston. *The Antimasonic Party in the United States, 1826-1843.* Lexington: University Press of Kentucky, 1983.

1425. Viola, Herman J. *Diplomats in Buckskins: A History of Indian Delegations in Washington City*. Washington: Smithsonian Institution Press, 1981.

1426. Walton, Brian G. "The Second Party System in Arkansas, 1836-1848." *Arkansas Historical Quarterly* 28 (Summer 1969): 120-55.

1427. Ward, Nathan. "Clay vs. Tyler." *American Heritage*, September 1991, 40. Asserts that the breakup of Tyler's cabinet on September 11, 1841, was over the direction of the Whig party, not the national banking issue.

1428. Warner, Lee H. "The Perpetual Crisis of Conservative Whigs: New York's Silver Grays." *New-York Historical Society Quarterly* 57 (July 1973): 213-36.

1429. Warren, Charles. *Bankruptcy in United States History*. Cambridge, Mass.: Harvard University Press, 1935; New York: Da Capo Press, 1972. Provides historical and legal background of bankruptcy legislation in the United States; discusses Webster's and Tyler's and efforts for bankruptcy legislation in 1841.

1430. Warren, Charles. *Congress, the Constitution, and the Supreme Court*. Boston: Little, Brown and Company, 1925, 1935; New York: Johnson Reprint Corporation, 1968. Explores judicial review of congressional legislation.

1431. Warren, Charles. *The Supreme Court in United States History*. 2 vols. Boston: Little, Brown, and Company, 1922, 1926, 1928, 1932, 1935, 1937, 1947.

1432. Watson, Harry L. *Jacksonian Politics and Community Conflict: The Emergence of the Second American Party System in Cumberland County, North Carolina*. Baton Rouge: Louisiana State University Press, 1981.

1433. Watson, Harry L. *Liberty and Power: The Politics of Jacksonian America*. New York: Hill and Wang, 1990. A standard survey of the period; has only one chapter covering the Van Buren-Harrison-Tyler presidencies.

1434. Webster, Donald B., Jr. "The Beauty and Chivalry of the United States Assembled ... ." *American Heritage* 17 (December 1965): 50-53, 87-90. Discusses the explosion aboard the *Princeton*.

1435. Wellington, Raynor G. *The Political & Sectional Influence of the Public Lands, 1828-1842*. Cambridge: Riverside Press, 1914; New York: Burt Franklin, 1970.

1436. "The Whig Regime at Washington." *United States Magazine and Democratic Review* 11 (July 1842): 95-97. Discusses the Whig party's "shuffling, shifting, shambling, and shameful manoeuvring."

1437. Williams, Max R. "The Foundations of the Whig Party in North Carolina." *North Carolina Historical Review* 47 (April 1970): 115-29.

1438. Wilson, Major L. *The Presidency of Martin Van Buren*. Lawrence: University Press of Kansas, 1984. Provides background to the political inheritance of the Harrison-Tyler presidencies.

1439. Wilson, Major L. *Space, Time and Freedom: The Quest for Nationality and the Irrepressible Conflict, 1815-1861*. Westport, Conn.: Greenwood Press, 1974. Collections of essays published in journals.

1440. Wood, Walter Kirk. "The Central Theme of Southern History: Republicanism, Not Slavery, Race, or Romanticism." *Continuity: A Journal of History* 9 (Fall 1984): 33-71.

1441. Wooster, Ralph A. *Politicians, Planters, and Plain Folk: Courthouse and Statehouse in the Upper South, 1850-1860*. Knoxville: University of Tennessee Press, 1975.

1442. Wooster, Ralph A. *The People in Power: Courthouse and Statehouse in the Lower South, 1850-1860*. Knoxville: University of Tennessee Press, 1969.

2. Social and Cultural Developments

1443. Abel, Ernest L. "'The Most Hated Man in America.'" *American History Illustrated* 22 (December 1987): 10-15, 48. Discusses Charles Dickens's 1842 visit to the United States.

1444. Ames, William E. *A History of the National Intelligencer*. Chapel Hill: University of North Carolina Press, 1972. Scholarly account of a major Washington newspaper devoted to the Whig cause.

1445. Billington, Ray Allen. *The Protestant Crusade, 1800-1860: A Study of the Origins of American Nativism*. New York: Macmillan Company, 1938; New York: Rinehart & Company, 1952; Gloucester, Mass.: Peter Smith, 1963; Chicago: Quadrangle Books, 1964.

1446. Bodo, John R. *The Protestant Clergy and Public Issues, 1812-1848*. Princeton: Princeton University Press, 1954.

1447. Braden, Waldo Warder. *The Oral Tradition in the South*. Baton Rouge: Louisiana State University Press, 1983.

1448. Braden, Waldo Warder, ed. *Oratory in the Old South, 1820-1860*. Prepared under the Auspices of the Speech Association of America. Baton Rouge: Louisiana State University Press, 1970.

1449. Brigance, William N., and Marie Kathryn Hochmuth, eds. *A History and Criticism of American Public Address*. 3 vols. New York: McGraw-Hill, 1943-1955; New York: Russell & Russell, 1971.

1450. Cash, Wilbur J. *The Mind of the South*. New York: A. A. Knopf, 1941; New York: Vintage Books, 1969.

1451. Coleman, Peter J. *Debtors and Creditors in America: Insolvency, Imprisonment for Debt, and Bankruptcy, 1607-1900*. Madison: State Historical Society of Wisconsin, 1974.

1452. Commager, Henry Steele. *The Era of Reform, 1830-1860*. Princeton, N.J.: D. Van Nostrand, 1960.

1453. Curti, Merle Eugene. *The American Peace Crusade, 1815-1860*. Durham, N.C.: Duke University Press, 1929.

1454. Dalzell, Robert F., Jr. *Enterprising Elite: The Boston Associates and the World They Made*. Cambridge, Mass.: Harvard University Press, 1987. Provides a brief discussion of the Associates' response to the Tyler administration.

1455. Demaree, Albert Lowther. *The American Press, 1819-1860*. New York: Columbia University Press, 1941; Philadelphia: Porcupine Press, 1974.

1456. Eaton, Clement. *The Growth of Southern Civilization, 1790-1860*. New York: Harper & Row, 1961.

1457. Eaton, Clement. *The Mind of the Old South*. Baton Rouge: Louisiana State University Press, 1964, 1967.

1458. Feldberg, Michael. *The Philadelphia Riots of 1844: A Study of Ethnic Conflict*. Westport, Conn.: Greenwood Press, 1975.

1459. Feldberg, Michael. *The Turbulent Era: Riot and Disorder in Jacksonian America*. New York: Oxford University Press, 1980.

1460. Fish, Carl Russell. *The Rise of the Common Man*. New York: Macmillan Company, 1927, 1944, 1950; Chicago: Quadrangle Books, 1971. Describes the social scene during the Tyler years.

1461. Friedman, Lawrence M. *A History of American Law.* New York: Simon and Schuster, 1973, 1985.

1462. Green, Constance McLaughlin. *Washington, Village and Capital, 1800-1878.* 2 vols. Princeton: Princeton University Press, 1962-63.

1463. Greenberg, Michael S. "Gentlemen Slaveholders: The Social Outlook of the Virginia Planter Class." Ph.D. diss., Rutgers University, 1972.

1464. Hale, Edward Everett. "Washington Then and Now." *Outlook* 79 (March 4, 1905): 542-55. Contrasts the Washington of 1844 with that of 1904.

1465. Hendricks, Rickey L. "Henry Clay and Jacksonian Indian Policy: A Political Anachronism." *Filson Club History Quarterly* 60 (April 1986): 218-38.

1466. Horwitz, Morton J. *The Transformation of American Law, 1780-1860.* Cambridge, Mass.: Harvard University Press, 1977. Explores changes and codification of American law.

1467. Kohl, Lawrence Frederick. *The Politics of Individualism: Parties and the American Character in the Jacksonian Era.* New York: Oxford University Press, 1989.

1468. Langley, Harold D. *Social Reform in the United States Navy, 1798-1862.* Urbana: University of Illinois Press, 1967.

1469. Nagel, Paul Chester. *One Nation Indivisible: The Union in American Thought, 1776-1861.* New York: Oxford University Press, 1964. Treats the various notions of union.

1470. Nye, Russell B. *The Cultural Life of the New Nation, 1776-1830.* New York: Harper, 1960.

1471. Nye, Russel B. *Society and Culture in America, 1830-1860.* New York: Harper & Row, 1974. A good survey of cultural developments in the antebellum United States.

1472. Pessen, Edward. *Riches, Class, and Power Before the Civil War.* Lexington, Mass.: D.C. Heath and Company, 1973.

1473. Phillips, Ulrich Bonnell. *Life and Labor in the Old South.* Boston: Little, Brown, and Company, 1929, 1930, 1948, 1957; New York: Grosset & Dunlap, 1929. An older classic, now outdated.

1474. Rezneck, Samuel. "The Social History of an American Depression, 1837-1843." *American Historical Review* 40 (July 1935): 662-87.

1475. Richards, Leonard L. *"Gentlemen of Property and Standing": Anti-Abolition Mobs in Jacksonian America.* New York: Oxford University Press, 1970. Discusses briefly Tyler's response to abolitionism.

1476. Satz, Ronald N. *American Indian Policy in the Jacksonian Era.* Lincoln: University of Nebraska Press, 1974.

1477. Somkin, Fred. *Unquiet Eagle: Memory and Desire in the Idea of American Freedom.* Ithaca: Cornell University Press, 1967.

1478. Stephenson, George M. *A History of American Immigration, 1820-1924.* Boston: Ginn and Company, 1926; New York: Russell & Russell, 1964.

1479. Tomlinson, Robert Hume. "The Origins and Editorial Policies of the *Richmond Whig and Public Advertiser*, 1824-1865." Ph.D. diss., Michigan State University, 1971.

1480. Tyler, Alice Felt. *Freedom's Ferment: Phases of American Social History from the Colonial Period to the Outbreak of the Civil War.* Minneapolis: The University of Minnesota Press, 1944; New York: Harper & Row, 1944, 1962; Freeport, N.Y.: Books for Libraries Press, 1970.

1481. Warren, Charles. *A History of the American Bar.* Boston: Little, Brown and Company, 1911, 1939; New York: Howard Fertig, 1966. Also available in *Microbook Library* [601]. Short discussion of Tyler's opinion of common law and on the *Batture* case.

1482. Whitehill, Walter Muir. "The Union of New England and Virginia." *Virginia Quarterly Review* 40 (Autumn 1964): 516-530. Explores the personal affection and intellectual compatibility between Massachusetts and Virginia.

1483. Wyatt-Brown, Bertram. *Southern Honor: Ethics and Behavior in the Old South.* New York: Oxford University Press, 1982.

3. Slavery and Abolitionism

1484. Barnes, Gilbert H. *The Antislavery Impulse, 1830-1844.* New York: D. Appleton-Century Company, 1933; Gloucester, Mass.: P. Smith, 1957, 1973; New York: Harcourt, Brace & World, 1964.

1485. Davis, David Brion. *The Slave Power Conspiracy and the Paranoid Style.* Baton Rouge: Louisiana State University Press, 1969.

1486. Dillon, Merton L. *Slavery Attacked: Southern Slaves and Their Allies, 1619-1865.* Baton Rouge: Louisiana State University Press, 1990.

1487. Dodd, William Edward. *The Cotton Kingdom: A Chronicle of the Old South.* New Haven: Yale University Press, 1919, 1921.

1488. Duignan, Peter, and Clarence C. Clindenen. *The United States and the African Slave Trade, 1619-1862.* Palo Alto, Calif.: Hoover Institution, Stanford University, 1963.

1489. Filler, Louis. *The Crusade Against Slavery, 1830-1860.* New York: Harper, 1960. Revised and published as *Crusade Against Slavery: Friends, Foes and Reforms, 1820-1860.* Algonac, Mich.: Reference Publications, 1986.

1490. Hoyt, Edwin Palmer. *The Amistad Affair.* London: Abelard-Schuman, 1970.

1491. Jenkins, William Sumner. *Pro-Slavery Thought in the Old South.* Chapel Hill: University of North Carolina Press, 1935.

1492. Jennings, Lawrence C. "French Views on Slavery and Abolitionism in the United States, 1830-1848." *Slavery & Abolitionism* 4 (May 1983): 19-40.

1493. Jervey, Edward D., and C. Harold Huber. "The *Creole* Affair." *Journal of Negro History* 65 (Summer 1980): 196-211.

1494. Jones, Howard. *Mutiny on the Amistad: The Saga of a Slave Revolt and Its Impact on American Abolition, Law, and Diplomacy.* New York: Oxford University Press, 1987.

1495. Jones, Howard. "The Mutiny on the *Amistad*." *This Constitution* 1 (Fall 1988): 46-50.

1496. Jones, Howard. "The Peculiar Institution and National Honor: The Case of the *Creole* Slave Revolt." *Civil War History* 21 (March 1975): 28-50. Discusses the 1841 slave mutiny, Tyler's handling of the event, and its impact on domestic politics and British-American relations.

1497. Lloyd, Arthur Young. *The Slavery Controversy, 1831-1860.* Chapel Hill: University of North Carolina Press, 1939.

1498. Martin, Christopher. *The Amistad Affair.* London: Abelard-Schuman, 1970.

1499. McFaul, John M. "Expediency vs. Morality: Jacksonian Politics and Slavery." *Journal of American History* 62 (June 1975): 24-39.

1500. Merk, Frederick, and Lois Bannister Merk. *Slavery and the Annexation of Texas.* New York: Knopf, 1972.

1501. Nye, Russel B. *Fettered Freedom: Civil Liberties and the Slavery Controversy, 1830-1860.* East Lansing: Michigan State University Press, 1949, 1963; Urbana: University of Illinois Press, 1972.

1502. Sewell, Richard H. *Ballots for Freedom: Antislavery Politics in the United States, 1837-1860.* New York: Oxford University Press, 1976.

1503. Shalhope, Robert E. "Race, Class, Slavery and the Antebellum Southern Mind." *Journal of Southern History* 37 (November 1971): 557-74.

1504. Smith, Elbert B. *The Death of Slavery: The United States, 1837-1865.* Chicago: University of Chicago Press, 1967.

1505. Staudenraus, Peter J. *The African Colonization Movement, 1816-1865.* New York: Columbia University Press, 1961; New York: Octagon Books, 1980.

1506. Wiecek, William M. "Slavery and Abolition Before the United States Supreme Court, 1820-1860." *Journal of American History* 65 (June 1978): 34-59.

4. Economic Issues

a) Tariff

1507. Baack, Bennett D., and Edward J. Ray. "Tariff Policy and Income Distribution: The Case of the United States, 1830-1860." *Explorations in Economic History* 11 (Winter 1973-74): 103-21.

1508. Carleton, William G. "Tariffs and the Rise of Sectionalism." *Current History* 42 (June 1962): 333-38.

1509. Dewey, Davis Rich. *Financial History of the United States.* New York: Longmans, Green & Company, 1907, 1928, 1931.

1510. McGowan, Daniel A. "The Tariff Controversy, 1830-1860: A Focal Point of Misunderstanding Which Led to Civil War." *Susquehanna University Studies* 9 (June 1971): 23-40.

1511. Stanwood, Edward. *American Tariff Controversies in the Nineteenth Century.* 2 vols. New York: Houghton, Mifflin and Company, 1903; New York: Russell & Russell, 1967. Also in *Microbook Library* [601].

1512. Taussig, Frank William. *The Tariff History of the United States*. New York: G. P. Putnam's Sons, 1885, 1888, 1892, 1897, 1910, 1914, 1923, 1931; New York: Capricorn Books, 1964; New York: A. M. Kelley, 1967. Also in *Microbook Library* [601].

b) Banking and Finance

1513. Catterall, Ralph C. H. *Second Bank of the United States*. Chicago: University of Chicago Press, 1902, 1903, 1960, 1968. Also in *Microbook Library* [601].

1514. "1840-1841." *United States Magazine and Democratic Review* 9 (November 1841): 496-501. Reviews the party situation in the United States and argues that both Harrison and Tyler had expressed opposition to a national bank.

1515. Hammond, Bray. *Banks and Politics in America from the Revolution to the Civil War*. Princeton: Princeton University Press, 1957.

1516. Jackson, John Byers. "John Tyler and the United States Bank." M.A. thesis, Ohio State University, 1938.

1517. Kinley, David. *The Independent Treasury of the United States and Its Relations to the Banks of the Country*. Washington: Government Printing Office, 1910; New York: A. M. Kelley, 1970. Also in *Microbook Library* [601].

1518. Macesich, George. "Sources of Monetary Disturbances in the United States, 1834-1845." *Journal of Economic History* 20 (September 1960): 407-34.

1519. McGrane, Reginald Charles. *Foreign Bondholders and American State Debts*. New York: Macmillan Company, 1935.

1520. McGrane, Reginald Charles. *The Panic of 1837: Some Financial Problems of the Jacksonian Era*. Chicago: University of Chicago Press, 1924, 1965.

1521. Miller, Harry E. *Banking Theories in the United States before 1860*. Cambridge: Harvard University Press, 1927; Clifton, N.J.: A. M. Kelley, 1972.

1522. "The Moral of the Veto." *United States Magazine and Democratic Review* 9 (September 1841): 295-98. Praises veto of the bank bill.

1523. Ng, Kenneth. "Free Banking Laws and Barriers to Entry in Banking, 1838-1860." *Journal of Economic History* 48 (December 1988): 877-89.

1524. Parry, Meredith. "John Tyler and the Bank of the United States." M.A. thesis, Ohio State University, 1938.

1525. Schweikart, Larry. "Banking in the American South, 1836-1865." *Journal of Economic History* 45 (June 1985): 465-67.

1526. Schweikart, Larry. *Banking in the American South from the Age of Jackson to Reconstruction.* Baton Rouge: Louisiana State University Press, 1987. Explores status of and attitudes toward banking.

1527. Schweikart, Larry. "Jacksonian Ideology, Currency Control and Central Banking: A Reappraisal." *Historian* 51 (November 1988): 78-102.

1528. Shade, William G. *Banks or No Banks: The Money Question in Western Politics, 1832-1865.* Detroit: Wayne State University Press, 1972.

1529. Sharp, James Roger. *The Jacksonians versus the Banks: Politics in the States after the Panic of 1837.* New York: Columbia University Press, 1970.

1530. Smith, Walter Buckingham. *Economic Aspects of the Second Bank of the United States.* Cambridge: Harvard University Press, 1953; New York: Greenwood Press, 1969.

1531. Taus, Esther Rogoff. *Central Banking Functions of the United States Treasury, 1789-1941.* New York: Columbia University Press, 1943; New York: Russell & Russell, 1967.

1532. Temin, Peter. "The Anglo-American Business Cycle, 1820-60." *Economic History Review* 27 (May 1974): 207-21.

1533. Temin, Peter. *The Jacksonian Economy.* New York: W. W. Norton & Company, 1969. Studies the economic crises and issues of the late 1830s.

1534. Timberlake, Richard H., Jr. "The Specie Circular and the Distribution of the Surplus." *Journal of Political Economy* 68 (April 1960): 109-17. Discusses economic recovery during the Tyler administration.

1535. Timberlake, Richard H., Jr. "The Specie Standard and Central Banking in the United States before 1860." *Journal of Economic History* 21 (September 1961): 318-41.

c) Other

1536. Brown, Thomas. "The Southern Whigs and Economic Development." *Southern Studies* 20 (Spring 1981): 20-38.

1537. Goldfield, David Reed. *Urban Growth in the Age of Sectionalism: Virginia, 1847-1861.* Baton Rouge: Louisiana State University Press, 1977.

1538. Goodrich, Carter. "The Virginia System of Mixed Enterprise: A Study of State Planning of Internal Improvements." *Political Science Quarterly* 64 (September 1949): 355-87.

1539. Gray, Lewis Cecil. *History of Agriculture in the Southern United States to 1860.* 2 vols. Washington: Carnegie Institution of Washington, 1933; Gloucester, Mass.: Peter Smith, 1958. Also available in *Microbook Library* [601].

1540. Hite, James C., and Ellen J. Hall. "The Reactionary Evolution of Economic Thought in Antebellum Virginia." *Virginia Magazine of History and Biography* 80 (October 1972): 476-88.

1541. Myers, Margaret G. *A Financial History of the United States.* New York: Columbia University Press, 1970.

1542. North, Douglass C. *The Economic Growth of the United States, 1790-1860.* Englewood Cliffs, N.J.: Prentice-Hall, 1961; New York: W.W. Norton, 1966.

1543. Robert, Joseph C. *The Tobacco Kingdom: Plantation, Market, and Factory in Virginia and North Carolina, 1800-1860.* Durham: Duke University Press, 1938; Gloucester, Mass.: P. Smith, 1965.

1544. Russell, Robert R. *Economic Aspects of Southern Sectionalism, 1840-1861.* Urbana: University of Illinois Press, 1924.

1545. Sioussat, St. George L. "Memphis as a Gateway to the West: A Study in the Beginnings of Railway Transportation in the Old Southwest." *Tennessee Historical Magazine* 3 (March 1917): 1-27. Discusses briefly Tyler's position on the rivers and harbors bill of 1844.

B. FOREIGN POLICY

1. General Studies

1546. Corwin, Edward S. *The President's Control of Foreign Relations.* Princeton: Princeton University Press, 1917.

1547. De Conde, Alexander. *The American Secretary of State: An Interpretation.* New York: Praeger, 1962; Westport, Conn.: Greenwood Press, 1975. One of the major studies of the role and influence of the secretary of state in the executive department and in diplomatic negotiations.

1548. De Conde, Alexander, ed. *Encyclopedia of American Foreign Policy: Studies of the Principal Movements and Ideas.* 3 vols. New York: Scribner, 1978.

1549. Goetzmann, William H. *When the Eagle Screamed: The Romantic Horizon in American Diplomacy, 1800-1860.* New York: Wiley, 1966.

1550. May, Ernest R. *The Making of the Monroe Doctrine.* Cambridge: Harvard University Press, 1975. Explores influence of the doctrine on nineteenth-century United States foreign policy.

1551. Merk, Frederick, and Lois Bannister Merk. *Manifest Destiny and Mission in American History: A Reinterpretation.* New York: Knopf, 1963.

1552. Merk, Frederick, and Lois Bannister Merk. *The Monroe Doctrine and American Expansionism, 1843-1849.* New York: Knopf, 1966.

1553. Nichols, Roy F. *Advance Agents of American Destiny.* Philadelphia: University of Pennsylvania Press, 1956.

1554. Paullin, Charles Oscar. *Diplomatic Negotiations of American Naval Officers, 1778-1883.* Baltimore: Johns Hopkins Press, 1912; Gloucester, Mass.: P. Smith, 1967. Also in *Microbook Library* **[601]**.

1555. Perkins, Dexter. *The Monroe Doctrine, 1826-1867.* Baltimore: Johns Hopkins Press, 1933. An older study of the importance the Monroe Doctrine in the determination of nineteenth-century American foreign policy.

1556. Reeves, Jesse Siddall. *American Diplomacy under Tyler and Polk.* Baltimore: Johns Hopkins Press, 1907; Gloucester, Mass.: P. Smith, 1967. Also in *Microbook Library* **[601]**. Examines the northeastern boundary controversy, the Ashburton treaty, the *Creole* and *Caroline* cases, the Texas question and relations with Mexico.

1557. Schroeder, John Herman. *Shaping a Maritime Empire: The Commercial and Diplomatic Role of the American Navy, 1829-1861.* Westport, Conn.: Greenwood Press, 1985.

1558. Stephanson, Anders. *Manifest Destiny: American Expansionism and the Empire of Right.* New York: Hill and Wang, 1995.

1559. Varg, Paul A. *New England and Foreign Relations, 1789-1850.* Hanover: University Press of New England, 1983.

1560. Varg, Paul A. *United States Foreign Relations, 1820-1860.* East Lansing: Michigan State University Press, 1979.

1561. Weinberg, Albert Katz. *Manifest Destiny: A Study of Nationalist Expansion in American History.* Baltimore: Johns Hopkins Press, 1935; Chicago: Quadrangle Books, 1963.

1562. Wriston, Henry M. *Executive Agents in American Foreign Relations.* Baltimore: John Hopkins Press, 1929. Discusses briefly Tyler's opinion on the use of agents, particularly in Japan, Texas, Santo Domingo, Hungary, Latin America, Canada, and Great Britain.

2. Texas and Mexico

1563. Adams, Ephraim Douglass. *British Interests and Activities in Texas, 1836-1846.* Baltimore: Johns Hopkins Press, 1910; Gloucester, Mass.: P. Smith, 1963. Also in *Microbook Library* [601].

1564. Ambler, Charles Henry, ed. "Virginia and Texas." *John P. Branch Historical Papers of Randolph-Macon College* 4 (1913): 116-37. Consists of a series of letters Thomas Ritchie received in April and May 1844 regarding Virginia's attitude on Tyler's annexation of Texas.

1565. Barker, Eugene C. "The Annexation of Texas." *Southwestern Historical Quarterly* 50 (July 1946): 49-74.

1566. Binkley, William C. *The Expansionist Movement in Texas, 1836-1850.* Berkeley: University of California Press, 1925; New York: Da Capo Press, 1970. Discusses in part the Santa Fe prisoners and negotiations for their release.

1567. Binkley, William C. *The Texas Revolution.* Baton Rouge: Louisiana State University Press, 1952; Austin: Texas State Historical Association, 1979.

1568. Brooke, George M., Jr. "The Vest Pocket War of Commodore Jones." *Pacific Historical Review* 31 (August 1962): 217-33. Explores Thomas ap Catesby Jones's seizure and restoration of Monterey and the Tyler administration's handling of the matter.

1569. Callahan, James M. *American Foreign Policy in Mexican Relations.* New York: Macmillan Company, 1932; New York: Cooper Square Publishers, 1967.

1570. Chase, Mary Catherine. *Negociations de la Republique du Texas en Europe, 1837-1845.* Paris: Champion, 1932.

1571. Chavez, Thomas Esteban. "The Trouble with Texans: Manuel Alvarez and the 1841 'Invasion.'" *New Mexico Historical Review* 53 (April 1978): 133-44.

1572. Day, James M. *Black Beans & Goose Quills: Literature of the Texan Mier Expedition.* Waco: Texian Press, 1970. Study of the writings on the expedition, includes bibliography.

1573. Eisenhower, John S. D. *So Far from God: The U.S. War with Mexico, 1846-1848.* New York: Random House, 1989.

1574. Gapp, Frank W. "The 'Capture' of Monterey in 1842." *Proceedings of the U.S. Naval Institute* 105 (March 1979): 46-54.

1575. Hanks, Robert J. "Commodore Jones and His Private War with Mexico." *American West* 16 (1979): 30-33, 60-63. Examines Thomas ap Catesby Jones's seizure of Monterey.

1576. Haynes, Sam W. *Soldiers of Misfortune: The Somervell and Mier Expeditions.* Austin: University of Texas Press, 1990.

1577. Laurent, Pierre Henri. "Belgium's Relations with Texas and the United States, 1839-1844." *Southwestern Historical Quarterly* 68 (October 1964): 220-36. Discusses briefly Tyler's response to Belgian interests and schemes in Texas.

1578. Marshall, Thomas Maitland. "Commercial Aspects of the Texan Santa Fe Expedition." *Southwestern Historical Quarterly* 20 (January 1917): 242-59. Explores the background of the expedition.

1579. McClendon, R. Earl. "Daniel Webster and Mexican Relations: The Santa Fe Prisoners." *Southwestern Historical Quarterly* 36 (April 1933): 288-311. Explores the efforts of Webster and Tyler on behalf of the Santa Fe prisoners.

1580. McClure, Charles R. "The Texan Santa Fe Expedition of 1841." *New Mexico Historical Review* 48 (January 1973): 45-56.

1581. Merk, Frederick. "A Safety Valve Thesis and Texan Annexation." *Journal of American History* 49 (December 1962): 413-36.

1582. Merk, Frederick, and Lois Bannister Merk. *Slavery and the Annexation of Texas.* New York: Alfred A. Knopf, 1972.

1583. Nance, Joseph Milton. "The Flag Incident of the Texas Mier Expedition of 1842-1844." *West Texas Historical Association Yearbook* 65 (1989): 5-23.

1584. Nance, Joseph Milton. "Was There a Mier Expedition Flag?" *Southwestern Historical Quarterly* 92 (April 1989): 543-57.

1585. Pletcher, David M. *The Diplomacy of Annexation: Texas, Oregon, and the Mexican War.* Columbia: University of Missouri Press, 1973.

1586. Reynolds, Curtis R. "The Deterioration of Mexican-American Diplomatic Relations, 1833-1845." *Journal of the West* 11 (April 1972): 213-24.

1587. Rippy, J. Fred. *The United States and Mexico.* New York: Alfred A. Knopf, 1926.

1588. Rives, George L. *The United States and Mexico, 1821-1848.* 2 vols. New York: Charles Scribner's Sons, 1913.

1589. Saxon, Gerald D. "The Politics of Expansion: Texas as an Issue in National Politics, 1819-1845." Ph.D. diss., North Texas State University, 1979.

1590. Schmitz, Joseph William. *Texas Statecraft, 1836-1845.* San Antonio: Naylor Company, 1941.

1591. Schroeder, John H. "Annexation or Independence: The Texas Issue in American Politics, 1836-1845." *Southwestern Historical Quarterly* 89 (October 1985): 137-64. Traces the history of the question of annexation between 1836 and 1843, when Tyler made it a campaign election issue.

1592. Schroeder, John H. "To Give 'Aid and comfort': American Opposition to the Mexican War, 1846-1848." Ph.D. diss., University of Virginia, 1971.

1593. Schroeder, John H. *Mr. Polk's War: American Opposition and Dissent, 1846-1848.* Madison: University of Wisconsin Press, 1973.

1594. Siegel, Stanley. *A Political History of the Texas Republic, 1836-1845.* Austin: University of Texas Press, 1956; New York: Haskell House, 1973.

1595. Smith, Justin H. *The Annexation of Texas.* New York: Barnes and Noble, 1941.

1596. Smothers, Marion B. "Tennesseans' Participation in the Annexation of Texas, 1836-1845." *West Tennessee Historical Society Papers* 33 (October 1979): 5-28.

1597. Stenberg, Richard R. "Intrigue for Annexation." *Southwest Review* 25 (October 1939): 58-69. Prints reports from Commodore Robert F. Stockton to Secretary of the Navy George Bancroft, 1845, shortly after Polk took office, regarding his diplomatic mission to the Republic of Texas.

1598. Struve, Walter. "German Merchants, German Artisans, and Texas During the 1830s and 1840s." *Yearbook of German-American Studies* 23 (1988): 91-104.

1599. Tutorow, Norman E. "The Old Northwest and the Texas Annexation Treaty." *East Texas Historical Journal* 7 (October 1969): 67-77.

1600. Tutorow, Norman E. *Texas Annexation and the Mexican War: A Political Study of the Old Northwest.* Palo Alto: Chadwick House, 1978.

1601. Tutorow, Norman E. "The Whigs of Ohio and Texas Annexation." *Northwest Ohio Quarterly* 43 (Winter 1971): 23-33.

1602. Tutorow, Norman E. "Whigs of the Old Northwest and Texas Annexation, 1836-April 1844." *Indiana Magazine of History* 66 (March 1970): 56-69.

1603. Tutorow, Norman E. "Whigs of the Old Northwest and the Mexican War." Ph.D. diss., Stanford University, 1967.

1604. Tyler, Lyon Gardiner. "The Annexation of Texas." *Magazine of American History* 8 (June 1882): 377-99. Discusses Tyler's stand on the bank question, his relations with Congress, and the motives behind his actions on Texas annexation.

1605. Tyler, Lyon Gardiner. "The Annexation of Texas." *Tyler's Quarterly Historical and Genealogical Magazine* 6 (October 1924): 81-97. Declares that the annexation of Texas "was an *important assertion* of the Monroe Doctrine against the intrigues and interferences of Great Britain and France."

1606. Tyler, Lyon Gardiner. "Honor Where Honor Is Due." *Confederate Veteran* 35 (September 1927): 325. Asserts that it was Tyler, not Polk, who added Texas to the Union; prints Tyler's letter of February 28, 1856, to Thomas J. Green, discussing the matter.

1607. Vásquez, Josefina Zoraida. "The Texas Question in Mexican Politics, 1836-1845." *Southwestern Historical Quarterly* 89 (January 1986): 309-44.

1608. West, Elizabeth Howard. "Southern Opposition to the Annexation of Texas." *Southwestern Historical Quarterly* 18 (July 1914): 74-82.

1609. Williams, Elgin. *The Animating Pursuits of Speculation: Land Traffic and the Annexation of Texas.* New York: Columbia University Press, 1949; New York: AMS Press, 1968. Discusses the role of the Galveston Bay and Texas Land Company in the Texas annexation drive.

1610. Winston, James E. "Texas Annexation Sentiment in Mississippi, 1835-1844." *Southwestern Historical Quarterly* 23 (July 1919): 1-19.

1611. Yoakum, Henderson. *History of Texas, from Its First Settlement in 1685 to Its Annexation to the United States in 1846.* 2 vols. New York: Redfield, 1856; Austin: Steck-Vaughn Company, 1935. Also in *Microbook Library* **[601]**.

3. Great Britain

1612. Adams, Ephraim Douglass. "English Interests in the Annexation of California." *American Historical Review* 14 (July 1909): 744-63.

1613. Allen, Harry C. *Conflict and Concord: The Anglo-American Relationship since 1783.* New York: St. Martin's Press, 1959.

1614. Allen, Harry C. *Great Britain and the United States: A History of Anglo-American Relations, 1783-1952.* London: Odhams Press, 1954; New York: St. Martin's Press, 1955; Hamden, Conn.: Archon Books, 1969.

1615. Arndt, J. Chris. "Maine in the Northeastern Boundary Controversy: States' Rights in Antebellum New England." *New England Quarterly* 62 (June 1989): 205-23.

1616. Baldwin, J. R. "Ashburton-Webster Boundary Settlement." *Canadian Historical Association Reports* 19 (1938): 120-33.

1617. Bartlett, C. J. *Great Britain and Sea Power, 1815-1853.* Oxford: Clarendon Press, 1963.

1618. Bourne, Kenneth. *Britain and the Balance of Power in North America, 1815-1908.* Berkeley: University of California Press, 1967; London: Longmans, Green and Company, 1967.

1619. Brauer, Kinley J. "The United States and British Imperial Expansion, 1815-1860." *Diplomatic History* 12 (Winter 1988): 19-37.

1620. Brown, Roger H. *The Struggle for the Indian Stream Territory.* Cleveland: Press of Western Reserve University, 1955. Discusses the northeastern boundary and the head of the Connecticut River.

1621. Burrage, Henry S. *Maine in the Northeastern Boundary Controversy.* Portland: Marks Printing House, 1919.

1622. Callahan, James M. *American Foreign Policy in Canadian Relations*. New York: Macmillan Company, 1937; New York: Cooper Square Publishers, 1967. Chapter 8 is especially useful for the Tyler years.

1623. Campbell, Charles S. *From Revolution to Rapprochement: The United States and Great Britain, 1783-1900*. New York: John Wiley & Sons, 1974. Sees the Treaty of Washington as a "monument to British-American good sense."

1624. Crook, David Paul. *American Democracy in English Politics, 1815-1850*. Oxford: Clarendon Press, 1965.

1625. Current, Richard N. "Webster's Propaganda and the Ashburton Treaty." *Mississippi Valley Historical Review* 34 (September 1947): 187-200.

1626. Dunning, William A. *The British Empire and the United States: A Review of Their Relations during the Century of Peace Following the Treaty of Ghent*. New York: Charles Scribner's Sons, 1914.

1627. Duram, James C. "A Study of Frustration: Britain, the USA, and the African Slave Trade, 1815-1870." *Social Science* 40 (October 1965): 220-25.

1628. Foote, Andrew Hull. *The African Squadron, Ashburton Treaty, Consular Sea Letters*. Philadelphia: William F. Geddes, 1855.

1629. Gill, George J. "Edward Everett and the Northeastern Boundary Controversy." *New England Quarterly* 42 (June 1969): 201-13. Discusses Everett's role in the Jared Sparks-Webster map controversy at the time of the Webster-Ashburton treaty negotiations.

1630. Hill, Charles Edward. *Leading American Treaties*. New York: Macmillan, 1922. Discusses historical setting and main provisions of the Webster-Ashburton treaty.

1631. Huth, David C. "Disinformation and Daniel Webster: The Maine Boundary Dispute." *Gnosis* 1 (Spring 1987): 1-20.

1632. Johnson, C. T. "Lord Ashburton and Old Oregon." *Washington Historical Quarterly* 1 (October 1906): 209-16.

1633. Johnson, Clifton H. "The Creole Affair." *Crisis* 78 (October 1971): 248-50. Argues that the Tyler administration's attitude toward the 1841 revolt was that the issue was a matter of comity between nations rather than the question of freedom for slaves.

1634. Jones, Howard. "Anglophobia and the Aroostook War." *New England Quarterly* 48 (December 1975): 519-39.

1635. Jones, Howard. "The *Caroline* Affair." *Historian* 38 (May 1976): 485-502. Explores the events surrounding the incident.

1636. Jones, Howard. *To the Webster-Ashburton Treaty: A Study in Anglo-American Relations, 1783-1843.* Chapel Hill: University of North Carolina Press, 1977. Carefully and skillfully assesses the background and negotiations that led to the Treaty of Washington.

1637. Jones, Wilbur D. *The American Problem in British Diplomacy, 1841-1861.* Athens: University of Georgia Press, 1974.

1638. Jones, Wilbur D. "The Influence of Slavery on the Webster-Ashburton Negotiations." *Journal of Southern History* 22 (February 1956): 45-58. Argues that slavery and the slave trade issue almost wrecked the treaty negotiations between Great Britain and the United States.

1639. Kurtz, Henry I. "The Undeclared War between Britain and America, 1837-1842." *History Today* 12 (November 1962): 773-83, 12 (December 1962): 872-80. Discusses the northeastern boundary and the Treaty of Washington, 1842.

1640. LeDuc, Thomas. "The Maine Frontier and the Northeastern Boundary Controversy." *American Historical Review* 53 (October 1947): 30-41.

1641. LeDuc, Thomas. "The Webster-Ashburton Treaty and the Minnesota Iron Ranges." *Journal of American History* 51 (December 1964): 476-81.

1642. Lillibridge, George D. *Beacon of Freedom: The Impact of American Democracy upon Great Britain, 1830-1870.* Philadelphia: University of Pennsylvania Press, 1955.

1643. Martin, Lawrence, and Samuel F. Bemis. "Franklin's Red-Line Map Was a Mitchell." *New England Quarterly* 10 (March 1937): 105-11. Attempts to identify Benjamin Franklin's "red-line" map, found by Jared Sparks and used in the negotiations of the Webster-Ashburton treaty.

1644. Mathieson, William Law. *Great Britain and the Slave Trade, 1839-1865.* New York: Longmans, Green and Company, 1929.

1645. McNeilly, Earl E. "The United States and the Suppression of the West African Slave Trade, 1819-1862." Ph.D. diss., Case Western Reserve University, 1973.

1646. Merk, Frederick. *Albert Gallatin and the Oregon Problem: A Study in Anglo-American Diplomacy.* Cambridge: Harvard University Press, 1950.

1647. Merk, Frederick. "The British Corn Crisis of 1845-46 and the Oregon Treaty." *Agricultural History* 8 (July 1934): 95-123.

1648. Merk, Frederick, and Lois Bannister Merk. *Fruits of Propaganda in the Tyler Administration.* Cambridge: Harvard University Press, 1971. Explores Tyler's and Webster's use of special agents and the secret service fund.

1649. Merk, Frederick. *The Oregon Question: Essays in Anglo-American Diplomacy and Politics.* Cambridge: Harvard University Press, 1967. Discusses the reasons Webster and Ashburton failed to resolve the dispute over the Oregon territory.

1650. Miller, Hunter. "A Point of Punctuation." *American Journal of International Law* 29 (January 1935): 118-23. Discusses changes in interpretation of the Webster-Ashburton treaty as a result of faulty punctuation in printing.

1651. Mills, Dudley. "British Diplomacy and Canada: The Ashburton Treaty." *United Empire: Royal Colonial Institute Journal,* New Series 2 (October 1911): 681-712. Supports Gallatin's evidence and argument regarding the Treaty of Washington.

1652. Nelson, Bernard H. "The Slave Trade as a Factor in British Foreign Policy, 1815-1862." *Journal of Negro History* 27 (April 1942): 192-209.

1653. Shewmaker, Kenneth E. "Daniel Webster and the Oregon Question." *Pacific Historical Review* 51 (May 1982): 195-201.

1654. Shewmaker, Kenneth E. "The 'War of Words': The Cass-Webster Debate of 1842-43." *Diplomatic History* 5 (Spring 1981): 151-64. Examines the debate between Webster and Cass over the right of search.

1655. Soulsby, Hugh G. *The Right of Search and the Slave Trade in Anglo-American Relations, 1814-1862.* Baltimore: Johns Hopkins Press, 1933.

1656. Sprague, John F. *The Northeastern Boundary and the Aroostook War.* Dover: Observer Press, 1910.

1657. Tyler, Lyon Gardiner. "Important Features of the Ashburton Treaty." *Confederate Veteran* 24 (February 1916): 54-55. Credits Tyler with important role in drafting and negotiating treaty. Article also published in *William and Mary College Quarterly Historical Magazine.*

1658. Van Alstyne, Richard W. "The British Right of Search and the African Slave Trade." *Journal of Modern History* 2 (March-December 1930): 37-47.

1659. Williams, Mary Wilhelmine. *Anglo-American Isthmian Diplomacy, 1815-1915.* Washington: American Historical Association, 1916; Gloucester, Mass., P. Smith, 1965; New York: Russell & Russell, 1965.

1660. Willis, William. *A History of the Law, the Courts, and the Lawyers of Maine.* Portland: Bailey & Noyes, 1863. Also in *Legal Treatises* [**606**]. Discusses Albert Smith and the northeastern boundary.

1661. Willson, Beckles. *America's Ambassadors to England (1785-1928): A Narrative of Anglo-American Diplomatic Relations.* London: John Murray, 1928.

1662. Willson, Beckles. *Friendly Relations: A Narrative of Britain's Ministers and Ambassadors to America, 1791-1930.* Boston: Little, Brown & Company, 1934.

1663. Winters, Herbert D. "Tyler, Webster, and the Oregon Question." *New York State Historical Association Journal* 11 (October 1930): 311-23.

4. Pacific Region

1664. Bradley, Harold Whitman. *The American Frontier in Hawaii: The Pioneers, 1789-1843.* Stanford: Stanford University Press, 1942. Explores the development of American interests in Hawaii.

1665. Callahan, James M. *American Relations in the Pacific and Far East, 1784-1900.* Baltimore: Johns Hopkins Press, 1901; New York: Praeger, 1969.

1666. Dennett, Tyler. *Americans in Eastern Asia: A Critical Study of the Policy of the United States with Reference to China, Japan, and Korea in the 19th Century.* New York: Macmillan, 1922.

1667. Donahue, William J. "The Caleb Cushing Mission." *Modern Asian Studies* 16 (April 1982): 193-216. A basic study on the background and the consequences of the mission to China.

1668. Henson, Curtis T., Jr. *Commissioners and Commodores: The East India Squadron and American Diplomacy in China.* University: University of Alabama Press, 1982.

1669. Huebner, Jon W. "The Unequal Treaties and United States Policy in China, 1842-68." *Asian Profile* 14 (August 1986): 409-17.

1670. Johnson, Robert E. *Far China Station: The U.S. Navy in Asian Waters, 1800-1898.* Annapolis: Naval Institute Press, 1979.

1671. Johnson, Robert E. *Thence Round Cape Horn: The Story of the United States Naval Forces in the Pacific Station, 1818-1923.* Annapolis: U.S. Naval Institute Press, 1963.

1672. Kuo, Ping-chia. "Caleb Cushing and the Treaty of Wanghai, 1844." *Journal of Modern History* 5 (March 1933): 34-54. Reconstructs the negotiation of the treaty based on Chinese official documents.

1673. Kuo, Ping-chia. *Some Oriental Influences on Western Culture: Canton and Salem: The Impact of Chinese Culture upon New England during the Post-Revolutionary Era.* [New York]: American Council, Institute of Pacific Relations, 1931.

1674. Kuykendall, Ralph S. "American Interests and American Influence in Hawaii in 1842." *Annual Report of the Hawaiian Historical Society* 39 (1931).

1675. Kuykendall, Ralph S. *The Hawaiian Kingdom, 1778-1854.* 3 vols. Honolulu: University of Hawaii, 1938-67. Discusses persecution of Catholics and the origin of the Tyler doctrine.

1676. Latourette, Kenneth Scott. *The History of Early Relations between the United States and China, 1784-1844.* New Haven: Yale University Press, 1917.

1677. Paullin, Charles Oscar. *American Voyages to the Orient, 1690-1865: An Account of Merchant and Naval Activities in China, Japan, and the Various Pacific Islands.* Annapolis: U.S. Naval Institute, 1971. First published as series of articles in the *United States Naval Institute Proceedings,* 1910-11.

1678. Rea, Kenneth W., ed. *Early Sino-American Relations, 1841-1912: The Collected Articles of Earl Swisher.* Boulder, Colo.: Westview Press, 1977.

1679. Shewmaker, Kenneth E. "Forging the 'Great Chain': Daniel Webster and the Origins of American Foreign Policy toward East Asia and the Pacific, 1841-1852." *Proceedings of the American Philosophical Society* 129 (1985): 225-59.

1680. Stevens, Sylvester K. *American Expansion in Hawaii, 1842-1898.* Harrisburg, Pa.: Archives Publishing Company, 1945.

1681. Swisher, Earl. *China's Management of the American Barbarians: A Study of Sino-American Relations, 1841-1861, with Documents.* New Haven: Far Eastern Association, Yale University, 1953; New York: Octagon Books, 1972. An English translation of those sections of Ch'ou pan i wu shih mo dealing with the United States, 1841-61.

1682. Tate, E. Mowbray. "American Merchant and Naval Contacts with China, 1784-1850." *American Neptune* 31 (July 1971): 177-91.

1683. Tong, Te-kong. *United States Diplomacy in China, 1844-1860.* Seattle: University of Washington Press, 1964.

1684. Woodward, William H. "America Meets China, 1839-1846: Politics, Expansion, and the Formal Beginnings of Sino-American Relations." Ph.D. diss., Georgetown University, 1978. Of particular importance for the Cushing mission to China.

5. Caribbean Region, Central and South America

1685. Brescia, Anthony M. "'Defences Strong Enough to Defy the World': The Visit of a U.S. State Department Special Agent to Bermuda in 1841." *Bulletin of the Institute of Maritime History and Archaeology* 10 (December 1987): 11-12, 14, 16, 25-26.

1686. Callahan, James M. *Cuba and Anglo-American Relations.* Washington: Government Printing Office, 1898.

1687. Callahan, James M. *Cuba and International Relations: A Historical Study in American Diplomacy.* Baltimore: Johns Hopkins Press, 1899; New York: AMS Press, 1972.

1688. Clayton, Lawrence A. "Private Matters: The Origins and Nature of United States-Peruvian Relations, 1820-1850." *The Americas* 42 (April 1986): 377-417.

1689. Foner, Philip S. *A History of Cuba and Its Relations with the United States.* 2 vols. New York: International Publishers, 1962-63.

1690. Langley, Lester D. "Slavery, Reform, and American Policy in Cuba, 1823-1878." *Revue de Histoire de Americas* 65/66 (1968): 71-84.

1691. Langley, Lester D. *Struggle for the American Mediterranean: United States-European Rivalry in the Gulf-Caribbean, 1776-1904.* Athens: University of Georgia Press, 1976.

1692. Logan, Rayford W. *The Diplomatic Relations of the United States with Haiti, 1776-1891.* Chapel Hill: University of North Carolina Press, 1941.

1693. Parks, E. Taylor. *Colombia and the United States, 1765-1934*. Durham: Duke University Press, 1935; New York: Greenwood Press, 1968.

1694. Peterson, Harold F. *Argentina and the United States, 1810-1960*. Albany: State University of New York, 1964. Also published as *La Argentina y los Estados Unidos, 1810-1960*. Buenos Aires: Editorial Universitaria de Buenos Aires, 1970.

1695. Randall, Robert W. "Captains and Diplomats: Americans in the Rio de la Plata, 1843-1846." *American Neptune* 46 (Fall 1986): 230-39.

1696. Rauch, Basil. *American Interest in Cuba, 1848-1855*. New York: Columbia University Press, 1948.

1697. Tansill, Charles Callan. *The United States and Santo Domingo, 1798-1873: A Chapter in Caribbean Diplomacy*. Baltimore: Johns Hopkins Press, 1938.

6. Canada

1698. Bonham, Milledge L. "Alexander McLeod: Bone of Contention." *New York History* 18 (April 1937): 189-217. Discusses the legal and diplomatic features of the *Caroline* case.

1699. Clark, S. D. *Movements of Political Protest in Canada, 1640-1840*. Toronto: University of Toronto Press, 1959. Provides background to the developments during Tyler's administration.

1700. Corey, Albert B. *The Crisis of 1830-1842 in Canadian-American Relations*. New Haven: Yale University Press, 1941. Covers the *Caroline*-McLeod affair.

1701. Corey, Albert B. "Public Opinion and the McLeod Case." *Canadian Historical Association Report* (1936): 53-64. Discusses attitudes toward the case.

1702. Creighton, D. G. "The Economic Background of the Rebellions of Eighteen Thirty-Seven." *Canadian Journal of Economics and Political Science* 3 (1937): 322-34.

1703. Dent, John C. *The Last Forty Years: Canada Since the Union of 1841*. 2 vols. Toronto: George Virtue, 1881.

1704. Dent, John C. *The Story of the Upper Canadian Rebellion, Largely Derived from Original Sources and Documents*. 2 vols. Toronto: C. B. Robinson, 1885.

1705. Dunham, Aileen. *Political Unrest in Upper Canada, 1815-1836.* London: Longmans, Green, and Company, 1927. Provides background to the developments in the Tyler administration.

1706. Ganong, William F. "Boundaries of New Brunswick." *Proceedings and Transactions of the Royal Society of Canada,* Second Series, 7 (May 1901): Section 2: 137-449. Traces the history of the boundaries and gives some attention to the question of maps, particularly those used in drafting the Webster-Ashburton treaty.

1707. Guillet, Edwin C. *The Lives and Times of the Patriots: An Account of the Rebellion in Upper Canada, 1837-38, and of the Patriot Agitation in the United States, 1837-1842.* Toronto: T. Nelson & Sons, 1938.

1708. Hand, Augustus N. "Local Incidents of the Papineau Rebellion." *New York History* 15 (October 1934): 376-87.

1709. Hitsman, J. Mackay. *Safeguarding Canada, 1763-1871.* Toronto: University of Toronto Press, 1968. Chapters 6 and 7 discuss the northeastern boundary question.

1710. Humphries, Charles W. "The Capture of York." *Ontario History* 51 (1959): 1-21.

1711. Kinchen, Oscar A. *The Rise and Fall of the Patriot Hunters.* New York: Bookman Associates, 1956.

1712. McInnes, Edgar W. *The Unguarded Frontier: A History of American-Canadian Relations.* Garden City, N.Y.: Doubleday, Doran, 1942.

1713. Ryerson, Stanley B. *Unequal Union: Confederation and the Roots of Conflict in the Canadas, 1815-1873.* New York: International Publishers, 1968.

1714. Schull, Joseph. *Rebellion: The Rising in French Canada, 1837.* Toronto: Macmillan of Canada, 1971.

1715. Stevens, Kenneth R. "The 'Caroline' Affair: Anglo-American Relations and Domestic Politics, 1837-1842." Ph.D. diss., Indiana University, 1982.

1716. Stevens, Kenneth R. "James Grogan and the Crisis in Canadian-American Relations, 1837-1842." *Vermont History* 50 (Fall 1982): 219-26. Discusses the background of the Grogan affair and the negotiations between Webster, Governor Silas H. Jenison of Vermont, and Canadian officials for extradition.

1717. Stevens, Kenneth R. *Border Diplomacy: The "Caroline" and McLeod Affairs in Anglo-American-Canadian Relations, 1837-1842.* Tuscaloosa: University of Alabama Press, 1989.

1718. Tiffany, Orrin E. *The Relations of the United States to the Canadian Rebellion of 1837-38.* Buffalo: Buffalo Historical Society, 1905.

1719. Watt, Alastair. "The Case of Alexander McLeod." *Canadian Historical Review* 12 (June 1931): 145-67. Endeavors to separate fact from fiction in the McLeod-*Caroline* incident; discusses Webster's efforts and Tyler's disagreements over procedures and policies for resolution.

1720. Zorn, Roman J. "Criminal Extradition Menaces the Canadian Haven for Fugitive Slaves, 1841-1861." *Canadian Historical Review* 38 (December 1957): 284-94. Discusses the Nelson Hacket case.

7. Continental Europe and the Mediterranean Area

1721. Bailey, Thomas A. *America Faces Russia: Russian-American Relations from Early Times to Our Day.* New York: Cornell University Press, 1950.

1722. Blumenthal, Henry. *A Reappraisal of Franco-American Relations, 1830-1871.* Chapel Hill: University of North Carolina Press, 1959.

1723. Field, James A., Jr. *America and the Mediterranean World, 1776-1883.* Princeton: Princeton University Press, 1969.

1724. Finnie, David H. *Pioneers East: The Early American Experience in the Middle East.* Cambridge: Harvard University Press, 1967. Discusses American missionaries (especially Eli Smith) in Syria and their impact on American foreign policy.

1725. Grabill, Joseph L. *Protestant Diplomacy and the Near East: Missionary Influence on American Policy, 1810-1927.* Minneapolis: University of Minnesota Press, 1971.

1726. Larrabee, Stephen A. *Hellas Observed: The American Experience of Greece, 1775-1865.* New York: New York University Press, 1957.

1727. Willson, Beckles. *America's Ambassadors to France (1777-1927): A Narrative of Franco-American Diplomatic Relations.* London: John Murray, 1928.

C. EXPLORATION AND WESTWARD EXPANSION

1728. Barnett, Steve. "U.S. Army Explorers of the American West, 1803-1861." *Manuscripts* 40 (Fall 1988): 269-90.

1729. Billington, Ray Allen. *The Far Western Frontier, 1830-1860*. New York: Harper, 1956, 1962.

1730. Billington, Ray Allen. *Westward Expansion: A History of the American Frontier*. New York: Macmillan Company, 1949, 1960, 1967, 1974, 1982.

1731. Burnett, Kevin. "Tippecanoe and Taylor Too." *Journal of the West* 31 (July 1992): 44-50. Part of a series of articles exploring presidents and the opening of the West.

1732. Carstensen, Vernon, ed. *The Public Lands: Studies in the History of the Public Domain*. Madison: University of Wisconsin Press, 1962, 1963. Collection of important essays.

1733. Eblen, Jack Ericson. *The First and Second United States Empires: Governors and Territorial Government, 1784-1912*. Pittsburgh: University of Pittsburgh Press, 1968.

1734. Fehrenbacher, Don E. *The Era of Expansion, 1800-1848*. New York: John Wiley & Sons, 1969.

1735. Foreman, Grant. *Indian Removal: The Emigration of the Five Civilized Tribes of Nations*. Norman: University of Oklahoma Press, 1932, 1933, 1956, 1972, 1976.

1736. Foreman, Grant. *The Five Civilized Tribes: Advancing the Frontier, 1830-1860*. Norman: University of Oklahoma Press, 1934, 1966, 1972, 1989.

1737. Garrison, George Pierce. *Westward Extension, 1841-1850*. New York: Harper & Brothers, 1906; New York: Haskell House, 1968: New York: Greenwood Press, 1969. Holds view that Tyler "was actuated in the main by courage and consistency."

1738. Goetzmann, William H. *Army Exploration in the American West, 1803-1863*. New Haven: Yale University Press, 1959; Lincoln: University of Nebraska Press, 1979; Austin: Texas State Historical Association, 1991.

1739. Goetzmann, William H. *Exploration and Empire: The Explorer and the Scientist in the Winning of the American West*. New York: Knopf, 1966; New York: Norton, 1978.

1740. Goetzmann, William H., and Glyndwr Williams. *The Atlas of North American Exploration, from the Norse to the Race to the Pole*. New York: Prentice Hall General Reference, 1992.

1741. Goodwin, Cardinal. *The Trans-Mississippi West, 1803-1853: A History of Its Acquisition and Settlement*. New York: D. Appleton, 1922; New York: Russell & Russell, 1967.

1742. Graebner, Norman A. *Empire on the Pacific: A Study in American Continental Expansion.* New York: Ronald Press, 1955.

1743. Henry, Robert S. "West by South." *Journal of Southern History* 24 (February 1958): 3-15. Explores briefly Tyler's role in westward expansion.

1744. Hibbard, Benjamin H. *A History of Public Land Policies.* New York: Macmillan, 1924; New York: Peter Smith, 1939; Madison: University of Wisconsin Press, 1965. Also in *Microbook Library* **[601]**.

1745. Josephy, Alvin M. *The Indian Heritage of America.* New York: Alfred A. Knopf, 1968, 1974, 1991.

1746. Lumpkin, Wilson. *The Removal of the Cherokee Indians from Georgia.* New York: Dodd, Mead & Company, 1907; New York: Arno Press, 1969; New York: A. M. Kelley, 1971. Also in *Microbook Library* **[601]**. Includes some of Lumpkin's speeches and correspondence on the removal question.

1747. Lundeberg, Philip K., and Dana M. Wegner. "'Not for Conquest But Discovery': Rediscovering the Ships of the Wilkes Expedition." *American Neptune* 49 (Summer 1989): 151-67.

1748. Majors, Harry M. "Wilkes on the Olympic Coast, April 28–May 1, 1841." *Northwest Discovery* 8 (October 1988): 1-100. Prints document relating to expedition.

1749. McReynolds, Edwin C. *The Seminoles.* Norman: University of Oklahoma Press, 1957.

1750. Merk, Frederick. *History of the Westward Movement.* New York: Knopf, 1978.

1751. Nathans, Sydney H. "The Southern Connection: Slaveholders and Antebellum Expansion." *Reviews in American History* 1 (September 1973): 389-95.

1752. Prucha, Francis Paul. *Atlas of Indian Affairs.* Lincoln: University of Nebraska Press, 1990.

1753. Prucha, Francis Paul. *Broadax and Bayonet: The Role of the United States Army in the Development of the Northwest, 1815-1860.* Madison: State Historical Society of Wisconsin, 1953; Lincoln: University of Nebraska Press, 1967.

1754. Prucha, Francis Paul. *A Guide to the Military Posts of the United States, 1789-1895.* Madison: State Historical Society of Wisconsin, 1964.

1755. Prucha, Francis Paul. *The Sword of the Republic: The United States Army on the Frontier, 1783-1846.* New York: Macmillan, 1969.

1756. Robbins, Roy M. *Our Landed Heritage: The Public Domain, 1776-1936.* Princeton: Princeton University Press, 1942; New York: Peter Smith, 1950; Gloucester, Mass.: Peter Smith, 1960; Lincoln: University of Nebraska Press, 1962, 1976.

1757. Stanton, William Ragan. *The Great United States Exploring Expedition of 1838-1842.* Berkeley: University of California Press, 1975.

1758. Stephenson, George M. *The Political History of the Public Lands from 1840 to 1862: From Pre-Emption to Homestead.* Boston: R. G. Badger, 1917; New York: Russell & Russell, 1967.

1759. Tyler, David Budlong. *The Wilkes Expedition: The First United States Exploring Expedition, 1838-1842.* Philadelphia: American Philosophical Society, 1968.

1760. Viola, Herman J. "The Wilkes Expedition on the Pacific Coast." *Pacific Northwest Quarterly* 80 (January 1989): 21-31.

1761. Viola, Herman J., and Carolyn Margolis, eds. *Magnificent Voyagers: The U.S. Exploring Expedition, 1838-1842.* Washington: Smithsonian Institution Press, 1967.

1762. Westerberg, Joshua F. "Hawaii: Overland Mail Via Mexico, 1842-46." *Collectors Club Philatelist* 34 (January 1955): 3-16. Discusses United States postal service to Hawaii.

X

Presidential Election of 1844

A. GENERAL STUDIES

1763. Anderson, James L., and W. Edwin Hemphill. "The 1843 Biography of John C. Calhoun: Was R. M. T. Hunter Its Author?" *Journal of Southern History* 38 (August 1972): 470-74. Argue that Hunter did write the biography.

1764. "The Baltimore Convention." *United States Magazine and Democratic Review* 13 (October 1843): 339-45. Predicts Clay's nomination by the Whigs; explores Democratic prospects for victory.

1765. Belohlavek, John M. "The Democracy in a Dilemma: George M. Dallas, Pennsylvania, and the Election of 1844." *Pennsylvania History* 41 (October 1974): 391-411.

1766. Carton, Stanley. "Cassius Marcellus Clay, Antislavery Whig in the Presidential Campaign of 1844." *Register of the Kentucky Historical Society* 68 (January 1970): 17-36.

1767. Curry, Roy Watson. "James A. Seddon, A Southern Prototype." *Virginia Magazine of History and Biography* 63 (April 1955): 123-50. Provides a brief biographical sketch of Tyler's colleague, his role in the election of 1840, at the 1861 Washington Peace Convention, and in the Provisional Congress of the Confederacy.

1768. Everett, Robert B. "James K. Polk and the Election of 1844 in Tennessee." *West Tennessee Historical Society Papers* 16 (1962): 5-28.

1769. Fitzsimons, Matthew A. "Calhoun's Bid for the Presidency, 1841-1844." *Mississippi Valley Historical Review* 38 (June 1951): 39-60.

1770. Grant, Clement L. "Cave Johnson and the Presidential Campaign of 1844." *East Tennessee Historical Society's Publications* 25 (1953): 54-73. Explores Johnson's role in the nomination of Polk.

1771. Persinger, Clark Edmund. *The "Bargain of 1844" as the Origin of the Wilmot Proviso.* Washington: Government Printing Office, 1913.

1772. Rayback, Joseph G. "The Presidential Ambitions of John C. Calhoun, 1844-1848." *Journal of Southern History* 14 (August 1948): 331-56.

1773. Redard, Thomas E. "The Election of 1844 in Louisiana: A New Look at the Ethnocultural Approach." *Louisiana History* 22 (Fall 1981): 419-33.

1774. Van der Linden, Frank. *Dark Horse.* San Antonio: Naylor Company, 1944. Deals with the annexation of Texas and Polk's nomination and election.

1775. Volpe, Vernon L. "The Liberty Party and Polk's Election, 1844." *Historian* 53 (Summer 1991): 691-710.

1776. Walmsley, J. E. "Presidential Campaign of 1844 in Mississippi." *Mississippi Historical Society Publications* 9 (1906): 179-97.

1777. Washburn, Clara Bracken. "Some Aspects of the 1844 Presidential Campaign in Tennessee." *Tennessee Historical Quarterly* 4 (March 1945): 58-74.

B. CAMPAIGN BIOGRAPHIES

1. Democratic Ticket

John C. Calhoun

1778. *The Calhoun Textbook...* New York: Herald Office; Philadelphia: G. B. Zieber & Company; Boston: Redding & Company; Charleston: Babcock & Company, Samuel Hart, Sr.; New Orleans: Bravo and Morgan; Mobile: J. M. Sumwalt and Company, 1843.

1779. [Hunter, Robert M. T.]. *Life of John C. Calhoun. Presenting a Condensed History of Political Events from 1811 to 1843.* New York: Harper & Brothers, 1843.

1780. *Life and Character of the Hon. John C. Calhoun, With Illustrations: Containing Notices of His Father and Uncles, and Their Brave Conduct During Our Struggle for Independence, in the American Revolutionary War.* New York: New World Press, 1843.

1781. *Life of John C. Calhoun, Presenting a Condensed History of Political Events from 1811 to 1843, Together with a Selection from His Speeches, Reports, and Other Writings Subsequent to His Election as Vice-President of the United States, Including His Leading Speech on the Late War Delivered in 1811.* New York: Harper & Brothers, 1843. Several editions with minor variations in title and contents.

Lewis Cass

1782. *Biography of General Lewis Cass, Including a Voice from a Friend.* New York: New World Press, 1843.

1783. [Rush, Richard]. *Biography of General Lewis Cass.* New York: J. Winchester, 1843. Published under pseudonym, "A Voice from a Friend."

1784. *Sketch of the Life and Services of General Lewis Cass, of Ohio.* Harrisburg: n.p., 1842.

James K. Polk

1785. *Biographical Sketches of the Democratic Candidates for the Presidency and Vice Presidency: James K. Polk, of Tennessee. From the Democratic Review for May 1838.* [n.p.: 1844?].

1786. [Hickman, George H.]. *The Life and Public Services of the Hon. James Knox Polk, With a Compendium of His Speeches on Various Public Measures. Also, a Sketch of the Life of the Hon. George Mifflin Dallas.* Baltimore: N. Hickman, 1844. Went through at least three editions.

1787. *Political Biography: Polk, Dallas, & Shunk.* Philadelphia: Mifflin & Parry, 1844.

1788. *The Political and Public Character of James K. Polk, of Tennessee.* Boston: Eastburn's Press, 1844. Went through several editions.

2. Democratic Republican Ticket

John Tyler

1789. Abell, Alexander G. *Life of John Tyler, President of the United States, Up to the Close of the Second Session of the Twenty-Seventh Congress, Including Some of His Most Important Speeches While a Member of the House of Representatives and of the Senate of the United States, and His Principal Messages and Other Public Papers as Chief Magistrate of the Union.* New York: Harper & Brothers, 1843; New York: Harper & Brothers, 1844.

1790. *A Brief Sketch of the Life of John Tyler: President of the United States, Compiled from Authentic Sources.* Philadelphia: J. R. Colon, 1842. Also in *Pamphlets* **[603]**.

1791. *A Defence of the President against the Attacks of Mr. Botts and the Clay Party.* [Washington]: Madisonian, 1844.

1792. *John Tyler: His History, Character, and Position, with a Portrait.* New York: Harper & Brothers, 1843. Also in *Goldsmiths'* **[600]**.

3. Liberty Ticket

James G. Birney

1793. Green, Beriah. *Sketches of the Life and Writings of James Gillespie Birney.* Utica: Jackson & Chaplin, 1844. Also in *Microbook Library* **[601]**.

1794. Tucker, J. N. T. *The Liberty Almanac ... No. Two. 1845 ...* Syracuse: Tucker & Kinney, [1844]. Contains short biographical sketch of Birney, pp. 19-23.

4. Whig Ticket

Henry Clay

1795. Anti-Junius (pseudonym). *The Tap of the Drum; or, A Few Words about John Tyler.* New York: J. and H. G. Langley, 1843. No. 1 of Political Tracts for the Times. Anti-Tyler.

1796. Anti-Junius (pseudonym). *Who and What Is John Tyler?* New York: J. and H. Langley, 1843. Also in *Pamphlets* **[603]**.

1797. Brownlow, William Gannaway. *A Political Register, Setting Forth the Principles of the Whig and Locofoco Parties in the United States, With the Life and Public Services of Henry Clay.* Jonesborough, Tenn.: Jonesborough Whig, 1844; Spartanburg, S.C.: Reprint Company, 1974.

1798. "Clay in the Field Again!" *United States Magazine and Democratic Review* 11 (August 1842): 205-8.

1799. [Collins, George C.]. *Fifty Reasons Why the Honorable Henry Clay Should Be Elected President of the United States.* Baltimore: The Author, 1844. Went through several editions.

1800. [Colton, Calvin]. *Life of Henry Clay, by Junius* ... New York: Greeley & McElrath; Philadelphia: Godey & McMichael, 1843.

1801. Graham, F. B. *Clay and Frelinghuysen Almanac.* New York: Turner & Fisher, [1844].

1802. *The Henry Clay Almanac, for the Year of Our Lord 1843 ... Containing Songs and Anecdotes and a Biographical Sketch of Henry Clay* ... Philadelphia: Grigg & Elliot, [c1842]. Several editions by various printers in Philadelphia and New York.

1803. *John, the Traitor; or, the Force of Accident. A Plain Story, by One Who Has Whistled at the Plow* ... New York: n.p.: 1843.

1804. *John Tyler; or, Honesty the Best Policy.* New York: Henry Langley, 1844.

1805. Life of Henry Clay. [Washington: Expositor, n.d.].

1806. *The Life and Public Services of Henry Clay.* [n.p.: 1844].

1807. Littell, John Stockton. *The Clay Minstrel; or, National Songster. To Which Is Prefixed a Sketch of the Life, Public Services, and Character of Henry Clay.* Philadelphia: Turner & Fisher, 1842; New York: Greeley & McElrath; Philadelphia: Thomas, Cowperthwait and Company, 1844.

1808. Mallory, Daniel, ed. *The Life and Speeches of the Hon. Henry Clay.* 2 vols. New York: Robert P. Bixby & Co, 1843; New York: Van Amringe and Bixby, 1844. Went through several editions.

1809. Sargent, Epes. *The Life and Public Services of Henry Clay ... Brought Down to the Year 1844.* New York: Greeley & McElrath, 1844.

1810. [Sargent, Epes?]. *Life and Public Services of Henry Clay.* New York: The New World, [c1842].

1811. [Sargent, Nathan]. *Brief Outline of the Life of Henry Clay.* Washington: John T. Towers, [1844]. Published under pseudonym "Oliver Oldschool."

1812. [Sargent, Nathan]. *A Sketch of the Life and Public Services of Henry Clay.* [Baltimore: American Whig, 1844?].

1813. [Sargent, Nathan]. *Life of Henry Clay.* [Philadelphia: R. G. Bedford, 1844?]. Several different editions.

1814. [Swain, J. B.], ed. *The Life and Speeches of Henry Clay*. 2 vols. New York: Greeley & McElrath, 1843, 1844.

1815. Vandenhoff, G., ed. *The Clay Code; or, Text-Book of Eloquence, a Collection of Axioms, Apothegms, ... Gathered from the Public Speeches of Henry Clay ...* New York: C. Shepard, 1844.

1816. *Whig Almanac and United States Register for 1843*. New York: Greeley and McElrath, [1842?]. Contains essay by Greeley and short sketch of Clay by Henry J. Raymond.

C. CAMPAIGN SPEECHES AND GENERAL PAMPHLETS

1817. Adams, Charles Francis. *Texas and the Massachusetts Resolutions*. Boston: Eastburn's Press, 1844. Opposes Texas annexation.

1818. *The Andover Husking; A Political Tale, Suited to the Circumstances of the Present Time, and Dedicated to the Whigs of Massachusetts ...* Boston: J. H. Eastburn, 1842. Anti-Tyler.

1819. [Atwater, Caleb]. Citizen of Ohio. *Mysteries of Washington City, During Several Months of the Session of the 28th Congress*. Washington: G. A. Sage, 1844. Also in *Selected Americana* [602]. Contrasts the Washington of 1844 with 1834, the moral climate, politics, political leaders; discusses briefly the Tyler administration and Tyler's relations with his cabinet.

1820. *The Campaign for 1844*. Election serial touting the Whig cause in Kentucky, published by Hodges, Todd & Pruett of Frankfort.

1821. Child, David Lee. *An Appeal from David L. Child, Editor of the Anti-Slavery Standard, to the Abolitionists*. N.p: 1844. Also in *Texas* [607].

1822. Child, David Lee. *The Taking of Naboth's Vineyard; or, History of the Texas Conspiracy, and an Examination of the Reasons Given by the Hon. J. C. Calhoun, Hon. R. J. Walker, and Others, for the Dismemberment and Robbery of the Republic of Mexico*. New York: S. W. Benedict & Company, 1845. Also in *Texas* [607].

1823. Child, David Lee. *The Texan Resolution, Republished with Additions from the Northampton (Massachusetts) Gazette, to Which is Added a Letter from Washington on the Annexation of Texas, and the Late Outrage in California*. Washington: Northampton, 1842; Washington: J. & G.S. Gideon, 1843. Also in *Texas* [607].

1824. Citizen of Pennsylvania. *A Few Plain Facts, Addressed to the People of Pennsylvania.* Philadelphia: J. Crissy, 1844.

1825. Clay, Henry. *Mr. Clay's Speech, Delivered in the City of Raleigh, N.C. April 13, 1844.* New York: Central Clay Committee, 1844.

1826. [Colton, Calvin]. *The Junius Tracts: No. 1. The Test, or Parties Tried by Their Acts; No. 2. The Currency; No. 3. The Tariff; No. 4. Life of Henry Clay; No. 5. Political Abolition; No. 6. Democracy; No. 7. Labor and Capital; No 8. The Public Lands; No. 9. Annexation of Texas. No. 10. The Tariff Triumphant.* New York: Greeley & McElrath, 1844: New York: Garland Publishers, 1974. 1844 Whig campaign publications under the pseudonym of "Junius."

1827. Democratic Party (Va.) State Central Committee. *Fincastle Democrat—Extra: Republicans of Botetourt! To Your Posts!! To Your Posts!! On the First Monday in November Next ... You ... Must Decide at the Polls Who Will be President and Vice President ...* n.p., [1844]. Supports Polk's candidacy.

1828. Green, Willis. *Address of the Hon. Willis Green, of Kentucky, before the Alexandria Clay Club.* n.p., [1844?].

1829. [Lee, Charles Carter]. *Song: On the Occasion of Raising the Clay Banner at Moorefield, Hardy County, Virginia, (on the 3d of August, 1844), Adorned with an Eagle, and Inscribed with the Names of Clay and Frelinghuysen.* n.p., [1844].

1830. *The Madisonian Pamphlet.* [Washington: n.p., 1844]. Contains letter from Tyler, August 20, 1844, to friends throughout the Union, essays on Webster and Clay, letter from Andrew Jackson, and one from J. K. Polk. Supports Tyler.

1831. *Republican Sentinel, Devoted to the Support of the Rights of the Union, of the States and of the People, as Defined by Strict Construction of the Written Constitution.* Richmond. A weekly serial published from March 16 to October 30, 1844, in support of Democratic candidates for office.

1832. Ritchie, Thomas. "More Misrepresentations!" in *John P. Branch Historical Papers of Randolph-Macon College* 3 (1911): 271-79. Responds to the Richmond Whig's endorsement of Calhoun for the presidency.

1833. Rives, William Cabell. *Letter of Hon. William C. Rives, (U.S. Senator from Virginia) Giving His Reasons for Preferring Mr. Clay to Mr. Van Buren for the Next President.* [New York: Office of the Tribune], 1844.

1834. *Southern State Rights, Free Trade and Anti-Abolition Tract No. 1.* Charleston: Walker & Burke, 1844. Also in *Texas* **[607]**.

1835. Stockton, R. F. *Speech of Capt. R. F. Stockton Delivered at the Great Democratic Meeting at New Brunswick, New Jersey, Wednesday, September 24, 1844.* New York: J. W. Bell, 1844. Also in *Goldsmiths'* **[600]**. Democratic campaign publication.

1836. [Stuart, Moses]. *Mr. Webster's Andover Address and His Political Course While Secretary of State: The Publishers Have No Authority to Designate the Authorship of the Following Pages, but from Various Circumstances, They Infer the Probability, that They Were Written by Prof. Stuart, of Andover.* Essex County, Mass.: n.p., 1844. Also in *Pamphlets* **[603]**. Published under pseudonym "Civis."

1837. *The Tariff, a Tract for the Times, By a Citizen of Virginia, Prepared by Order of Hon. Willis Green, Chairman of the Executive Committee of the Whig Members of Congress.* [Washington: n.p.: 1844]. Also in *Goldsmiths'* **[600]**.

1838. *Tract No. 4. Providential Dispensations: Omens—Results of 1840.* [n.p.: 1843?].

1839. Tyler, John, Jr. *Address of John Tyler, Jr. Esq., Delivered before the Democratic Association of Portsmouth, Virginia, During the Canvass of 1844.* Washington: J. E. Dow and Company, [1845]. Argues against a bank of the United States and strongly defends the Tyler administration.

1840. Washington, D.C. Democratic Tyler Meeting, 1844. *Democratic Tyler Meeting at Washington...* [Washington: n.p.: 1844].

1841. Webster, Daniel. *Speech of Daniel Webster of Massachusetts Delivered at the Great Whig Mass Convention Held at Philadelphia on the 1st Day of October, 1844.* Philadelphia: n.p., 1844. Also in *Legal Treatises* **[606]**.

1842. Whig Congressional Committee. *Prospect before Us; or, Locofoco Impositions Exposed to the People of the United States.* Washington: Gideon's, 1844. Whig campaign pamphlet.

1843. *Whig Congressional Committee. Tariff Doctrine.* Washington: Gideon's Office, [1844].

1844. *Whig State Convention.* Richmond: P. D. Bernard, 1844. Held in Clay Club House, 7 February 1844. Denounced Van Buren, supported Clay.

1845. *Whig Text Book; or, Democracy Unmasked: To the People of the United States.* Washington: Gideon's Office, 1844.

XI

Associates of Tyler

A. COLLECTIVE BIOGRAPHIES

1846. Garraty, John A., and Jerome L. Sternstein, eds. *Encyclopedia of American Biography*. New York: Harper and Row, 1974.

1847. Harrison, Frederick G. *Biographical Sketches of Pre-Eminent Americans*. 4 vols. Boston: Walker, 1892-93. Contains sketches and portraits of many of Tyler's contemporaries.

1848. Johnson, Allen, and Dumas Malone, eds. *Dictionary of American Biography*. 23 vols. New York: C. Scribner's, 1928-58. A major collection of biographical sketches of prominent figures.

1849. *The National Cyclopædia of American Biography ...* 63 vols to date. New York: J. T. White Co., 1893– . An important collection of biographical sketches.

1850. Sobel, Robert. *Biographical Directory of the United States Executive Branch, 1774-1971*. Westport, Conn.: Greenwood Publishing Co., 1971. Has brief thumbnail sketches of Tyler and members of his cabinet.

1851. Wilson, James Grant, and John Fiske, eds. *Appleton's Cyclopedia of American Biography*. 6 vols. New York: Appleton, 1886-89 (and numerous other editions).

B. MEMBERS OF CABINET

1852. *Attorneys General of the United States, 1789-1979*. [Washington]: U.S. Dept. of Justice, 1980, 1985. Has portraits and short biographical sketches.

1853. Bell, William Gardner. *Secretaries of War and Secretaries of the Army: Portraits and Biographical Sketches*. Washington: Center for Military History, United States Army, 1982. Brief sketches with color-reproduced portraits.

1854. Bemis, Samuel F., ed. *American Secretaries of State and Their Diplomacy*. 10 vols. New York: Alfred A. Knopf, 1927-29; New York: Cooper Square Publishers, 1963. Volumes 3-6 especially important for Tyler's colleagues and cabinet.

1855. Burke, Lee H., and Jan K. Herman. *The Secretaries of State: Portraits and Biographical Sketches*. Washington: Bureau of Public Affairs, Office of Public Communication, 1978.

1856. Coletta, Paolo E., ed. *The American Secretaries of the Navy*. Annapolis: U.S. Naval Institute, 1980.

1857. Ingersoll, Lurton Dunham. *A History of the War Department of the United States, with Biographical Sketches of the Secretaries*. Washington: Francis B. Mohun, 1879. Also available in *Microbook Library* **[601]**.

1858. *Official Arrangements for the Funeral Solemnities and Interment of Abel P. Upshur ... Thomas W. Gilmer ... Beverly Kennon ... Virgil Maxcy ... and David Gardiner*. Washington: n.p., 1844. Covers briefly lives of members of Tyler's cabinet and friends killed on board the *Princeton*.

1859. Roberts, William C. *The Leading Orators of Twenty-Five Campaigns, From the First Presidential Canvass to the Present Time: Portraits, Reminiscences and Biographical Sketches of America's Distinguished Political Speakers*. New York: L. K. Strouse & Co., 1884.

1860. Smith, William Henry. *History of the Cabinet of the United States of America, from President Washington to President Coolidge ...* Baltimore: Industrial Printing Co., 1925.

1861. *Two Hundredth Anniversary of the Office of the Attorney General*. [Washington]: U.S. Dept. of Justice, [1990].

1862. Vexler, Robert I. *The Vice-Presidents and Cabinet Members: Biographies Arranged Chronologically by Administration*. 2 vols. Dobbs Ferry, N.Y.: Oceana Publications, 1975.

George E. Badger, Secretary of the Navy

1863. Graham, William A. *Discourse in Memory of the Life and Character of the Honorable George E. Badger.* Raleigh: Nichols, Gorman and Neathery, 1866.

1864. Jessup, Rachel Dean. "George Edmund Badger: Unionist and Disunionist." M.A. thesis, Wake Forest University, 1963.

John Bell, Secretary of War

1865. Grim, Mark Sillers. "The Political Career of John Bell." M.A. thesis, University of Tennessee, 1930. Offers a brief introduction, with bibliography, to Bell's career both in Tennessee and in Washington.

1866. Parks, Joseph Howard. *John Bell of Tennessee.* Baton Rouge: Louisiana State University Press, [1950]. The standard biography of Bell, contains an extensive bibliography.

George M. Bibb, Secretary of the Treasury

1867. "Bibb, George M." *Biographical Encyclopedia of the Commonwealth of Kentucky.* Easley, S.C.: Genealogical Publishing Co., 1980.

1868. Goff, John S. "The Last Leaf: George Mortimer Bibb." *Register of the Kentucky Historical Society* 59 (October 1961): 331-42.

John C. Calhoun, Secretary of State

1869. Bancroft, Frederic. *Calhoun and the South Carolina Nullification Movement.* Baltimore: Johns Hopkins University Press, 1928; Gloucester, Mass.: P. Smith, 1966.

1870. Bartlett, Irving H. *John C. Calhoun: A Biography.* New York: W. W. Norton & Co., 1993.

1871. Capers, Gerald M. *John C. Calhoun—Opportunist: A Reappraisal.* Gainesville: University of Florida Press, 1960.

1872. Coit, Margaret L. *John C. Calhoun, American Portrait.* Boston: Houghton Mifflin, 1950; Englewood Cliffs, N.J.: Prentice-Hall, 1970.

1873. Current, Richard N. *John C. Calhoun.* New York: Washington Square Press, 1963.

1874. Lander, Ernest McPherson. *Reluctant Imperialists: Calhoun, the South Carolinians, and the Mexican War*. Baton Rouge: Louisiana State University Press, 1979.

1875. Meigs, William Montgomery. *The Life of John Caldwell Calhoun*. 2 vols. New York: G. E. Stechert, 1917; New York: Da Capo Press, 1970.

1876. Niven, John. *John C. Calhoun and the Price of Union: A Biography*. Baton Rouge: Louisana State University Press, 1988.

1877. Silbey, Joel H. "John C. Calhoun and the Limits of Southern Congressional Unity, 1841-1850." *Historian* 30 (November 1967): 58-71.

1878. Wiltse, Charles M. *John C. Calhoun*. 3 vols. Indianapolis: Bobbs-Merrill, 1944-51; New York: Russell & Russell, 1968.

John J. Crittenden, Attorney General

1879. Kelly, Jack. "John J. Crittenden and the Constitutional Union Party." *Filson Club Historical Quarterly* 48 (July 1974): 265-76.

1880. Kirwan, Albert D. *John J. Crittenden: The Struggle for the Union*. Lexington: University of Kentucky Press, 1962.

Thomas Ewing, Secretary of the Treasury

1881. Gilbert, Abby L. "Thomas Ewing, Sr.: Ohio's Advocate for a National Bank." *Ohio History* 82 (Winter/Spring 1973): 4-24. Explores Ewing's efforts after Jackson's veto of the bank bill.

1882. Miller, Paul Ingersoll. "Thomas Ewing, Last of the Whigs." Ph.D. diss., Ohio State University, 1933.

Hugh Swinton Legaré, Attorney General and Secretary of State

1883. Cain, Marvin R. "Return of Republicanism: A Reappraisal of Hugh Swinton Legaré and the Tyler Presidency." *South Carolina Historical Magazine* 79 (October 1978): 264-80. Explores the pivotal role that Legaré played in the reorganized Tyler cabinet, 1841-43.

1884. Davis, Richard Beale. "The Early American Lawyer and the Profession of Letters." *Huntington Library Quarterly* 12 (1948-49): 191-205. Examines the careers of Legaré and Francis W. Gilmer.

1885. O'Brien, Michael. *A Character of Hugh Swinton Legaré.* Knoxville: University of Tennessee Press, 1985.

1886. Preston, William Campbell. *Eulogy on Hugh Swinton Legaré, Delivered at the Request of the City of Charleston by W. C. Preston, Nov. 7, 1843.* Charleston: n.p., [1843]. Also in *Legal Treatises* **[606]**.

1887. Rhea, Linda. *Hugh Swinton Legaré: A Charleston Intellectual.* Chapel Hill: University of North Carolina Press, 1934.

John Y. Mason, Secretary of the Navy

1888. "John Young Mason Papers." *Virginia Historical Society, Occasional Bulletin* 31 (October 1975): 1-4. Describes the Society's collection of Mason papers, including Tyler, Polk, and Buchanan letters.

1889. Lauzac, Henry. "John Young Mason." *Southern Literary Messenger* 28 (1859): 72-73.

1890. Williams, Frances Leigh. "The Heritage and Preparation of a Statesman, John Young Mason, 1799-1859." *Virginia Magazine of History and Biography* 75 (July 1967): 305-30.

James M. Porter, Secretary of War

1891. Friedman, Jean E., and William G. Shade. "James M. Porter: A Conservative Democrat in the Jacksonian Era." *Pennsylvania History* 42 (1975): 189-204. Also describes Tyler's courtship of the Pennsylvania Democrats in 1843-44.

Abel P. Upshur, Secretary of the Navy and Secretary of State

1892. Carpenter, William S. *The Development of American Political Thought.* Princeton: Princeton University Press, 1930, pp. 132-33. Discusses Upshur's interpretation of majority rights as developed in speech before the Virginia Constitutional Convention, 1829-30.

1893. Hall, Claude H. "Abel P. Upshur and the Navy as an Instrument of Foreign Policy." *Virginia Magazine of History and Biography* 69 (July 1961): 290-99.

1894. Hall, Claude H. "Abel Parker Upshur, An Eastern Shoreman Reforms the United States Navy." *Virginia Cavalcade* 23 (Spring 1974): 29-37.

1895. Hall, Claude H. *Abel Parker Upshur, Conservative Virginian, 1790-1844.* Madison: State Historical Society of Wisconsin, 1964.

1896. Hall, Claude H. "Abel Parker Upshur." Ph.D. diss., University of Virginia, 1954.

1897. Hall, Claude H. "The Early Life of Abel Parker Upshur, 1790-1841." M.A. thesis, University of Virginia, 1949.

1898. Miller, Russell E. "Abel Parker Upshur: A Study in Ante-Bellum Social and Political Philosophy." Ph.D. diss., Princeton University, 1951.

1899. Mitchell, Donald W. "Abel Upshur, Forgotten Prophet of the Old Navy." *United States Naval Institute Proceedings* 75 (December 1949): 1367-75.

1900. Sturges, Mary Jane Stith (Upshur). "Abel Parker Upshur, Secretary of State of the United States, 1842-1844." *Magazine of American History* 1 (1877): 542-48.

Daniel Webster, Secretary of State

1901. Bartlett, Irving H. *Daniel Webster*. New York: Norton, [1978].

1902. Baxter, Maurice Glen. *One and Inseparable: Daniel Webster and the Union.* Cambridge, Mass.: Harvard University Press, 1984.

1903. Curtis, George Ticknor. "Mr. Webster as a Diplomatist." *North American Review* 68 (January 1849): 1-41.

1904. Curtis, George Ticknor. *Life of Daniel Webster.* 2 vols. New York: D. Appleton, 1870, 1872, 1889, 1893. Also in *Legal Treatises* [**606**]. An early, but important account of Webster by one of his literary executors; prints many significant letters and documents.

1905. Dalzell, Robert F., Jr. *Daniel Webster and the Trial of American Nationalism, 1843-1852.* Boston: Houghton Mifflin, 1973. One of the best studies of Webster's later political career.

1906. Fuess, Claude Moore. *Daniel Webster.* 2 vols. Boston: Little, Brown and Co., 1930; Hamden, Conn.: Archon Books, 1958; New York: Da Capo Press, 1968.

1907. Nathans, Sydney H. "Daniel Webster and the Whig Party, 1828-1844." Ph.D. diss., Johns Hopkins University, 1969.

1908. Nathans, Sydney H. "Daniel Webster, Massachusetts Man." *New England Quarterly* 39 (June 1966): 161-81. Explores reasons for his support of Tyler.

1909. Nathans, Sydney H. *Daniel Webster and Jacksonian Democracy*. Baltimore: Johns Hopkins University Press, 1973.

1910. Peterson, Merrill D. *The Great Triumvirate: Webster, Clay, and Calhoun*. New York: Oxford University Press, 1987.

1911. Porter, David L. "The Ten Best Secretaries of State—and the Worst Five." *American Heritage* 33 (December 1981): 78-80. Rates Webster among the best.

1912. Shewmaker, Kenneth E. "'Congress only can declare war' and 'the President is Commander in Chief': Daniel Webster and the War Power." *Diplomatic History* 12 (Fall 1988): 383-409.

1913. Shewmaker, Kenneth E. "Daniel Webster and the Oregon Question." *Pacific Historical Review* 51 (May 1982): 195-201. Offers a corrective to previous scholarship on Webster and the "tripartite plan" as a solution to the settlement of the northwestern boundary.

1914. Shewmaker, Kenneth E. "Daniel Webster and the Politics of Foreign Policy." *Journal of American History* 63 (September 1976): 303-15.

1915. Shewmaker, Kenneth E. "Daniel Webster: A Lesser-Known Great Secretary of State." *Dartmouth College Library Bulletin* 12 (November 1971): 29-36.

1916. Shewmaker, Kenneth E., ed. *Daniel Webster: "The Completest Man."* Hanover: University Press of New England, 1990. Contains overview of Webster's oratorical skills by William H. Rehnquist and documents and scholarly evaluations of Webster the politician by Richard N. Current, of the orator and writer by Irving H. Bartlett, of the lawyer by Maurice G. Baxter, of the diplomatist by Howard Jones, and of Webster's legacy by Shewmaker.

William Wilkins, Secretary of War

1917. Slick, S. E. "The Life of William Wilkins." Ph.D. diss., University of Pittsburgh, 1931.

C. MEMBERS OF CONGRESS

1. Collective Biographies

1918. *Biographical Directory of the United States Congress, 1774-1989.* Washington: Government Printing Office, 1989. Lists executive officers, officers of Congress, and delegates; provides thumbnail biographical sketches of congressmen with occasional references to other biographical materials.

1919. Dyer, Oliver. *Great Senators of the United States Forty Years Ago (1848 and 1849), with Personal Recollections and Delineations of Calhoun, Benton, Clay, Webster, General Houston, Jefferson Davis, and Other Distinguished Statesmen of that Period.* New York: Robert Bonner's Sons, 1889. A Senate reporter, Dyer provides personal glimpses of many of Tyler's senatorial associates.

1920. Goldman, Perry M., and J. S. Young, eds. *The United States Congressional Directories, 1789-1840.* New York: Columbia University Press, 1973. Provides congressional committee listings and addresses of living quarters.

1921. *Portraits of United States Senators, With a Biographical Sketch of Each.* Claremont, N. H.: Tracy, Kenney & Co., 1856. Contains primitive engravings and thumbnail sketches of the lives of many of Tyler's senatorial colleagues.

2. Individual Studies

John Quincy Adams, Massachusetts Representative

1922. Bemis, Samuel F. *John Quincy Adams and the Foundations of American Foreign Policy.* New York: Alfred A. Knopf, 1949, 1950.

1923. Bemis, Samuel F. *John Quincy Adams and the Union.* New York: Alfred A. Knopf, 1956.

1924. Richards, Leonard L. *The Life and Times of Congressman John Quincy Adams.* New York: Oxford University Press, 1986.

William Allen, Ohio Representative and Senator

1925. McGrane, Reginald Charles. *William Allen: A Study in Western Democracy.* Columbus: Ohio State Archaeological and Historical Society, 1925.

Nathan Appleton, Massachusetts Representative

1926. Gregory, Francis W. *Nathan Appleton: Merchant and Entrepreneur, 1779-1861.* Charlottesville: University Press of Virginia, 1975.

1927. Winthrop, Robert Charles. *Memoir of the Hon. Nathan Appleton, LL.D.* Boston: J. Wilson and Son, 1861; Westport, Conn.: Greenwood Press, 1969.

David R. Atchison, Missouri Senator

1928. Atchison, Theodore. "David R. Atchison: A Study in American Politics." *Missouri Historical Review* 24 (July 1930): 502-15.

1929. Parrish, William Earl. *David Rice Atchison of Missouri: Border Politician.* Columbia: University of Missouri Press, 1961.

Arthur Pendleton Bagby, Alabama Senator

1930. Martin, John M. "The Senatorial Career of Arthur Pendleton Bagby." *Alabama Historical Quarterly* 42 (Fall/Winter 1980): 124-56.

Daniel Dewey Barnard, New York Representative

1931. Penney, Sherry. "Dissension in the Whig Ranks: Daniel Dewey Barnard versus Thurlow Weed." *New-York Historical Society Quarterly* 59 (January 1975): 71-92.

1932. Penney, Sherry. *Patrician in Politics: Daniel Dewey Barnard of New York.* Port Washington, N.Y.: Kennikat Press, 1974.

Thomas Hart Benton, Missouri Senator

1933. Chambers, William N. *Old Bullion Benton: Senator from the New West.* Boston: Little, Brown, 1956.

1934. Meigs, William Montgomery. *The Life of Thomas Hart Benton.* Philadelphia: J. B. Lippincott Co., 1904; New York: Da Capo Press, 1970.

1935. Roosevelt, Theodore. *Life of Thomas Hart Benton.* Boston: Houghton, Mifflin, 1887, 1899; New York: AMS Press, 1972.

1936. Smith, Elbert B. *Magnificent Missourian: The Life of Thomas Hart Benton.* Philadelphia: Lippincott, 1958.

John Macpherson Berrien, Georgia Senator

1937. McCrary, Royce, Jr. "John Macpherson Berrien of Georgia: A Political Biography." Ph.D. diss., University of Georgia, 1971.

Horace Binney, Pennsylvania Representative

1938. Binney, Charles C. *Life of Horace Binney.* Philadelphia: J. B. Lippincott, 1903.

John Minor Botts, Virginia Representative

1939. Painter, Simon M. "Political Career of John Minor Botts." M.A. thesis, Washington and Lee University, 1934.

1940. Webster, Clyde C. "John Minor Botts, Anti-Secessionist." *Richmond College Historical Papers* 1 (1915-16): 9-37.

Sidney Breese, Illinois Senator

1941. McNulty, John W. "Sidney Breese: His Early Career in Law and Politics in Illinois." *Journal of the Illinois State Historical Society* 61 (Summer 1968): 164-81.

James Buchanan, Pennsylvania Senator

1942. Binder, Frederick Moore. "James Buchanan: Jacksonian Expansionist." *Historian* 55 (Autumn 1992): 69-84. Discusses views and attitudes of Buchanan and Webster toward England, 1841-43.

1943. Curtis, George Ticknor. *Life of James Buchanan.* 2 vols. New York: Harper and Brothers, 1883.

1944. Klein, Philip S. *President James Buchanan, A Biography.* University Park: Pennsylvania State University Press, 1962.

William O. Butler, Kentucky Representative

1945. Roberts, G. F. "William O. Butler." M.A. thesis, University of Kentucky, 1962.

Rufus Choate, Massachusetts Representative and Senator

1946. Brown, Samuel Gilman. *The Life of Rufus Choate.* Boston: Little, Brown and Co., 1870.

1947. Fuess, Claude Moore. *Rufus Choate, the Wizard of the Law*. New York: Minton, Balch & Co., 1928.

1948. Matthews, Jean V. *Rufus Choate, the Law and Civic Virtue*. Philadelphia: Temple University Press, 1980.

1949. Walker, David Bradstreet. "Rufus Choate, An American Whig." Ph.D. diss., Brown University, 1956.

Clement C. Clay, Alabama Representative and Senator

1950. Nuermberger, Ruth Anna. *The Clays of Alabama: A Planter-Lawyer-Politician Family*. Lexington: University of Kentucky Press, 1958.

Henry Clay, Kentucky Senator

1951. Baxter, Maurice Glen. *Henry Clay and the American System*. Lexington: University Press of Kentucky, 1995.

1952. Colton, Calvin. *The Life and Times of Henry Clay*. 2 vols. New York: A. S. Barnes & Co., 1846. Published later as first two volumes of *The Life, Correspondence, and Speeches of Henry Clay*, 6 vols., 1852.

1953. Eaton, Clement. *Henry Clay and the Art of American Politics*. Boston: Little, Brown and Co., 1957.

1954. Jones, Thomas B. "Henry Clay and Continental Expansion, 1820-1844." *Register of the Kentucky Historical Society* 73 (July 1975): 241-62.

1955. Mayo, Bernard. *Henry Clay, Spokesman of the New West*. Boston: Houghton Mifflin Co., 1937; Hamden, Conn.: Archon Books, 1966.

1956. Poage, George Rawlings. *Henry Clay and the Whig Party*. Chapel Hill: University of North Carolina Press, 1936; Gloucester, Mass.: Peter Smith, 1965. Adopts a favorable view of Tyler.

1957. Remini, Robert V. *Henry Clay: Statesman for the Union*. New York: W. W. Norton & Co., 1991. A long, lively study.

1958. Schurz, Carl. *Life of Henry Clay*. 2 vols. Boston: Houghton Mifflin Co., 1887, 1915.

1959. Van Deusen, Glyndon G. *The Life of Henry Clay*. Boston: Little, Brown and Co., 1937.

Nathan Clifford, Maine Representative

1960. Clifford, Philip G. *Nathan Clifford, Democrat, 1803-1881.* New York: G. P. Putnam's Sons, 1922.

Duncan L. Clinch, Georgia Representative

1961. Patrick, Rembert Wallace. *Aristocrat in Uniform: General Duncan L. Clinch.* Gainesville: University of Florida Press, 1963.

Thomas L. Clingman, North Carolina Representative and Senator

1962. Jeffrey, Thomas E. "Thunder from the Mountains: Thomas Lanier Clingman and the End of Whig Supremacy in North Carolina." *North Carolina Historical Review* 56 (October 1979): 366-95.

1963. Kruman, Marc W. "Thomas L. Clingman and the Whig Party: A Reconsideration." *North Carolina Historical Review* 64 (January 1987): 1-18.

Howell Cobb, Georgia Representative

1964. Boykin, Samuel, ed. *A Memorial Volume of the Hon. Howell Cobb, of Georgia.* Philadelphia: J. B. Lippincott & Co., 1870.

1965. Gannon, Nell Upshaw. "Howell Cobb: a Political Biography." Ph.D. diss., University of California, 1933.

1966. Simpson, John Eddins. *Howell Cobb: The Politics of Ambition.* Chicago: Adams Press, 1973.

Walter Colquitt, Alfred Cuthbert, William C. Dawson, Georgia Representatives and Senators

1967. Mellinchamp, Josephine. *Senators from Georgia.* Huntsville, Ala.: Strode Publishers, Inc., 1976.

George W. Crawford, Georgia Representative

1968. Cleveland, Len G. "George W. Crawford of Georgia, 1798-1872." Ph.D. diss., University of Georgia, 1974.

Caleb Cushing, Massachusetts Representative

1969. Fuess, Claude Moore. *The Life of Caleb Cushing.* 2 vols. New York: Harcourt, Brace & World, 1923; Hamden, Conn.: Archon Books, 1965. Most complete biographical study of Cushing.

1970. Hodgson, Sister Michael Catherine. *Caleb Cushing, Attorney General of the United States, 1853-1857.* Washington: Catholic University of America Press, 1955.

John Adams Dix, New York Senator

1971. Lichterman, Martin. "John Adams Dix, 1789-1879." Ph.D. diss., Columbia University, 1952.

Augustus C. Dodge, Iowa Delegate and Senator

1972. Pelzer, Louis. *Augustus Caesar Dodge.* Iowa City: State Historical Society of Iowa, 1908.

Henry Dodge, Wisconsin Delegate and Senator

1973. Clark, James I. *Henry Dodge, Frontiersman: First Governor of Wisconsin Territory.* Madison: State Historical Society of Wisconsin, 1957.

1974. Pelzer, Louis. *Henry Dodge.* Iowa City: State Historical Society of Iowa, 1911.

James Duane Doty, Wisconsin Delegate and Representative

1975. Smith, Alice E. *James Duane Doty: Frontier Promoter.* Madison: State Historical Society of Wisconsin, 1954.

Stephen A. Douglas, Illinois Representative and Senator

1976. Capers,Gerald M. *Stephen A. Douglas, Defender of the Union.* Boston: Little, Brown, [1959].

1977. Johannsen, Robert W. *The Frontier, the Union, and Stephen A. Douglas.* Urbana: University of Illinois Press, 1989.

1978. Johannsen, Robert W. *Stephen A. Douglas.* New York: Oxford University Press, 1973.

1979. Johannsen, Robert W. "Stephen A. Douglas and the South." *Journal of Southern History* 33 (February 1967): 26-50.

William Pitt Fessenden, Maine Representative and Senator

1980. Fessenden, Francis. *Life and Public Services of William Pitt Fessenden, United States Senator from Maine, 1854-1864 ...* 2 vols. New York: Houghton, Mifflin and Co., 1907; New York: Da Capo Press, 1970.

1981. Jellison, Charles A. *Fessenden of Maine: Civil War Senator.* Syracuse: Syracuse University Press, 1962.

Millard Fillmore, New York Representative

1982. Bailey, Howard. "Millard Fillmore: The Forgotten President." *American History Illustrated* 6 (June 1971): 26-35.

1983. Grayson, Benson Lee. *The Unknown President: The Administration of President Millard Fillmore.* Washington: University Press of America, 1981.

1984. Rayback, Robert J. "Biography of Millard Fillmore, 13th President of the United States." Ph.D. diss., University of Wisconsin, 1948.

1985. Rayback, Robert J. *Millard Fillmore: Biography of a President.* Buffalo: Buffalo Historical Society, 1959.

1986. Schelin, Robert C. "Millard Fillmore: Anti-Mason to Know-Nothing: A Moderate in New York State Politics, 1828-1856." Ph.D. diss., State University of New York, Binghampton, 1975.

1987. Stoddard, William Osborn. *Zachary Taylor, Millard Fillmore, Franklin Pierce, and James Buchanan.* New York: Stokes, 1888.

Hamilton Fish, New York Representative

1988. Nevins, Allan. *Hamilton Fish: The Inner History of the Grant Administration.* 2 vols. New York: Dodd, Mead & Co., 1936; New York: F. Ungar Publishing Co., 1957.

Joshua R. Giddings, Ohio Representative

1989. Gamble, Douglas A. "Joshua Giddings and the Ohio Abolitionists: A Study in Radical Politics." *Ohio History* 88 (Winter 1979): 37-56.

1990. Julian, George W. *The Life of Joshua R. Giddings.* Chicago: A.C. McClurg and Co., 1892.

1991. Solberg, Richard W. "Joshua Giddings: Politician and Idealist." Ph.D. diss., University of Chicago, 1952.

1992. Stewart, J. Brewer. *Joshua R. Giddings and the Tactics of Radical Politics.* Cleveland: Press of Case Western Reserve University, 1970.

William A. Graham, North Carolina Senator

1993. Williams, Max R. "The Education of William A. Graham." *North Carolina Historical Review* 40 (1963): 1-14.

1994. Williams, Max R. "William A. Graham, North Carolina Whig Party Leader, 1804-1849." Ph.D. diss., University of North Carolina at Chapel Hill, 1965.

William M. Gwin, Mississippi Representative

1995. Blattner, Helen Harland. "The Political Career of William McKendree Gwin." M.A. thesis, University of California, Berkeley, 1914.

1996. Stanley, Gerald. "Senator William Gwin: Moderate or Racist?" *California Historical Quarterly* 50 (September 1971): 243-55.

1997. Steele, Robert V. P. *Between Two Empires: The Life Story of California's First Senator, William McKendree Gwin.* Boston: Houghton Mifflin, 1969.

John P. Hale, New Hampshire Representative

1998. Sewell, Richard H. *John P. Hale and the Politics of Abolition.* Cambridge: Harvard University Press, 1965.

Hannibal Hamlin, Maine Representative

1999. Hamlin, Charles Eugene. *The Life and Times of Hannibal Hamlin.* Cambridge: Riverside Press, 1899; Port Washington, N.Y.: Kennikat Press, 1971.

2000. Hunt, H. Draper. *Hannibal Hamlin of Maine: Lincoln's First Vice President.* Syracuse: Syracuse University Press, 1969.

2001. Kazarian, Richard, Jr. "Working Radicals: The Early Political Careers of William Seward, Thaddeus Stevens, Henry Wilson, Charles Sumner, Salmon P. Chase and Hannibal Hamlin." Ph.D. diss., Brown University, 1981.

George Smith Houston, Alabama Representative

2002. *Memorial Addresses on the Life and Character of George S. Houston.* Washington: Government Printing Office, 1880.

Robert M. T. Hunter, Virginia Representative

2003. Crow, Jeffrey J. "R. M. T. Hunter and the Secession Crisis, 1860-1861: A Southern Plan for Reconstruction." *West Virginia History* 34 (April 1973): 273-90.

2004. Fisher, John E. "The Dilemma of a States' Rights Whig: The Congressional Career of R. M. T. Hunter, 1837-1841." *Virginia Magazine of History and Biography* 81 (October 1973): 387-404.

2005. Fisher, John E. "Statesman of the Lost Cause: The Career of R. M. T. Hunter, 1859-1887." M.A. thesis, University of Virginia, 1966.

2006. Fisher, John E. "Statesman of the Lost Cause: R. M. T. Hunter and the Sectional Controversy, 1847-1887." Ph.D. diss., University of Virginia, 1968.

2007. Scanlon, J. "A Life of Robert Hunter." Ph.D. diss., University of Virginia, 1969.

2008. Simms, Henry Harrison. *Life of Robert M. T. Hunter: A Study in Sectionalism and Secession.* Richmond: William Byrd Press, 1935.

Charles Jared Ingersoll, Pennsylvania Representative

2009. Meigs, William Montgomery. *The Life of Charles Jared Ingersoll.* Philadelphia: J. B. Lippincott Co., 1897; New York: Da Capo Press, 1970. Also in *Microbook Library* [601] and in *Legal Treatises* [606].

Andrew Johnson, Tennessee Representative

2010. McKitrick, Eric L. *Andrew Johnson: A Profile.* New York: Hill and Wang, 1969.

2011. Riches, William Terence Martin. "The Commoners: Andrew Johnson and Abraham Lincoln to 1861." Ph.D. diss., University of Tennessee, 1976.

2012. Steele, Robert V. P. *The First President Johnson: The Three Lives of the Seventeenth President of the United States of America.* New York: Morrow, 1968.

2013. Stryker, Lloyd Paul. *Andrew Johnson: A Study in Courage.* New York: Macmillan Co., 1929.

2014. Trefousse, Hans Louis. *Andrew Johnson: A Biography*. New York: Norton, 1989.

Cave Johnson, Tennessee Representative

2015. Grant, Clement L. "The Public Career of Cave Johnson." Ph.D. diss., Vanderbilt University, 1951.

John Pendleton Kennedy, Maryland Representative

2016. Bohner, Charles H. *John Pendleton Kennedy, Gentleman from Baltimore*. Baltimore: Johns Hopkins University Press, 1961.

2017. Gwathmey, Edward M. *John Pendleton Kennedy*. New York, T. Nelson and Sons, 1931.

2018. Ridgely, Joseph Vincent. *John Pendleton Kennedy*. New York: Twayne Publishers, 1966.

2019. Spelman, Georgia Peterman. "The Whig Rhetoric of John Pendleton Kennedy." Ph.D. diss., Indiana University, 1974.

2020. Tuckerman, Henry T. *The Life of John Pendleton Kennedy*. New York: G. P. Putnam & Sons, 1871.

Preston King, New York Representative

2021. Muller, Ernest. "Preston King: A Political Biography." Ph.D. diss., Columbia University, 1957.

Thomas Butler King, Georgia Representative

2022. Steel, Edward M., Jr. *T. Butler King of Georgia*. Athens: University of Georgia Press, 1964.

William Rufus King, Alabama Representative

2023. Martin, John M. "William Rufus King: Southern Moderate." Ph.D. diss., University of North Carolina, 1955.

Henry S. Lane, Indiana Representative

2024. Barringer, Graham. "The Life and Letters of Henry S. Lane." Ph.D. diss., University of Indiana, 1927.

Lewis F. Linn, Missouri Senator

2025. Husband, Michael B. "Senator Lewis F. Linn and the Oregon Question." *Missouri Historical Review* 66 (October 1971): 1-19.

2026. Linn, Elizabeth A. Relfe, and Nathan Sargent. *Life and Public Services of Dr. Lewis F. Linn, for Ten Years a Senator of the United States from the State of Missouri.* New York: D. Appleton and Co., 1857. Also available in *Selected Americana* [**602**].

Lucius Lyon, Michigan Delegate, Senator, and Representative

2027. Shirigian, John. "Lucius Lyon: His Place in Michigan History." Ph.D. diss., University of Michigan, 1961.

Willie P. Mangum, North Carolina Senator

2028. McDuffie, Penelope. *Chapters in the Life of Willie Person Mangum.* Durham: Duke University Press, 1925.

George Perkins Marsh, Vermont Representative

2029. Curtis, Jane, Will Curtis, and Frank Lieberman. *The World of George Perkins Marsh, America's First Conservationist and Environmentalist: An Illustrated Biography.* Woodstock, Vt.: Countryman Press, 1982.

2030. Lowenthal, David. *George Perkins Marsh, Versatile Vermonter.* New York: Columbia University Press, 1958.

George McDuffie, South Carolina Senator

2031. Green, Edwin. *George McDuffie.* Columbia, S.C.: State Co., 1936.

Robert Dale Owen, Indiana Representative

2032. Leopold, Richard William. *Robert Dale Owen: A Biography.* Cambridge: Harvard University Press, 1940.

2033. Pancoast, Elinor, and Anne E. Lincoln. *The Incorrigible Idealist: Robert Dale Owen in America.* Bloomington, Ind.: Principia Press, 1940.

James Alfred Pearce, Maryland Representative and Senator

2034. Steiner, Bernard C. "James Alfred Pearce." *Maryland Historical Magazine* 16 (1921): 319-39, 17 (1922): 33-47, 177-90, 269-83. 348-63; 18 (1923): 38-52, 134-50, 257-73, 341-57, 19 (1924): 13-29, 162-78.

Francis W. Pickens, South Carolina Representative

2035. Edmunds, John B., Jr. *Francis W. Pickens and the Politics of Destruction.* Chapel Hill: University of North Carolina Press, 1986.

Franklin Pierce, New Hampshire Senator

2036. Gara, Larry. *The Presidency of Franklin Pierce.* Lawrence: University Press of Kansas, 1991.

2037. Hawthorne, Nathaniel. *The Life of Franklin Pierce.* Boston: Ticknor, Reed & Fields, 1852; New York: Garrett Press, 1970.

2038. Nichols, Roy F. *Franklin Pierce: Young Hickory of the Granite Hills.* Philadelphia: University of Pennsylvania Press, 1931, 1958.

John Pope, Kentucky Representative

2039. Baylor, Orval. *John Pope, Kentuckian: His Life and Times.* Cynthiana, Ky.: Hobson Press, 1943.

Samuel Prentiss, Vermont Senator

2040. Binney, Charles. *Memoirs of Judge Samuel Prentiss of Montpelier, Vermont, and His Wife.* Boston: n.p., 1883.

Seargent Smith Prentiss, Mississippi Representative

2041. Prentiss, George L., ed. *A Memoir of S. S. Prentiss.* 2 vols. New York: Charles Scribner, 1855, 1856, 1858, 1861. Also in *Legal Treatises* [606].

2042. Shields, Joseph D. *Life and Times of Seargent Smith Prentiss.* Philadelphia: J. B. Lippincott, 1883.

William Campbell Preston, South Carolina Senator

2043. Green, Edwin. *William Campbell Preston.* Columbia: n.p., 1946.

Alexander Ramsey, Pennsylvania Representative

2044. Tyland, William Jesse. *Alexander Ramsey: A Study of a Frontier Politician and the Transition of Minnesota from Territory to State.* Philadelphia: Harris and Partridge Co., 1941.

John Reynolds, Illinois Representative

2045. Harper, Josephine L. "John Reynolds: The 'Old Ranger' of Illinois, 1788-1865." Ph.D. diss., University of Illinois at Urbana—Champaign, 1949.

Robert Barnwell Rhett, South Carolina Representative

2046. White, Laura Amanda. *Robert Barnwell Rhett, Father of Secession.* New York: Century Co., 1931; Gloucester, Mass.: P. Smith, 1965.

William Cabell Rives, Virginia Representative and Senator

2047. Cooper, Frances Harlee. "William Cabell Rives, A Southern Statesman." M.A. thesis, Duke University, 1943.

2048. Dingledine, Raymond C. "The Early Life of William Cabell Rives, 1793-1832." M.A. thesis, University of Virginia, 1941.

2049. Dingledine, Raymond C. "The Political Career of William Cabell Rives." Ph.D. diss., University of Virginia, 1947.

2050. Harned, Ray Alton. "William Cabell Rives and the Expunging Resolutions." M.A. thesis, University of Richmond, 1935.

2051. Louthan, Henry Thompson. "Congressional Career of William Cabell Rives of Virginia." M.A. thesis, University of Chicago, 1911.

2052. Sowle, Patrick. "The Trials of a Virginia Unionist: William Cabell Rives and the Secession Crisis, 1860-1861." *Virginia Magazine of History and Biography* 80 (January 1972): 3-20.

2053. Thomas, Mary Elizabeth, ed. "William Cabell Rives and the British Abolitionists." *Virginia Magazine of History and Biography* 89 (January 1981): 64-66.

2054. Wingfield, Russell Stewart. "William Cabell Rives, A Biography." *Richmond College Historical Papers* 1 (June 1915): 57-72.

Robert C. Schenck, Ohio Representative

2055. Joyner, Fred B. "Robert Cumming Schenck: First Citizen and Statesman of the Miami Valley." *Ohio State Archaeological and Historical Quarterly* 58 (July 1949): 286-97.

Ambrose Hundley Sevier, Arkansas Senator

2056. Walton, Brian. "Ambrose Hundley Sevier in the United States Senate, 1836-1848." *Arkansas Historical Quarterly* 32 (Spring 1973): 25-60.

John Slidell, Louisiana Representative

2057. Diket, Albert L. *Senator John Slidell and the Community He Represented in Washington, 1853-1861.* Washington: University Press of America, 1982.

2058. Sears, Louis. *John Slidell.* Durham: Duke University Press, 1925.

Caleb B. Smith, Indiana Representative

2059. Bochin, Hal W. "Caleb B. Smith's Opposition to the Mexican War." *Indiana Magazine of History* 69 (June 1973): 95-114.

2060. Thomas, Richard J. "Caleb Blood Smith: Whig Orator and Politician—Lincoln's Secretary of Interior." Ph.D. diss., Indiana University, 1969.

William Smith, Virginia Representative

2061. Fahrner, Alvin A. "The Public Career of William 'Extra Billy' Smith." Ph.D. diss., University of North Carolina, 1953.

Samuel L. Southard, New Jersey Senator

2062. Birkner, Michael J. "Politics, Law and Enterprise in Jacksonian America: The Career of Samuel Lewis Southard, 1787-1842." Ph.D. diss., University of Virginia, 1981.

2063. Birkner, Michael J. *Samuel L. Southard, Jeffersonian Whig.* Rutherford, N.J.: Fairleigh Dickinson University Press, 1984.

2064. Ershkowitz, Herbert. "Samuel L. Southard: A Case Study of Whig Leadership in the Age of Jackson." *New Jersey History* 88 (Spring 1970): 5-24.

Edward Stanly, North Carolina Representative

2065. Brown, Norman D. "Edward Stanly: First Republican Candidate for Governor of California." *California Historical Quarterly* 47 (September 1968): 251-72.

2066. Brown, Norman D. *Edward Stanly: Whiggery's Tarheel "Conqueror."* University: University of Alabama Press, 1974.

Alexander H. Stephens, Georgia Representative

2067. Richardson, Eudora Ramsay. *Little Aleck: A Life of Alexander H. Stephens, the Fighting Vice-President of the Confederacy.* Indianapolis: Bobbs-Merrill Co., 1932.

2068. Schott, Thomas Edwin. *Alexander H. Stephens of Georgia: A Biography.* Baton Rouge: Louisiana State University Press, 1988.

2069. Von Abele, Rudolph R. *Alexander H. Stephens: A Biography.* New York: Knopf, 1946.

William H. Stiles, Georgia Representative

2070. Harwell, Christopher L. "William Stiles: Georgia Gentleman-Politician." Ph.D. diss., Emory University, 1959.

Alexander H. H. Stuart, Virginia Representative

2071. Robertson, Alexander. *Alexander Hugh Holmes Stuart, 1807-1891: A Biography.* Richmond: William Byrd Press, 1925.

Richard W. Thompson, Indiana Representative

2072. Neely, Mark E., Jr. "Richard W. Thompson: The Persistent Know Nothing." *Indiana Magazine of History* 72 (June 1976): 95-122.

2073. Roll, Charles. *Colonel Dick Thompson: The Persistent Whig.* Indianapolis: Indiana Historical Bureau, 1948.

Joseph R. Underwood, Kentucky Representative

2074. Priest, Nancy L. "Joseph Rogers Underwood: Nineteenth Century Kentucky Orator." *Register of the Kentucky Historical Society* 75 (October 1977): 286-303.

Robert J. Walker, Mississippi Senator

2075. Dodd, William Edward. *Robert J. Walker, Imperialist.* Chicago: Chicago Literary Club, 1914; Gloucester, Mass.: P. Smith, 1967.

2076. Jordan, H. Donaldson. "A Politician of Expansion, Robert J. Walker." *Mississippi Valley Historical Review* 19 (December 1932): 362-81.

2077. Shenton, James P. *Robert John Walker: A Politician from Jackson to Lincoln.* New York: Columbia University Press, 1961.

John Wentworth, Illinois Representative

2078. Fehrenbacher, Don Edward. *Chicago Giant: A Biography of Long John Wentworth.* Madison: American History Research Center, 1957.

Robert Charles Winthrop, Massachusetts Representative

2079. Winthrop, Robert Charles, Jr. *A Memoir of Robert C. Winthrop.* Boston: Little, Brown, and Co., 1897. Also available in *Legal Treatises* [606].

Henry A. Wise, Virginia Representative

2080. Adkins, Edwin Payne. "Henry A. Wise in Sectional Politics, 1833-1860." Ph.D. diss., Ohio State University, 1948.

2081. Atkins, Paul Alexander. "Henry A. Wise and the Virginia Secession Convention, February 13–April 17, 1861." M.A. thesis, University of Virginia, 1950.

2082. Eaton, Clement. "Henry A. Wise, A Liberal of the Old School." *Journal of Southern History* 7 (November 1941): 482-94.

2083. Eaton, Clement. "Henry A. Wise: A Study in Virginia Leadership, 1850-1861." *West Virginia History* 3 (April 1942): 187-204.

2084. Simpson, Craig Michael. "Henry A. Wise in Antebellum Politics, 1850-1861." Ph.D. diss., Stanford University, 1972.

2085. Simpson, Craig Michael. *A Good Southerner: The Life of Henry A. Wise.* Chapel Hill: University of North Carolina Press, 1985.

2086. Wise, Barton H. *The Life of Henry A. Wise of Virginia, 1806-1876.* New York: Macmillan Co., 1899. Also available in *Microbook Library* [601].

Fernando Wood, New York Representative

2087. Anbinder, Tyler G. "Fernando Wood and New York City's Secession From the Union: A Political Reappraisal." *New York History* 68 (January 1987): 67-92.

2088. Mushkat, Jerome. *Fernando Wood: A Political Biography.* Kent, Ohio: Kent State University Press, 1990.

2089. Pleasants, Samuel A. *Fernando Wood of New York.* New York: Columbia University Press, 1948.

William Woodbridge, Michigan Senator

2090. Lanman, Charles. *The Life of William Woodbridge.* Washington: Blanchard and Mohun, 1867.

Levi Woodbury, New Hampshire Senator

2091. Capowski, Vincent. "The Making of a Jacksonian Democrat: Levi Woodbury, 1789-1851." Ph.D. diss., Fordham University, 1966.

Silas Wright, New York Senator

2092. Chancellor, William Estabrook. *A Life of Silas Wright, 1795-1847, United States Senator from New York, 1833-1844, Governor of the State of New York, 1844-1846.* New York: W. C. O'Donnell, Jr., 1913.

2093. Garraty, John A. *Silas Wright.* New York: Columbia University Press, 1949.

2094. Gillet, Ransom H. *The Life and Times of Silas Wright.* 2 vols. Albany: The Argus Co., 1874. Also available in *Microbook Library* [601].

2095. Hammond, Jabez D. *Life and Times of Silas Wright, Late Governor of the State of New York.* Syracuse: Hall & Dickson, 1848; New York: A.S. Barnes & Co., 1848. Also available in *Selected Americana* [602].

William Lowndes Yancey, Alabama Representative

2096. Draughon, Ralph Brown, Jr. "William Lowndes Yancey: From Unionist to Secessionist, 1814-1852." Ph.D. diss., University of North Carolina at Chapel Hill, 1968.

2097. Du Bose, John Witherspoon. *The Life and Times of William Lowndes Yancey: A History of Political Parties in the United States, from 1834-1864, Especially as to the Origin of the Confederate States.* Birmingham: Roberts & Son, 1892.

2098. Mitchell, Rexford S. "William Lowndes Yancey: Orator of Southern Constitutional Rights." Ph.D. diss., University of Wisconsin, 1937.

David Levy Yulee, Florida Territorial Delegate and Senator

2099. Adler, Joseph G. "The Public Career of Senator David Levy Yulee." Ph.D. diss., Case Western Reserve University, 1973.

2100. Thompson, Arthur W. "David Yulee: A Study of 19th Century American Thought and Enterprise." Ph.D. diss., Columbia University, 1954.

D. SUPREME COURT JUSTICES

1. Collective Biographies

2101. Blaustein, Albert P. *The First One Hundred Justices: Statistical Studies on the Supreme Court of the United States.* New York: Archon Books, 1978. Analyzes decisions of court, provides biographies and information on the selection process, and rates justices.

2102. Campbell, Tom Walter. *Four Score Forgotten Men: Sketches of the Justices of the U.S. Supreme Court.* Little Rock: Pioneer Publishing Co., 1950.

2103. Chase, Harold, et al. *Biographical Dictionary of the Federal Judiciary.* Detroit: Gale Publishing Co., 1976.

2104. Choper, Jesse H., ed. *The Supreme Court and Its Justices.* Chicago: American Bar Association, 1987. Brief biographical sketches.

2105. Cox, Joseph. *United States Supreme Court: Its Organization and Judges to 1835.* [Cincinnati: n.p., 1890]. Also available in *Legal Treatises* **[606]**.

2106. Ewing, Cortez Arthur Milton. *The Judges of the Supreme Court, 1789-1937: A Study of Their Qualifications.* Minneapolis: University of Minnesota Press, [1938].

2107. Flanders, Henry. *The Lives and Times of the Chief Justices of the Supreme Court of the United States.* 2 vols. Philadelphia: Lippincott, Grambo & Co., 1855-58; Buffalo: W. S. Hein, [1971]. Also available in *Legal Treatises* **[606]**. Covers through John Marshall's incumbency.

2108. Friedman, Leon, and Fred L. Israel, eds. *The Justices of the United States Supreme Court, 1789-1969: Their Lives and Major Opinions.* 5 vols. New York: Chelsea House, 1969-1978.

2109. Schmidhauser, John Richard. *United States Supreme Court Justices Biographical Data, 1789-1958.* Ann Arbor: Inter-University Consortium for Political and Social Research, 1972.

2110. Umbreit, Kenneth Bernard. *Our Eleven Chief Justices: A History of the Supreme Court in Terms of Their Personalities.* 2 vols. New York: Harper and Brothers, 1938; Port Washington, N.Y., Kennikat Press. 1969.

2111. Van Santvoord, George. *Sketches of the Lives and Judicial Services of the Chief Justices of the Supreme Court of the United States.* New York: C. Scribner, 1854. Also available in *Microbook Library* [**601**]. Contains biographies of John Jay, John Rutledge, Oliver Ellsworth, John Marshall, and Roger B. Taney.

2. Individual Studies

Henry Baldwin

2112. Taylor, Flavia M. "The Political and Civic Career of Henry Baldwin, 1799-1830." *Western Pennsylvania Historical Magazine* 24 (March 1941): 37-50.

Philip Pendleton Barbour

2113. Cynn, P. P. "Philip Pendleton Barbour." *John P. Branch Historical Papers of Randolph-Macon College* 4 (1913): 67+.

John Catron

2114. Caldwell, Joshua W. *Sketches of the Bench and Bar of Tennessee.* Knoxville: Ogden Brothers, 1898.

2115. Gass, Edmund C. "The Constitutional Opinions of Justice John Catron." *East Tennessee Historical Society's Publications* 8 (1936): 54-73. Discusses opinions by Catron involving habeas corpus under provisions of the Webster-Ashburton Treaty, *Ex parte Dorr* and the Dorr rebellion in Rhode Island.

Peter V. Daniel

2116. Brown, Henry Billings. "The Dissenting Opinions of Mr. Justice Daniel." *American Law Review* 21 (November–December 1887): 869-900. Also available in *Legal Treatises* [**606**].

2117. Burnette, Lawrence, Jr. "Peter V. Daniel, Agrarian Justice." *Virginia Magazine of History and Biography* 62 (July 1954): 289-305.

2118. Frank, John P. *Justice Daniel Dissenting: A Biography of Peter V. Daniel, 1784-1869.* Cambridge: Harvard University Press, 1964.

John Marshall

2119. Beveridge, Albert J. *The Life of John Marshall.* 4 vols. Boston; Houghton Mifflin, 1916-19, 1944.

2120. Cuneo, John R. *John Marshall, Judicial Statesman.* New York: McGraw-Hill, 1974.

2121. Newmyer, R. Kent. *The Supreme Court under Marshall and Taney.* New York: Thomas Y. Crowell, 1968.

2122. Stites, Francis N. *John Marshall: Defender of the Constitution.* Boston: Little, Brown & Co., 1981.

John McLean

2123. Weisenburger, Francis Phelps. *The Life of John McLean, A Politician on the United States Supreme Court.* Columbus: Ohio State University Press, 1937; New York: Da Capo Press, 1971.

Samuel Nelson

2124. United States. Circuit Court (2nd Circuit). *Proceedings by the Bar of the United States Courts for the Second Circuit On the Retirement of Mr. Justice Nelson from the Supreme Court of the United States.* New York: F. Hart, 1873. Also available in *Legal Treatises* [**606**].

Joseph Story

2125. Dunne, Gerald T. *Justice Joseph Story and the Rise of the Supreme Court.* New York: Simon and Schuster, 1970.

2126. McClellan, James. *Joseph Story and the American Constitution: A Study in Political and Legal Thought with Selected Writings.* Norman: University of Oklahoma Press, 1971, 1990.

2127. Newmyer, R. Kent. "The Lost Legal World of Joseph Story." *This Constitution* 4 (Winter 1992): 58-65.

2128. Newmyer, R. Kent. "A Note on the Whig Politics of Justice Joseph Story." *Mississippi Valley Historical Review* 48 (December 1961): 480-91.

2129. Newmyer, R. Kent. *Supreme Court Justice Joseph Story: Statesman of the Old Republic.* Chapel Hill: University of North Carolina Press, 1985.

Roger B. Taney

2130. Armstrong, Walter P. "The Rehabilitation of Roger B. Taney." *Tennessee Law Review* 14 (June 1936): 205-18.

2131. Boudin, Louis B. "John Marshall and Roger B. Taney." *Georgetown Law Journal* 24 (May 1936): 864-909.

2132. Fehrenbacher, Don E. "Roger B. Taney and the Sectional Crisis." *Journal of Southern History* 43 (November 1977): 555-66.

2133. Harris, Robert J. "Chief Justice Taney: Prophet of Reform and Reaction." In *American Constitutional Law: Historical Essays,* ed. Leonard W. Levy. New York: Harper and Row, 1966.

2134. Lewis, Walker. *Without Fear or Favor: A Biography of Chief Justice Roger Brooke Taney.* Boston: Houghton Mifflin, 1965.

2135. Mendelsohn, Wallace. "Chief Justice Taney, Jacksonian Judge." *Pitt Law Review* 12 (1951): 381-93.

2136. Smith, Charles W., Jr. *Roger B. Taney, Jacksonian Jurist.* Chapel Hill: University of North Carolina Press, 1936.

2137. Steiner, Bernard C. *Life of Roger Brooke Taney, Chief Justice of the United States Supreme Court.* Baltimore: Williams & Wilkins Co., 1922; Westport, Conn.: Greenwood Press, 1970.

2138. Swisher, Carl Brent. *Roger B. Taney.* New York: Macmillan Co., 1935, 1936; Hamden, Conn.: Archon Books, 1961.

2139. Wiecek, William M. "Chief Justice Taney and His Court." *This Constitution* 6 (Spring 1985): 19-24.

Smith Thompson

2140. Roper, Donald Malcolm. *Mr. Justice Thompson and the Constitution.* New York: Garland, 1987.

James Moore Wayne

2141. Lawrence, Alexander A. *James Moore Wayne, Southern Unionist.* Chapel Hill: University of North Carolina Press, 1943; Westport, Conn.: Greenwood Press, [1970].

E. DIPLOMATS AND OTHER OFFICIALS

1. Collective Biographies

2142. Burns, Gerald. "A Collective Biography of Consular Officers, 1828-1861." Ph.D. diss., University of Pittsburgh, 1973.

2143. Findling, John E. *Dictionary of American Diplomatic History.* Westport, Conn.: Greenwood Publishing Co., 1980, 1989.

2. Individual Studies

2144. Adams, Ephraim Douglass. "Lord Ashburton and the Treaty of Washington." *American Historical Review* 17 (July 1912): 764-82.

2145. Baker, Elizabeth Feaster. *Henry Wheaton, 1785-1848.* Philadelphia: University of Pennsylvania Press, 1937; New York: Da Capo Press, 1971.

2146. Bell, Herbert C. F. *Lord Palmerston.* 2 vols. Hamden, Conn.: Archon Books, 1966.

2147. Bourne, Kenneth. *Palmerston: The Early Years, 1784-1841.* New York: Macmillan, 1982; London: Allen Lane, 1982.

2148. Bryson, Thomas A. *An American Consular Officer in the Middle East in the Jacksonian Era: A Biography of William Brown Hodgson, 1801-1871.* Atlanta: Resurgens Publications, 1979. Appointed by Tyler as consul to Tunis.

2149. Chamberlain, Muriel E. *Lord Aberdeen: A Political Biography.* London: Longmans, 1983.

2150. Cobb, Edwin L. "Powhatan Ellis of Mississippi." *Journal of Mississippi History* 30 (May 1968): 91-110. Discusses release of Santa Fe prisoners.

2151. Dougall, Richardson, and Mary P. Chapman. *United States Chiefs of Mission, 1778-1973.* Washington: U.S. Department of State, 1973.

2152. Frothingham, Paul Revere. *Edward Everett, Orator and Statesman.* Boston: Houghton Mifflin Co., 1925.

2153. Gardner, Eugene Norfleet. "Andrew Stevenson." *Richmond College Historical Papers* 1 (June 1916): 259-308.

2154. Gash, Norman. *The Life of Sir Robert Peel after 1830.* London: Rowman and Littlefield, 1972.

2155. Gulick, Edward V. *Peter Parker and the Opening of China.* Cambridge: Harvard University Press, 1973.

2156. Hewlett, Richard G. "Lewis Cass in National Politics, 1842-1861." Ph.D. diss., University of Chicago, 1952.

2157. Iremonger, Lucille. *Lord Aberdeen: A Biography of the Fourth Earl of Aberdeen, K.G., K.T., Prime Minister, 1852-1855.* London: Collins, 1978.

2158. Klunder, Willard Carl. "Lewis Cass, 1782-1866: A Political Biography." Ph.D. diss., University of Illinois at Urbana—Champaign, 1981.

2159. Klunder, Willard Carl. "Lewis Cass and Slavery Expansion: 'The Father of Popular Sovereignty' and Ideological Infanticide." *Civil War History* 32 (December 1986): 293-317.

2160. Lander, Ernest M., Jr. "General Waddy Thompson, A Friend of Mexico during the Mexican War." *South Carolina Historical Magazine* 78 (January 1977): 32-42.

2161. McLaughlin, Andrew C. *Lewis Cass.* Boston: Houghton Mifflin and Co., 1891, 1899, 1919; New York: AMS Press, 1972. The 1891 edition is also in *Microbook Library* **[601]**.

2162. Oeste, George Irvin. *John Randolph Clay: America's First Career Diplomat.* Philadelphia: University of Pennsylvania Press, 1966.

2163. Ridley, Jasper. *Lord Palmerston.* New York: E. P. Dutton & Co., 1971.

2164. Siegel, Stanley. *The Poet President of Texas: The Life of Mirabeau B. Lamar, President of the Republic of Texas.* Austin: Jenkins Publishing Co., 1977.

2165. Southgate, Donald. *"The Most English Minister ...": The Policies and Politics of Palmerston.* New York: St. Martin's Press, 1966.

2166. Stevens, Walter W. "Lewis Cass and the Presidency." *Michigan History* 49 (June 1965): 123-34.

2167. Thompson, Henry Tazewell. *Waddy Thompson, Jr.: Member of Congress, 1835-1841, Minister to Mexico, 1842-44.* [Columbia, S.C.: n.p.], 1929.

2168. Varg, Paul A. *Edward Everett: The Intellectual in the Turmoil of Politics.* Selinsgrove, Pa.: Susquehanna University Press, 1992.

2169. Wayland, Francis Fry. *Andrew Stevenson, Democrat and Diplomat, 1785-1857.* Philadelphia: University of Pennsylvania Press, 1949.

2170. Woodford, Frank B. *Lewis Cass: The Last Jeffersonian.* New Brunswick: Rutgers University Press, 1950; New York: Octagon Books, 1973.

2171. Young, William T. *Sketch of the Life and Public Services of General Lewis Cass, With the Pamphlet on the Right of Search, and Some of His Speeches on the Great Political Questions of the Day.* Detroit: Markham & Elwood, 1852; Philadelphia: E. H. Butler & Co., 1853.

F. MILITARY FIGURES

2172. Barrows, Edward M. *The Great Commodore: The Exploits of Matthew Calbraith Perry.* Indianapolis: Bobbs-Merrill Co., 1935; Freeport, N.Y.: Books for Libraries Press, 1972.

2173. Bauer, K. Jack. *Zachary Taylor: Soldier, Planter, Statesman of the Old Southwest.* Baton Rouge: Louisiana State University Press, 1985.

2174. Bradley, Udolpho Theodore. "The Contentious Commodore: Thomas ap Catesby Jones of the Old Navy, 1788-1858." Ph.D. diss., Cornell University, 1933.

2175. Bradley, Udolpho Theodore. "Thomas ap Catesby Jones, A Personality of the Days of Sail." *United States Naval Institute Proceedings* 59 (August 1933): 1154-56.

2176. Davis, Varina. *Jefferson Davis, Ex-President of the Confederate States of America: A Memoir.* 2 vols. New York: Belford Co., 1890.

2177. Davis, William C. *Jefferson Davis: The Man and His Hour.* New York: Harper Collins, 1991.

2178. Dyer, Brainerd. *Zachary Taylor.* Baton Rouge: Louisiana State University Press, 1946; New York: Barnes & Noble, 1967.

2179. Eaton, Clement. *Jefferson Davis.* New York: Free Press, 1977.

2180. Eckenrode, Hamilton James. *Jefferson Davis, President of the South.* New York: Macmillan Co., 1923.

2181. Elliott, Charles Winslow. *Winfield Scott: The Soldier and the Man.* New York: Macmillan Co., 1937.

2182. Hamilton, Holman. *The Three Kentucky Presidents: Lincoln, Taylor, Davis.* Lexington: University Press of Kentucky, 1978.

2183. Hamilton, Holman. *Zachary Taylor.* 2 vols. Indianapolis: Bobbs-Merrill, 1941; Hamden, Conn.: Archon Books, 1966. Volume 1, military career; volume 2, the White House.

2184. Long, David F. *Nothing Too Daring: A Biography of Commodore David Porter, 1780-1843.* Annapolis: United States Naval Institute Press, 1970.

2185. McKinley, Silas Bent. *Old Rough and Ready.* New York: Vanguard Press, 1946.

2186. Maloney, Linda M. *The Captain from Connecticut: The Life and Naval Times of Isaac Hull.* Boston: Northeastern University Press, 1986.

2187. Morison, Samuel Eliot. *"Old Bruin": Commodore Matthew C. Perry, 1794-1858.* Boston: Little, Brown and Co., 1967.

2188. Scott, Florence Johnson. *Old Rough and Ready on the Rio Grande.* San Antonio: Naylor Co., 1935; Waco: Texian Press, 1969. Mier expedition.

2189. Smith, Arthur D. Howden. *Old Fuss and Feathers.* New York: Greystone Press, 1937. Biography of Winfield Scott.

2190. Strode, Hudson. *Jefferson Davis.* 3 vols. New York: Harcourt, Brace, 1955-64.

2191. Williams, Frances Leigh. *Matthew Fontaine Maury: Scientist of the Sea.* New Brunswick: Rutgers University Press, 1963.

G. JOURNALISTS

2192. Ambler, Charles Henry. *Thomas Ritchie: A Study in Virginia Politics.* Richmond: Bell Book & Stationery Co., 1913.

2193. Anderson, Sterling P., Jr. "Edmund Ruffin, Editor and Publisher." *Virginia Cavalcade* 17 (Summer 1967): 32-38.

2194. Boney, Francis Nash. "Rivers of Ink, A Stream of Blood: The Tragic Career of John Hampden Pleasants." *Virginia Cavalcade* 18 (Summer 1968): 33-39.

2195. Copeland, Fayette. *Kendall of the Picayune, Being His Adventures in New Orleans, on the Texan Santa Fe Expedition, in the Mexican War, and in the Colonization of the Texas Frontier.* Norman: University of Oklahoma Press, 1943. George Wilkins Kendall of the *New Orleans Times-Picayune.*

2196. Craven, Avery Odelle. *Edmund Ruffin, Southerner: A Study in Secession.* New York: D. Appleton and Co., 1932; Hamden, Conn.: Archon Books, 1964; Baton Rouge: Louisiana State University Press, 1966.

2197. Crouthamel, James L. *Bennett's New York Herald and the Rise of the Popular Press.* Syracuse: Syracuse University Press, 1989.

2198. Crouthamel, James L. *James Watson Webb: A Biography.* Middletown, Conn.: Wesleyan University Press, 1969.

2199. Dillon, Merton L. *Elijah P. Lovejoy, Abolitionist Editor.* Urbana: University of Illinois Press, 1961. Ohio newspaperman and martyr to the abolitionist cause.

2200. Ford, Edwin H., and Edwin Emery, eds. *Highlights in the History of the American Press.* Minneapolis: University of Minnesota Press, 1954. Contains biographical sketches of major newspapermen of the period.

2201. Goldberg, Isaac. *Major Noah: American Jewish Pioneer.* New York: Jewish Publications Society, 1936.

2202. Green, Fletcher M. "Duff Green, Militant Journalist of the Old School." *American Historical Review* 52 (January 1947): 247-64.

2203. Griffin, Barbara Jean. "Thomas Ritchie: Other Dimensions." *Richmond Literature and History Quarterly* 2 (Summer 1979): 29-33. Explores Ritchie's life apart from his editorial duties.

2204. Griffin, Barbara Jean, ed. "Thomas Ritchie and the Code Duello." *Virginia Magazine of History and Biography* 92 (1984): 71-95.

2205. Hallock, Judith Lee. "The Agricultural Apostle and His Bible: Edmund Ruffin and the *Farmers' Register*." *Southern Studies* 23 (Fall 1984): 205-15.

2206. Harris, William C. *William Woods Holden, Firebrand of North Carolina Politics*. Baton Rouge: Louisiana State University Press, 1987.

2207. James, Bessie Rowland. *Anne Royall's U.S.A.* New Brunswick: Rutgers University Press, 1972. Discusses briefly Royall's views and treatment of Tyler.

2208. Moore, David Wayne. "Duff Green and the South, 1824-45." Ph.D. diss., Miami University, 1983. Some discussion of the foreign policy of the Tyler administration.

2209. Mutersbaugh, Bert Marsh. "Jeffersonian Journalist: Thomas Ritchie and the Richmond Enquirer, 1804-1820." Ph.D. diss., University of Missouri—Columbia, 1982.

2210. Osthaus, Carl. R. "An Affair of Honor—Not an Honorable Affair: The Ritchie-Pleasants Duel and the Press." *Virginia Cavalcade* 26 (Winter 1977): 110-23.

2211. Parker, John A. *"The Missing Link": What Led to the War; or, The Secret History of the Kansas-Nebraska Bill, with an Appendix Containing Sketches and Reminiscences of "The Richmond Enquirer" and "Whig" and Their Editors, and an Introductory Note by Waldorf H. Phillips*. Washington: Gray and Clarkson, 1886. Reprinted from the *National Quarterly Review* for July 1880.

2212. Porter, Sarah Harvey. *The Life and Times of Anne Royall*. Cedar Rapids: Torch Book Press Shop. 1908. Appendixes provide guide to pen portraits in Royall's publications.

2213. Sarna, Jonathan D. *Jacksonian Jew: The Two Worlds of Mordecai Noah*. New York: Holmes & Meier, 1981. Brief discussions of the relationship between Tyler and Webster and Noah, as editor of the pro-Tyler *Union*.

2214. Seaton, Josephine. *William Winston Seaton of the "National Intelligencer": A Biographical Sketch*. Boston: J P. Osgood and Co., 1871.

2215. Shoptaugh, Terry L. "Amos Kendall: A Political Biography." Ph.D. diss., University of New Hampshire, 1984.

2216. Smith, Elbert B. *Francis Preston Blair*. New York: Free Press, 1980. Democratic editor of the *Washington Globe*.

2217. Smith, Kenneth L. "Duff Green and the *United States Telegraph*, 1826-1837." Ph.D. diss., College of William and Mary, 1981.

2218. Smith, William E. "Francis P. Blair, Pen-Executive of Andrew Jackson." *Mississippi Valley Historical Review* 17 (March 1931): 543-56.

2219. Smith, William E. *The Francis Preston Blair Family in Politics*. 2 vols. New York: Macmillan Co., 1933; New York: Da Capo Press, 1969.

2220. Thrift, Charles Tinsley. "Thomas Ritchie." *John P. Branch Historical Papers of Randolph-Macon College* 3 (1911): 170-87.

2221. Van Deusen, Glyndon G. *Thurlow Weed, Wizard of the Lobby*. Boston: Little, Brown and Co., 1947; New York: Da Capo Press, 1969.

2222. Weisberger, Bernard A. "Horace Greeley: Reformer as Republican." *Civil War History* 23 (March 1977): 5-25.

2223. Weisenburger, Francis Phelps. *A Life of Charles Hammond, The First Great Journalist of the Old Northwest*. Columbus: [Ohio State University Press], 1934.

H. OTHERS

1. Collective Biographies

2224. Dodson, Edward Griffith. *Speakers and Clerks of the Virginia House of Delegates*. Richmond: E. Griffith Dodson, 1956. Sketches of Tyler's colleagues.

2225. Gaines, William H., Jr. *Biographical Register of Members: Virginia State Convention of 1861, First Session*. Richmond: Virginia State Library, 1969. Provides brief outline of Tyler's career, pp. 77-78.

2226. Kallenbach, Joseph Ernest. *American State Governors, 1776-1976*. 3 vols. Dobbs Ferry, N.Y.: Oceana Publications, 1977-82. Arranged by states, contains electoral and biographical data.

2227. Kvasnicka, Robert M., and Herman J. Viola, eds. *The Commissioners of Indian Affairs, 1824-1897*. Lincoln: University of Nebraska Press, 1979.

2228. Tyler, Lyon Gardiner, ed. *Encyclopedia of Virginia Biography.* 5 vols. New York: Lewis Historical Publishing Co., 1915.

2229. Tyler, Lyon Gardiner, et al. *History of Virginia.* 6 vols. Chicago: American Historical Society, 1924. Volume 2, entitled *Federal Period, 1763-1861,* is most useful for the Tyler years; Volumes 4-6 contain Virginia biographies.

2230. Warner, Ezra J., and W. Buck Yearns. *Biographical Register of the Confederate Congress.* Baton Rouge: Louisiana State University Press, 1975.

2. Individual Studies

2231. Adams, Charles Francis. *Richard Henry Dana, A Biography.* 2 vols. Boston: Houghton, Mifflin and Co., 1890, 1891; Detroit: Gale Research Co., 1968. Also available in *Microbook Library* **[601]**.

2232. Alexander, Holmes Moss. *The American Talleyrand: The Career and Contemporaries of Martin Van Buren, Eighth President.* New York: Harper, 1935; New York: Russell & Russell, 1958, 1962, 1968.

2233. Ammon, Harry. *James Monroe: The Quest for National Identity.* New York: McGraw-Hill, 1971.

2234. Anderson, Dice R. *William Branch Giles: A Study in the Politics of Virginia and the Nation from 1790 to 1830.* Menasha: George Banta, 1915. Brief discussion of Giles's relations with Tyler.

2235. Auchampaugh, Philip Gerald. "John W. Forney, Robert Tyler, and James Buchanan." *Tyler's Quarterly Historical and Genealogical Magazine* 15 (October 1933): 71-90. Discusses Tyler's dislike of Forney.

2236. Auchampaugh, Philip Gerald. *Robert Tyler, Southern States Rights Champion, 1847-1866: A Documentary Study Chiefly of Antebellum Politics.* Duluth: H. Stein, 1934.

2237. Bassett, John Spencer. *The Life of Andrew Jackson.* 2 vols. Garden City, N.Y.: Doubleday, Page and Co., 1911; New York: Macmillan Co., 1916, 1925, 1928; Hamden, Conn.: Archon Books, 1967 (2 vols. in 1).

2238. Belohlavek, John M. *George Mifflin Dallas: Jacksonian Patrician.* Philadelphia: Pennsylvania State University Press, 1977.

2239. Birney, William. *James G. Birney and His Times: The Genesis of the Republican Party.* New York: D. Appleton and Co., 1890; New York: Negro Universities Press, 1969; New York: Bergman Publishers [1969]. Available in *Microbook Library* [**601**].

2240. Boney, Francis Nash. "John Letcher, Civil War Governor of Virginia." M.A. thesis, University of Virginia, 1960.

2241. Boney, Francis Nash. "The Life of John Letcher, Virginia's Civil War Governor." Ph.D. diss., University of Virginia, 1963.

2242. Brant, Irving. *James Madison.* 6 vols. Indianapolis: Bobbs-Merrill, 1941-61.

2243. Braverman, Howard. "David Campbell and Virginia Politics, 1837-1840." M.A. thesis, Duke University, 1945.

2244. Brugger, Robert J. *Beverley Tucker: Heart over Head in the Old South.* Baltimore: Johns Hopkins University Press, 1978.

2245. Bugg, James L. "The Political Career of James Murray Mason: The Legislative Phase." Ph.D. diss., University of Virginia, 1950.

2246. Cain, Marvin R. "William Wirt Against Andrew Jackson: Reflections of an Era." *Mid-America* 47 (April 1965): 113-38.

2247. Cauble, Frank P. "William Wirt and His Friends: A Study in Southern Culture, 1772-1832." Ph.D. diss., University of North Carolina, 1934.

2248. Chamberlain, Georgia S. "Ferdinand Pettrich, Sculptor of the President Tyler Indian Peace Medal." *Numismatist* 70 (April 1957): 387-90.

2249. Christian, A. K. *Mirabeau Buonaparte Lamar.* Austin: Von Boeckmann-Jones, 1922. Also published in *Southwestern Historical Quarterly*, January 1920–April 1921. Discussion on the Santa Fe expedition.

2250. Cleaves, Freeman. *Old Tippecanoe: William Henry Harrison and His Times.* New York: Charles Scribner's Sons, 1939; Port Washington, N.Y.: Kennikat Press, 1969.

2251. Cohen, Henry. *Business and Politics in America from the Age of Jackson to the Civil War: The Career Biography of W. W. Corcoran.* Westport, Conn.: Greenwood Publishing Corp., 1971.

2252. Cole, Donald B. *Martin Van Buren and the American Political System.* Princeton: Princeton University Press, 1984.

2253. Coleman, Elizabeth Tyler. *Priscilla Cooper Tyler and the American Scene, 1816-1899.* University: University of Alabama Press, 1955. Discusses Tyler's early life in New York, her work with her father as an actress, her marriage to Robert Tyler and her life as a member of the Tyler household.

2254. Collier, J. G. "The Political Career of James McDowell, 1830-1850." Ph.D. diss., University of North Carolina–Chapel Hill, 1963.

2255. Cook, Tony Stanley. "Historical Mythmaking: Richard Henry Dana and American Emigration to California, 1840-1850." *Southern California Quarterly* 68 (Summer 1986): 97-117.

2256. Crenshaw, Ollinger. "Christopher G. Memminger's Mission to Virginia, 1860." *Journal of Southern History* 8 (August 1942): 334-49. Discusses mission to promote a southern convention.

2257. Cresson, William P. *James Monroe.* Chapel Hill: University of North Carolina Press, 1946.

2258. Curtis, James C. *Andrew Jackson and the Search for Vindication.* Boston: Little, Brown and Co., 1976.

2259. Curtis, James C. *The Fox at Bay: Martin Van Buren and the Presidency, 1837-1841.* Lexington: University Press of Kentucky, 1970.

2260. Duberman, Martin B. *Charles Francis Adams, 1807-1866.* Boston: Houghton Mifflin, 1961; Stanford: Stanford University Press, 1968.

2261. Duckett, Alvin L. *John Forsyth, Political Tactician.* Athens: University of Georgia Press, 1962.

2262. Duval, John C. *The Adventures of Big-Foot Wallace.* Macon, Ga.: J. W. Burke & Co., 1870, 1885, 1921; Lincoln: University of Nebraska Press, 1936, 1966. Biography of William Alexander Anderson Wallace, a participant in the Mier expedition, 1842.

2263. Eckhardt, Celia Morris. *Fanny Wright: Rebel in America.* Cambridge: Harvard University Press, 1984.

2264. Edwards, Ninian Wirt. *History of Illinois, from 1778-1833, and Life and Times of Ninian Edwards.* Springfield: Illinois State Journal Co., 1870; New York: Arno Press, 1975.

2265. Egerton, Douglas R. *Charles Fenton Mercer and the Trial of National Conservatism.* Jackson: University Press of Mississippi, 1989.

2266. Ellis, George Edward. *Memoir of Jared Sparks*. Cambridge: J. Wilson and Son, 1869.

2267. Ewing, Francis Howard. "The Senatorial Career of the Hon. Felix Grundy." *Tennessee Historical Magazine*, 2nd Series, 2 (1931): 3-27; (1932): 111-35, 220-24, 270-91.

2268. Faust, Drew Gilpin. *James Henry Hammond and the Old South: A Design for Mastery*. Baton Rouge: Louisiana State University Press, 1982.

2269. Findley, Paul. *A. Lincoln, the Crucible of Congress*. New York: Crown Publishers, 1979.

2270. Fladeland, Betty. *James Gillespie Birney: Slaveholder to Abolitionist*. Ithaca, N.Y.: Cornell University Press 1955; New York: Greenwood Press, 1969. Liberty Party candidate for the presidency in 1844.

2271. Friend, Llerena B. *Sam Houston: The Great Designer*. Austin: University of Texas Press, 1954, 1969.

2272. Gambrell, Herbert Pickens. *Anson Jones, the Last President of Texas*. Garden City, N.Y.: Doubleday, 1948; Austin: University of Texas Press, 1964.

2273. Gambrell, Herbert Pickens. *Mirabeau Buonaparte Lamar, Troubadour and Crusader*. Dallas: Southwest Press, 1934.

2274. Gatell, Frank Otto. *John Gorham Palfrey and the New England Conscience*. Cambridge: Harvard University Press, 1963.

2275. Gilliam, Will D., Jr. "Robert J. Breckenridge: Kentucky Unionist." *Register of the Kentucky Historical Society* 69 (October 1971): 362-85.

2276. Glenn, Virginia Louise. "James Hamilton, Jr., of South Carolina: A Biography." Ph.D. diss., University of North Carolina at Chapel Hill, 1964.

2277. Goebel, Dorothy Burne. *William Henry Harrison: A Political Biography*. Indianapolis: Historical Bureau of the Indiana Library and Historical Department, 1926; Philadelphia: Porcupine Press, 1974.

2278. Going, Charles B. *David Wilmot, Free-Soiler: A Biography of the Great Advocate of the Wilmot Proviso*. New York: D. Appleton and Co., 1924; Gloucester, Mass.: P. Smith, 1966.

2279. Gordon, Armistead Churchill. *William Fitzhugh Gordon, A Virginian of the Old School: His Life, Times and Contemporaries, 1787-1858.* New York: Neale, 1909.

2280. Govan, Thomas P. *Nicholas Biddle: Nationalist and Public Banker, 1786-1844.* Chicago: University of Chicago Press, 1959, 1975.

2281. Graham, Philip. *The Life and Poems of Mirabeau B. Lamar.* Chapel Hill: University of North Carolina Press, 1938.

2282. Green, James A. *William Henry Harrison: His Life and Times.* Richmond: Garrett and Massie, 1941.

2283. Gresham, L. Paul. "The Public Career of Hugh Lawson White." *Tennessee Historical Quarterly* 3 (December 1944): 291-318.

2284. Grigsby, Hugh Blair. *Discourse on the Life and Character of the Honorable Littleton Waller Tazewell* ... Norfolk: J. D. Ghiselin, Jr., 1860. Also available in *Selected Americana* **[602]** and in *Legal Treatises* **[606]**.

2285. Hall, Cline Edwin. "The Political Life of Benjamin Watkins Leigh." M.A. thesis, University of Richmond, 1959.

2286. Hickin, Patricia. "Gentle Agitator: Samuel M. Janney and the Antislavery Movement in Virginia, 1842-1851." *Journal of Southern History* 37 (May 1971): 159-90.

2287. Hickin, Patricia. "John C. Underwood and the Antislavery Movement in Virginia, 1847-1860." *Virginia Magazine of History and Biography* 73 (April 1965): 156-68.

2288. Hidy, Ralph W. *The House of Baring in American Trade and Finance: English Merchant Bankers at Work, 1763-1861.* Cambridge: Harvard University Press, 1938, 1949.

2289. Hobeika, John E. "Lyon Gardiner Tyler—The Sage of Lion's Den." *Tyler's Quarterly Historical and Genealogical Magazine* 18 (April 1937): 193-231. Reviews the life and writings of L. G. Tyler, one of John Tyler's sons.

2290. Ireland, John. "Andrew Drew, the Man Who Burned the *Caroline*." *Ontario History* 59 (September 1967): 137-56.

2291. Jacobs, David H. "Martin Van Buren: Political Genius or Failure?" *Concord Review* 1 (Spring 1989): 63-75.

2292. James, Marquis. *Andrew Jackson: The Border Captain*. New York: Grosset & Dunlap, 1933, 1959; New York: Literary Guild, 1933.

2293. James, Marquis. *Andrew Jackson: Portrait of a President*. New York: Grosset & Dunlap, 1937; New York: Garden City Publishing Co., 1940 (single-volume edition); Indianapolis: Bobbs-Merrill Co., 1937.

2294. James, Marquis. *The Raven: A Biography of Sam Houston*. Indianapolis: Bobbs-Merrill Co., 1929; New York: Grosset & Dunlap, 1929: New York: Blue Ribbon Books, 1936; Garden City, N.Y.: Halcyon House, 1949.

2295. Jervey, Theodore D. *Robert Y. Hayne and His Times*. New York: Macmillan, 1909; New York: Da Capo Press, 1970.

2296. Jones, Russell M. "A Friend at Court: Louis-Philippe, King of the French, 1830-1848." *Laurels* 59 (Winter 1988-89): 143-52.

2297. Jordan, Laylon Wayne. "Between Two Worlds: Christopher G. Memminger of Charleston and the Old South in Mid-Passage." *Proceedings of the South Carolina Historical Association* 51 (1981): 56-78.

2298. Katz, Irving. "Confidant at the Capital: William W. Corcoran's Role in Nineteenth-Century American Politics." *Historian* 29 (August 1967): 546-64.

2299. Kilbourn, William. *The Firebrand: William Lyon Mackenzie and the Rebellion in Upper Canada*. Toronto: Clarke, Irwin, 1956.

2300. Kreneck, Thomas H. "Sam Houston and the Jacksonian Frontier Personality." *Houston Review* 8 (1986): 104-34.

2301. Levy, Leonard. *The Law of the Commonwealth and Chief Justice Shaw: The Evolution of American Law, 1830-1860*. Cambridge: Harvard University Press, 1957; New York: Oxford University Press, 1986.

2302. Lowery, Charles Douglas. *James Barbour, A Jeffersonian Republican*. University: University of Alabama Press, 1984.

2303. Lynch, Denis T. *An Epoch and a Man: Martin Van Buren and His Times*. New York: H. Liveright, 1929; Washington, N.Y.: Kennikat Press, 1971.

2304. Macfarland, William H. *An Address on the Life, Character and Public Services of the Late Hon. Benjamin Watkins Leigh, Delivered before the Virginia Historical Society*. Richmond: Macfarlane & Fergusson, 1851. Also available in *Selected Americana* [602].

2305. Mackay, R. A. "The Political Ideals of William Lyon Mackenzie." *Canadian Journal of Economics and Political Science* 3 (1937): 1-22.

2306. Mansfield, Stephen. "Thomas Roderick Dew at William and Mary: 'A Main Prop of that Venerable Institution.'" *Virginia Magazine of History and Biography* 75 (October 1967): 429-42.

2307. McCormick, Eugene I. *James K. Polk: A Political Biography.* Berkeley: University of California Press, 1922.

2308. McIntosh, Linda. "William Wirt and the Election of 1832." M.A. thesis, Johns Hopkins University, 1973.

2309. McPherson, James M. "The Fight Against the Gag Rule: Joshua Leavitt and Antislavery Insurgency in the Whig Party, 1839-1842." *Journal of Negro History* 48 (July 1963): 177-95.

2310. Meyer, Leland W. *The Life and Times of Colonel Richard M. Johnson of Kentucky.* New York: Columbia University Press, 1932; New York: AMS Press, 1967.

2311. Middleton, Stephen. *Ohio and the Antislavery Activities of Attorney Salmon Portland Chase, 1830-1849.* New York: Garland Publishing, 1990.

2312. Mitchell, Norma Anne (Taylor). "The Political Career of Governor David Campbell of Virginia." Ph.D. diss., Duke University, 1967.

2313. Moore, Powell. "James K. Polk: Tennessee Politician." *Journal of Southern History* 17 (November 1951): 493-516.

2314. Morison, Samuel Eliot. *Harrison Gray Otis, 1765-1848: The Urbane Federalist.* Boston: Houghton Mifflin, 1969.

2315. Morison, Samuel Eliot. *The Life and Letters of Harrison Gray Otis, 1765-1848.* 2 vols. Boston: Houghton-Mifflin, 1913.

2316. Munroe, John A. *Louis McLane: Federalist and Jacksonian.* New Brunswick: Rutgers University Press, 1973.

2317. Niven, John. *Gideon Welles, Lincoln's Secretary of the Navy.* New York: Oxford University Press, 1973.

2318. Niven, John. *Martin Van Buren: The Romantic Age of American Politics.* New York: Oxford University Press, 1983.

2319. Nye, Russel B. *George Bancroft, Brahmin Rebel.* New York: A. A. Knopf, 1944.

2320. Oberg, Michael L. "William Wirt and the Trials of Republicanism." *Virginia Magazine of History and Biography* 99 (July 1990): 305-26.

2321. Pancake, John S. *Samuel Smith and the Politics of Business, 1752-1839.* University: University of Alabama Press, 1972.

2322. Parton, James. *Life of Andrew Jackson.* 3 vols. New York: Mason Brothers, 1860, 1861; New York: Johnson Reprint Corporation, 1967 (and many other editions). Also available in *Microbook Library* **[601]**. and in *Legal Treatises* **[606]**.

2323. Perling, Joseph Jerry. *President's Sons: The Prestige of Names in a Democracy.* New York: Odyssey Press, 1947; Freeport, N.Y.: Books for Libraries Press, 1971.

2324. Peterson, Norma Lois. *Littleton Waller Tazewell.* Charlottesville: University Press of Virginia, 1983.

2325. Ramsay, Jack C. *Thunder Beyond the Brazos: Mirabeau B. Lamar, A Biography.* Austin: Eakin Press, 1985.

2326. Rayback, Joseph G. "Martin Van Buren: His Place in the History of New York and the United States." *New York History* 64 (April 1983): 120-35.

2327. Remini, Robert V. *Andrew Jackson and the Course of American Democracy, 1833-1845.* New York: Harper & Row, 1984.

2328. Remini, Robert V. *Andrew Jackson and the Course of American Empire, 1767-1821.* New York: Harper & Row, 1977.

2329. Remini, Robert V. *Andrew Jackson and the Course of American Freedom, 1822-1832.* New York: Harper & Row, 1981.

2330. Rice, Harvey Mitchell. *The Life of Jonathan M. Bennett: A Study of the Virginias in Transition.* Chapel Hill: University of North Carolina Press, 1943.

2331. Riddle, Donald W. *Congressman Abraham Lincoln.* Urbana: University of Illinois Press, 1957.

2332. Riddle, Donald W. *Lincoln Runs for Congress.* New Brunswick: Rutgers University Press, 1948.

2333. Rippy, J. Fred. *Joel Roberts Poinsett, Versatile American.* Durham: Duke University Press, 1935.

2334. Robert, Joseph C. "William Wirt, Virginian." *Virginia Magazine of History and Biography* 80 (October 1972): 387-441. Discusses Tyler's opinion of Wirt's forensic achievements.

2335. Rosenthal, Herbert Hillel. "James Barbour, Virginia Politician, 1775-1842." M.A. thesis, University of Virginia, 1942.

2336. Sellers, Charles G. *James K. Polk, Continentalist: 1843-1848.* Princeton: Princeton University Press, 1966.

2337. Sellers, Charles G. *James K. Polk, Jacksonian, 1795-1843.* Princeton: Princeton University Press, 1957.

2338. Shallope, Robert E. *John Taylor of Caroline, Pastoral Republican.* Columbia: University of South Carolina Press, 1980.

2339. Shepard, Edward M. *Martin Van Buren.* Boston: Houghton, Mifflin, 1888, 1899, 1916. Also available in *Legal Treatises* **[606]**.

2340. Sibley, Marilyn McAdams. "James Hamilton, Jr., vs. Sam Houston: Repercussions of the Nullification Controversy." *Southwestern Historical Quarterly* 89 (October 1985): 165-80. Explores the longstanding contempt Hamilton and Houston had for each other and the political ramifications of that dislike as it affected Texas finances during the Tyler administration.

2341. Spencer, Ivor D. *The Victor and the Spoils: A Life of William L. Marcy.* Providence: Brown University Press, 1959.

2342. Stealey, John Edmund, III. "Gideon Draper Camden: A Whig of Western Virginia." *West Virginia History* 26 (October 1964): 13-30.

2343. Steiner, Bernard C. *Life of Reverdy Johnson.* Baltimore: The Norman, Remington Co., 1914; New York: Russell & Russell, 1970.

2344. Tanner, Carol Minor. "Joseph C. Cabell, 1788-1856." Ph.D. diss., University of Virginia, 1948.

2345. Turner, Charles W. "Virginia Agricultural Reform, 1815-1860, and Philip St. George Cocke." *Virginia Social Science Journal* 2 (April 1967): 44-67.

2346. Van Deusen, Glyndon G. *William Henry Seward.* New York: Oxford University Press, 1967.

2347. Walters, Raymond, Jr. *Albert Gallatin.* New York: Macmillan, 1957.

2348. Ward, John William. *Andrew Jackson: Symbol for an Age.* New York: Oxford University Press, 1955, 1962.

2349. Weddell, Alexander Wilbourne. "Samuel Mordecai, Chronicler of Richmond, 1786-1855." *Virginia Magazine of History and Biography* 53 (October 1945): 264-87. Discusses briefly Tyler's speech in Richmond in November 1858.

2350. West, Carroll Van. "Democratic Ideology and the Antebellum Historian: The Case of Henderson Yoakum." *Journal of the Early Republic* 3 (Fall 1983): 319-39.

2351. Williams, Gary M. "Colonel George Blow: Planter and Political Prophet of Antebellum Sussex." *Virginia Magazine of History and Biography* 90 (October 1982): 432-45. Provides a thumbnail biographical sketch of one of Tyler's college friends.

2352. Entry number skipped.

XII
Personal Life and Post-Presidential Years

A. CONGRESSIONAL WITNESS FOR DANIEL WEBSTER, 1846

2353. Eberling, Ernest J. *Congressional Investigations: A Study of the Origin and Development of the Power of Congress to Investigate and Punish for Contempt.* New York: Columbia University Press, 1928; New York: Octagon Books, 1973.

2354. "Ex-Presidents Who Testified—Tyler, Teddy Roosevelt Gave Facts to Congress." *U.S. News and World Report,* Nov. 27, 1953, 32. Discusses Tyler's appearance before a House committee investigating Webster.

2355. Jones, Howard. "The Attempt to Impeach Daniel Webster." *Capitol Studies* 3 (Fall 1975): 31-44. Carefully treats the efforts of Charles Jared Ingersoll to impeach Webster.

2356. Stathis, Stephen W. "Executive Cooperation: Presidential Recognition of the Investigative Authority of Congress and the Courts." *Journal of Law & Politics* 3 (1986): 183-294. Contrasts the claim of executive privilege with instances of executive cooperation with Congress.

2357. Stathis, Stephen W. "Former Presidents as Congressional Witnesses." *Presidential Studies Quarterly* 13 (Summer 1983): 458-81. Describes Tyler's appearance on Webster's behalf.

2358. Stevens, Kenneth R. "The Webster-Ingersoll Feud: Politics and Personality in the New Nation." *Historical New Hampshire* 37 (1982): 174-92. Recounts the longstanding disagreements and clashes between Webster and Ingersoll.

B.   WASHINGTON PEACE CONFERENCE, 1861

2359. Adams, Henry. *The Great Secession Winter of 1860-61 and Other Essays*, ed. George Hochfield. New York: Sagamore Press, 1958.

2360. Agar, Herbert. *The Price of Union.* Boston: Houghton Mifflin, 1950.

2361. Bell, Eva E. "Virginia during the Period of Secession." *Confederate Veteran* 35 (September 1927): 329-30. Discusses Virginia's role in and delegates to the peace convention.

2362. Bentley, Carrie Helen. "The Secession Convention of Virginia, 1861." M.A. thesis, University of Texas-Austin, 1932.

2363. Boisseau, Sterling. "The Virginia Convention of 1861." *Confederate Veteran* 32 (January 1924): 8-10. Briefly mentions Tyler in his discussion of the secession convention, February 13, 1861, in Richmond.

2364. Brown, Thomas. "Edward Everett and the Constitutional Union Party of 1860." *Historical Journal of Massachusetts* 11 (June 1983): 69-81.

2365. Chambers, Lenoir. "The South on the Eve of the Civil War." *North Carolina Historical Review* 39 (Spring 1962): 181-94.

2366. Craven, Avery Odelle. *The Coming of the Civil War.* Chicago: University of Chicago Press, 1942.

2367. Crenshaw, Ollinger. *The Slave States in the Presidential Election of 1860.* Baltimore: Johns Hopkins Press, 1945; Gloucester, Mass.: P. Smith, 1969.

2368. Fite, Emerson David. *The Presidential Campaign of 1860.* New York: Macmillan, 1911; Port Washington, N.Y.: Kennikat Press, 1967. Also available in *Microbook Library* [**601**].

2369. Goldfield, David Reed. "The Triumph of Politics over Society: Virginia, 1851-1861." Ph.D. diss., University of Maryland, 1970.

2370. Graebner, Norman A. "Thomas Corwin and the Sectional Crisis." *Ohio History* 86 (Autumn 1977): 229-47.

2371. Greeman, Betty Dix. "The Democratic Convention of 1860: Prelude to Secession." *Maryland Historical Magazine* 67 (Fall 1972): 225-53.

2372. Gunderson, Robert Gray. "The Old Gentlemen's Convention: The Peace Conference of 1861." *Civil War History* 7 (March 1961): 5-12. Notes that Tyler was the center of attention at the gathering.

2373. Gunderson, Robert Gray. *Old Gentlemen's Convention: The Washington Peace Conference of 1861.* Madison: University of Wisconsin Press, 1961.

2374. Hamilton, Holman. *Prologue to Conflict: The Crisis and Compromise of 1850.* New York: W. W. Norton, 1964.

2375. Henig, Gerald S. "Opposition to Secession in Virginia and North Carolina, 1860-1861." M.A. thesis, University of Wisconsin—Madison, 1965.

2376. Hoppin, William Warner. *The Peace Conference of 1861 at Washington, D.C.* Providence, R.I.: Standard Printing Co., 1891, 1903.

2377. Jeffrey, Thomas E. "The Secessionist Party at the Virginia Convention of 1861." M.A. thesis, Catholic University of America, 1970.

2378. Jermann, Peter D. "The Reluctant Nation? The Question of Southern Nationalism and Secession, 1860-1861." *Cithara* 21 (May 1982): 24-32.

2379. Keene, Jesse Lynn. *The Peace Convention of 1861.* Tuscaloosa: Confederate Publishing Co., 1961.

2380. Knoles, George H., ed. *The Crisis of the Union, 1860-61.* Baton Rouge: Louisiana State University Press, 1965.

2381. Largent, Robert J. "Virginia Takes the Road to Secession." *West Virginia History* 3 (January 1942): 120-46.

2382. Maddox, Robert Franklin. "The Presidential Election of 1860 in Western Virginia." *West Virginia History* 25 (April 1964): 211-27.

2383. Meerse, David E. "Buchanan, Corruption, and the Election of 1860." *Civil War History* 12 (June 1966): 116-31.

2384. Memminger, Christopher Gustavus. *The Mission of South Carolina to Virginia.* Baltimore: J. Lucas & Son, [1861]. Reprint of *De Bow's Review* article.

2385. Mering, John V. "Allies or Opponents? The Douglas Democrats and the Constitutional Unionists." *Southern Studies* 23 (Winter 1984): 376-85.

2386. Mering, John V. "The Constitutional Union Campaign of 1860: An Example of the Paranoid Style." *Mid-America* 60 (April–July 1978): 95-106.

2387. Mering, John V. "The Slave-State Constitutional Unionists and the Politics of Consensus." *Journal of Southern History* 43 (August 1977): 395-410.

2388. Moore, James Tice. "Secession and the States: A Review Essay." *Virginia Magazine of History and Biography* 94 (January 1986): 60-76.

2389. Nevins, Allan. *Ordeal of the Union.* 2 vols. New York: Scribner, 1947-50. Major study of the period 1847-57.

2390. Nichols, Roy F. *The Disruption of American Democracy.* New York: Macmillan Co., 1948; New York; Collier Books, 1962.

2391. Parry, Meredith. "John Tyler and Secession." M.A. thesis, West Virginia University, 1934.

2392. Potter, David. *The Impending Crisis, 1848-1861.* New York: Harper and Row, 1976.

2393. Rice, Philip Morrison. "The Know-Nothing Party in Virginia." *Virginia Magazine of History and Biography* 55 (1947): 61-75, 159-69.

2394. Shanks, Henry Thomas. "The Secession Movement in Virginia." Ph.D. diss., University of North Carolina—Chapel Hill, 1929.

2395. Simms, Henry Harrison. *A Decade of Sectional Controversy, 1851-1861.* Chapel Hill: University of North Carolina Press, 1942; Westport, Conn.: Greenwood Press, 1978.

2396. Stanley, Robert H. "Party Conflict and the Secessionist Alternative: The Virginia House of Delegates as a Test Case, 1850-1860." *Essays in History* 24 (1980): 5-28.

2397. Sweet, Leonard I. "The Reaction of the Protestant Episcopal Church in Virginia to the Secession Crisis: October 1859 to May 1861." *Historical Magazine of the Protestant Episcopal Church* 41 (June 1972): 137-51.

2398. Taylor, John Charles Randolph. "Virginia Know Nothings: Whigs in Search of a National Party." M.A. thesis, University of Virginia, 1974.

2399. Tyler, Lyon G., Jr. "Virginia's Call for Statesmanship: The Peace Convention of 1861." *Virginia Cavalcade* 10 (Autumn 1960): 12-18.

2400. Wilson, Clyde N., Jr. "Five Men in Dilemma." *Civil War Times Illustrated* 9 (October 1970): 20-27. Explores the attitudes and activities of five ex-presidents—Van Buren, Tyler, Pierce, Buchanan, and Fillmore—towards secession and the Civil War.

2401. Yoder, Thomas. "Illinois: The Old Northwest and the Peace Conference of 1861." M.S. thesis, Illinois State University, 1967.

C. CONFEDERATE CONGRESS

2402. Beringer, Richard E. "Political Factionalism in the Confederate Congress." Ph.D. diss., Northwestern University, 1966.

2403. Lewis, Albert L. "The Confederate Congress: A Study in Personnel." M.A. thesis, University of Southern California, 1955.

2404. Sikes, Enoch Walter. *The Confederate States Congress.* Raleigh, N.C.: Edwards & Broughton, 1903.

2405. Yearns, W. Buck. *The Confederate Congress.* Athens: University of Georgia Press, 1960.

2406. Yearns, W. Buck. *The Confederate Governors.* Athens: University of Georgia Press, 1985.

D. WHITE HOUSE HOST, HOSTESS, AND GENTLEMAN FARMER

2407. Aikman, Lonnelle. *The Living White House.* Washington: White House Historical Association, 1966.

2408. Barzman, Sol. *The First Ladies.* New York: Cowles Book Co, 1970.

2409. Boller, Paul F., Jr. *Presidential Wives.* New York: Oxford University Press, 1988. Explores the life and character of both Letitia Christian and Julia Gardiner Tyler, pp. 78-87.

2410. Bonnell, John Sutherland. *Presidential Profiles: Religion in the Life of American Presidents.* Philadelphia: Westminster Press, 1971.

2411. Bradshaw, Herbert Clarence. "A President's Bride at 'Sherwood Forest.'" *Virginia Cavalcade* 7 (Spring 1958): 30-39. Discusses the Tyler family home and the background and family of Julia Gardiner.

2412. Brown, Margaret W. *Dresses of the First Ladies of the White House.* Washington: Smithsonian Institution, 1952.

2413. Cannon, Poppy, and Patricia Brooks. *The Presidents' Cookbook: Practical Recipes from George Washington to the Present.* [New York]: Funk & Wagnalls, 1968.

2414. Caroli, Betty Boyd. *First Ladies.* New York: Oxford University Press, 1987. One of the few scholarly investigations of the role and influence of first ladies in the White House, including the Tyler wives.

2415. Caroli, Betty Boyd. *Inside the White House: America's Most Famous Home.* Garden City, N.Y.: Doubleday Book & Music Clubs, 1992.

2416. Chiles, Rosa Pendleton. "Book Returned to Tyler Family." *Tyler's Quarterly Historical and Genealogical Magazine* 31 (April 1950): 252-55. Book taken from the Tyler household during the Civil War.

2417. Crispell, Kenneth R., and Carlos F. Gomez. *Hidden Illness in the White House.* Durham: Duke University Press, 1988.

2418. Dale, Philip M. *Medical Biographies: The Ailments of Thirty-Three Famous Persons.* Norman: University of Oklahoma Press, 1952.

2419. Durant, John. *The Sports of Our Presidents.* New York: Hastings House Publishers, 1964.

2420. Eastman, John. *Who Lived Where: A Biographical Guide to Homes and Museums.* New York: Bonanza Books, 1983. Discusses the various properties Tyler owned and lived in.

2421. Ferris, Robert G., ed. *The Presidents from the Inauguration of George Washington to the Inauguration of Jimmy Carter: Historic Places Commemorating the Chief Executives of the United States.* Washington: U.S. Department of the Interior, National Park Service, 1977.

2422. Fuller, Edmund, and David E. Green. *God in the White House: The Faiths of American Presidents.* New York: Crown, 1968.

2423. Furman, Bess. *White House Profile: A Social History of the White House, Its Occupants and Its Festivities.* Indianapolis: Bobbs-Merrill, 1951.

2424. Gerlinger, Irene. *Mistresses of the White House: Narrator's Tale of a Pageant of First Ladies.* New York: French, 1950; Freeport, N.Y.: Books for Libraries Press, 1970.

2425. Gillette, Jane Brown. "Family Affair." *Historic Preservation* 45 (September/October 1993): 44-51, 97-99. An illustrated article on Sherwood Forest, retirement home of John Tyler.

2426. Gordon, Lydia L. *From First Lady Washington to Mrs. Cleveland.* Boston: Lee and Shephard, 1889; Freeport, N.Y.: Books for Libraries Press, 1972.

2427. Gotlieb, Howard, and Gail Grimes. "President Tyler and the Gardiners: A New Portrait." *Yale University Library Gazette* 34 (July 1959): 2-12. Discuss the Gardiner family papers in the Yale University Library.

2428. Hall, Grover C., Jr. "Tyler and His Horse." *Philadelphia Evening Bulletin,* July 10, 1970. Discusses Tyler's accession to the presidency, the horse he rode to Richmond to board the train for Washington, and the inscription on the marker over the horse's grave.

2429. Hall, Virginius Cornick, Jr. "Notes on Patrick Henry Portraiture." *Virginia Magazine of History and Biography* 71 (April 1963): 168-84. Discusses John Henry's contacts with Tyler in 1860 about portraits.

2430. Hampton, Vernon B. *The Religious Background of the White House.* Boston: Christopher, 1932.

2431. Hampton, William Judson. *Presidential Shrines from Washington to Coolidge.* Boston: Christopher, 1928.

2432. Healy, Diana Dixon. *America's First Ladies: Private Lives of the Presidential Wives.* New York: Atheneum, 1988.

2433. "Historical and Social Jottings." *Magazine of American History* 18 (July 1887): 88-89. Discusses courtship and marriage of Tyler and Julia Gardiner on July 26, 1844.

2434. Holloway, Laura C. *The Ladies of the White House ... 1789-1881.* Philadelphia: Bradley & Co., 1881.

2435. "Homes of Virginia-Born Presidents of the United States." *Virginia Journal of Education* 54 (September–November, 1960, January–May 1961). Includes discussion of Sherwood Forest.

2436. Isely, Bliss. *Presidents, Men of Faith.* Boston: Wilde, 1953.

2437. Jeffries, Ona Griffin. *In and Out of the White House, From Washington to the Eisenhowers: An Intimate Glimpse Into the Social and Domestic Aspects of Presidential*

Life. New York: W. Funk, 1960. Popular account of social life during the Tyler administration.

2438. Jensen, Amy La Follette. *The White House and Its Thirty-Five Families*. New York: McGraw-Hill, 1971.

2439. Jones, Cranston. *Homes of the American Presidents*. New York: McGraw-Hill, 1962.

2440. Jones, Robert, comp. *The President's Own White House Cookbook*. Chicago: Culinary Arts Institute, 1973.

2441. Kale, Wilford. "Tyler Country: A Family Nourishes Its Roots." *Virginia Genealogical Society Newsletter* 16 (November, December 1990): 1. Explores the Tyler background in Charles City County.

2442. Kirk, Elise K. *Music at the White House: A History of the American Spirit*. Urbana: University of Illinois Press, 1986.

2443. Klamkin, Marian. *White House China*. New York: Charles Scribner's Sons, 1972. Relates that Tyler did not purchase state china during his administration.

2444. Klapthor, Margaret Brown. *The First Ladies' Cook Book: Favorite Recipes of All the Presidents of the United States*. New York: Parents' Magazine Press, 1975.

2445. Lindop, Edmund. *White House Sportsmen*. Boston: Houghton Mifflin, 1964.

2446. Mann, Nancy Wilson. "Mrs. President Tyler in Richmond." *Richmond Quarterly* 10 (Summer, Fall, Winter 1987): 1-6. Discusses courtship and marriage of Tyler and Julia Gardiner and her life in Richmond following Tyler's death.

2447. Mann, Nancy Wilson. *Tyler and Gardiners on the Village Green: Williamsburg, Virginia, and East Hampton, Long Island*. New York: Vantage Press, 1983.

2448. Martin, Asa E. "The 'Rebel' at Sherwood Forest," in *After the White House*. State College, Pa.: Penns Valley Publishers, 1951.

2449. Marx, Rudolph. *The Health of the Presidents*. New York: Putnam, 1960.

2450. Middleton, Arthur Pierce. "President Tyler's Williamsburg Residence." *Tyler's Quarterly Historical and Genealogical Magazine* 31 (April 1950): 222-25. Discusses house that burned in 1873.

2451. National Museum of History and Technology. *The First Ladies' Hall.* Washington: Smithsonian Institution Press, 1955, 1973.

2452. Owen, Mrs. Marie Bankhead. "Raising the First Confederate Flag." *Confederate Veteran* 24 (May 1916): 199. Recounts the raising of the first Confederate flag in Montgomery, Alabama, by Letitia Christian Tyler, granddaughter of Tyler.

2453. Paletta, Lu Ann. *The World Almanac of First Ladies.* New York: World Almanac, 1990.

2454. Peckham, Stephen Farnum. "An Echo from the Civil War." *Journal of American History* 5, No. 4 (1911): 611-32. Discusses Tyler papers found by Union soldier on floor at Sherwood Forest in 1864.

2455. Perling, Joseph Jerry. *A President Takes a Wife.* Middleburg, Va.: Denlinger's, 1959. Historical novel on the marriage of John Tyler and Julia Gardiner.

2456. Perrine, William. "When an Actress Was Mistress of the White House." *Ladies Home Journal* 21 (October 1904): 15. Discusses Priscilla Cooper.

2457. Peterson, Helen Stone. "First Lady at 22." *Virginia Cavalcade* 11 (Winter 1961-62): 14-19. Provides a biographical sketch and anecdotes of Priscilla Cooper Tyler, White House hostess during the illness of Letitia Christian Tyler.

2458. "Plantation for a President: Sherwood Forest, Home of John Tyler in Charles City County, Virginia." *House and Garden* 151 (June 1979): 156-59.

2459. Pollard, John. "Jamestown Fifty Years Ago." *Confederate Veteran* 14 (November 1906): 520. Reminiscences about the 250th anniversary of the settlement and Tyler's speech on the occasion.

2460. *Presidential Inaugural Bibles: An Exhibition, November 17, 1968-February 23, 1969. Washington Cathedral: The Rare Book Library.* New York: Spiral Press, 1968. Reports that Tyler's inaugural Bible has not been identified.

2461. "The President's Marriage." *Magazine of American History* 18 (July 1887): 89. Discusses Tyler's courtship and marriage to Julia Gardiner.

2462. *The Presidents and Their Wives from Washington to Kennedy.* Washington: Haskin Service Co., 1961.

2463. Prindiville, Kathleen. *First Ladies.* New York: Macmillan Co., 1932, 1941.

2464. Pugh, Evelyn L. "Women and Slavery: Julia Gardiner Tyler and the Duchess of Sutherland." *Virginia Magazine of History and Biography* 88 (April 1980): 186-202. Explores the correspondence on antislavery and the public response to it.

2465. Quinn, Sandra L., and Sanford Kanter. *America's Royalty: All the President's Children*. Westport, Conn.: Greenwood Press, 1983.

2466. Rives, Ralph Hardee. "The Jamestown Celebration of 1857." *Virginia Magazine of History and Biography* 66 (July 1958): 259-71. Discusses Tyler's oration.

2467. Robbins, Peggy. "President Tyler's First Ladies." *American History Illustrated* 18 (January 1984): 9.

2468. Roos, Charles A. "Physicians to the Presidents and Their Patients: A Biobibliography." *Medical Library Association Bulletin* 49 (July 1961): 291-360.

2469. Rosenbach, Abraham Simon Wolf. "The Libraries of the Presidents of the United States." *Proceedings of the American Antiquarian Society*, New Series 44 (October 1934): 337-64. Briefly discusses Tyler's library, reproduces his bookplate.

2470. Rysavy, Francois, with Frances S. Leighton. *A Treasury of White House Cooking*. New York: G. P. Putnam, 1972.

2471. Schick, Frank Leopold. *Records of the Presidency: Presidential Papers and Libraries from Washington to Reagan*. Phoenix: Oryx Press, 1989.

2472. Seager, Robert, II. "John Tyler: The Planter of Sherwood Forest." *Virginia Cavalcade* 13 (Summer 1963): 4-11.

2473. Seale, William. *The President's House*. 2 vols. Washington: White House Historical Association, 1986.

2474. Shockley, Martin Staples. "Priscilla Cooper in the Richmond Theatre." *Virginia Magazine of History and Biography* 67 (April 1959): 180-85. Discusses her career in Richmond before her marriage to Robert Tyler in 1839.

2475. Singleton, Esther. *The Story of the White House*. 2 vols. New York: The McClure Co., 1907.

2476. Smith, Bessie White. *The Romances of the Presidents*. Boston: Lothrop, Lee & Shepard Co., 1932.

2477. Still, William. *The Underground Railroad: A Record of Facts, Authentic Narratives, Letters, &c...* . Cincinnati, Ohio: People's Publishing Co., 1871; Philadelphia: Porter & Coates, 1872; New York: Arno Press, 1968. Also available in *Microbook Library* [601]. Contains story of a slave of the Christian family and his life with Tyler.

2478. Taylor, John M. *From the White House Inkwell: American Presidential Autographs*. Rutland, Vt.: C. E. Tuttle, 1968.

2479. "The Three William and Mary Alumni Presidents of the United States." *DeBow's Review* 26 (June 1859): 664-68. Reports on Tyler's address in February 1859.

2480. "The Two Plum Puddings." *Magazine of American History* 12 (November 1884): 469. Relates anecdote of servants' presentation of dessert on an occasion when Jefferson dined with Tyler.

2481. Truett, Randle Bond. *The First Ladies in Fashion*. New York: Hastings House, 1954, 1965.

2482. Truett, Randle Bond. *The White House, Home of the Presidents*. New York: Hastings House, 1949.

2483. Tucker, R. Whitney. *The Descendants of the Presidents*. Charlotte, N.C.: Delmar Printing Co., 1975.

2484. Tyler, Julia Gardiner. "To the Duchess of Sutherland and the Ladies of England." *Southern Literary Messenger* 19 (February 1853): 126+. Discouraged foreign intervention in America's domestic affairs, particularly slavery.

2485. [Tyler, Lyon G.]. "Cedar Grove Farm, New Kent County, Virginia: Epitaphs from the Tombstones." *Tyler's Quarterly Historical and Genealogical Magazine* 12 (January 1931): 194-95. Provides epitaphs from the tombs of Letitia Christian, Tyler's first wife and several of their children, buried at the residence of Robert Christian, Letitia's father.

2486. [Tyler, Lyon G.?], ed. "Edmund Ruffin's Visit to John Tyler [November 1857]." *William and Mary College Quarterly Historical Magazine*, Series 1, 14 (January 1906): 193-211. Discusses Tyler's residence, character, physical appearance, accession to presidency, ideas on executive power, presidential administration, and Tyler's great respect for Webster, whom Ruffin holds in lower esteem than Tyler because of Webster's low morals.

2487. [Tyler, Lyon G.]. "John Tyler and the Ladies of Brazoria." *Tyler's Quarterly Historical and Genealogical Magazine* 11 (July 1929): 1-4. Asserts Tyler's central role in the annexation of Texas and prints exchange of correspondence between Tyler and the ladies of Brazoria, Texas, 1845-46, on the presentation of a silver pitcher to Tyler in appreciation for his efforts for Texan annexation.

2488. [Tyler, Lyon G.?]. "The Planter's Pride in His Slaves." *William and Mary College Quarterly Historical Magazine*, Series 1, 23 (April 1915): 225-26. Relates story told by Aaron Hilton, a black neighbor of the Tylers, of an incident at Sherwood Forest between an overseer and a slave and Tyler's handling of the matter.

2489. [Tyler, Mrs. Lyon G.?], ed. "When Ex-President Tyler and Mrs. Tyler Visited Petersburg, Va., in 1854." *Tyler's Quarterly Historical and Genealogical Magazine* 19 (January 1938): 132-39. Prints letters from Julia Gardiner Tyler to her mother and sister describing the trip and activities.

2490. Warren, Owen G. "To the President's Bride." *Southern Literary Messenger* 10 (November 1844): 666-67. Poem copied from the *New York Mirror* on the occasion of the marriage of John Tyler and Julia Gardiner.

2491. Whitton, Mary Ormsbee. *First First Ladies, 1789-1865: A Study of the Wives of the Early Presidents.* New York: Hastings House, 1948; Freeport, N.Y.: Books for Libraries Press, 1969.

2492. Williamson, David. *Debrett's Presidents of the United States of America.* London: Webb & Bower, 1989.

2493. Wold, Karl D. *Mr. President—How Is Your Health?* St. Paul, Minn.: Bruce Publishing Co., 1948.

2494. Woolfall, Lila G. A. *Presiding Ladies of the White House ...* Washington: Bureau of National Literature and Art, 1903.

2495. Zorn, Walter Lewis. *The Descendants of the Presidents of the United States of America.* Monroe, Mich.: 1954, 1955.

E. DEATH AND BURIAL

2496. Collins, Herbert R., and David B. Weaver. *Wills of the U.S. Presidents.* New York: Communication Channels, 1976.

2497. Confederate States of America. Congress of the Confederate States. *Proceedings on the Announcement of the Death of Hon. John Tyler, January 20th and 21st, 1862.* Richmond: Enquirer Book and Job Press, 1862.

2498. "Death of John Tyler." *Southern Literary Messenger* 34 (January 1862): 69-70. Reviews career.

2499. Laird, Archibald. *Monuments Marking the Graves of the Presidents: A Collection of Photographs and Inscriptions.* North Quincy, Mass.: Christopher Publishing House, 1971.

2500. Laird, Archibald. *The Near Great—Chronicle of the Vice Presidents: A Collection of Photographs and Inscriptions and a Record of Historical Events.* North Quincy, Mass.: Christopher Publishing House, 1980. Contains short biographical sketches, miscellaneous information, and monument inscriptions.

XIII

Historiographical Materials

A. ASSESSMENTS

2501. Bailey, Thomas A. *Presidential Greatness: The Image and the Man from George Washington to the Present.* New York: Appleton-Century, 1966.

2502. Bailey, Thomas A. *Presidential Saints and Sinners.* New York: Free Press, 1981.

2503. Bailey, Thomas A. *The Pugnacious Presidents: White House Warriors on Parade.* New York: Free Press, 1980.

2504. Bratton, Daniel L. "The Rating of Presidents." *Presidential Studies Quarterly* 13 (Summer 1983): 400-404.

2505. Cook, Blake C. "John Tyler, Stalwart Son of Old Virginia." *Tyler's Quarterly Historical and Genealogical Magazine* 24 (July 1942): 18-29. Speech in commemoration of 150th year of birth and 100th of presidency; prints Tyler's letter to China; reviews life and career.

2506. Hamilton, Holman. *White House Images and Realities.* Gainesville: University of Florida Press, 1958. Discusses briefly circumstances and career, fact and fiction, and responses to the Tyler and other administrations.

2507. Jennings, A. H. "John Tyler and Abraham Lincoln." *Confederate Veteran* 37 (June 1929): 212-14. Praises Lyon G. Tyler's assessment of Tyler.

2508. Kibler, J. Luther. "Highways and Milestones Through Seven Decades of United States History, 1775-1845: 'Honest John Tyler.'" *Tyler's Quarterly Historical and*

Genealogical Magazine 31 (January 1950): 143-46. Suggests topics for a study of Tyler, "one of our great American statesmen."

2509. Kynerd, Tom. "An Analysis of Presidential Greatness and 'President Rating.'" *Southern Quarterly* 9 (April 1971): 309-29.

2510. Laski, Harold J. *The American Presidency: An Interpretation.* New York: Grosset & Dunlap, 1940? Ranks Tyler as a strong president.

2511. Maranell, Gary M. "The Evaluation of Presidents: An Extension of the Schlesinger Polls." *Journal of American History* 57 (June 1970): 104-13.

2512. Murray, Robert M., and Tim H. Blessing. "The Presidential Performance Study: A Progress Report." *Journal of American History* 70 (December 1983): 535-55. Finds that Tyler's ranking as president has changed little since the Schlesinger report; Tyler's rank remains below average.

2513. Rossiter, Clinton. "The Presidents and the Presidency." *American Heritage* 7 (April 1956): 28-33, 94-95.

2514. Rossiter, Clinton. *The American Presidency.* New York: New American Library, 1956. Rates Tyler's performance as president on par with that of the two Adamses, Madison, Van Buren, McKinley, Taft, and Hoover, above Fillmore, Benjamin Harrison, and Coolidge.

2515. Schlesinger, Arthur M., Jr. "Historians Rate United States Presidents." *Life* 25 (November 25, 1948): 65-68, 73-74.

2516. Schlesinger, Arthur M., Jr. "Our Presidents: A Rating by Seventy-Five Historians." *New York Times Magazine,* July 29, 1962, pp. 12-13, 40-43. Updates 1948 poll; places Tyler in a below average category in presidential ranking.

2517. Sidey, Hugh. "The Presidency: What Links These Six?" *Time,* April 15, 1991, p. 35. Ranks Tyler, along with Taylor, Fillmore, Pierce, Coolidge, and Reagan, as "below average" presidents.

2518. Tyler, Lyon G. "Tyler versus Lincoln." *Tyler's Quarterly Historical and Genealogical Magazine* 10 (October 1928): 75-99. Responds to article in *Time.*

2519. "Tyler versus Lincoln." *Time,* April 9, 1928; response June 4, 1828.

2520. Tyler, Lyon Gardiner. "Highways and Milestones through Seven Decades of United States History, 1775-1845: 'Andrew Jackson and John Tyler.'" *Tyler's Quarterly*

Historical and Genealogical Magazine 30 (January–October 1949): 161-165, 235-239; 31 (January–October 1950): 1-5, 65-69.

2521. Tyler, Lyon Gardiner. *John Tyler and Abraham Lincoln: Who Was the Dwarf? A Reply to a Challenge*. Richmond: Richmond Press, 1929. Defends Tyler against charges that he was "historically a dwarf," a statement made in *Time*.

2522. [Tyler, Lyon G.?]. "John Tyler's Administration." *Tyler's Quarterly Historical and Genealogical Magazine* 14 (April 1933): 195-97. Reviews and praises the accomplishments of the Tyler presidency.

B. BIBLIOGRAPHIES

2523. American Historical Association. *Writings on American History*. 46 vols. Washington: Government Printing Office, 1902-64.

2524. Bemis, Samuel F., and Grace G. Griffin. *Guide to the Diplomatic History of the United States, 1775-1921*. Washington: Government Printing Office, 1935. Provides a convenient guide to literature on foreign policy issues of the Tyler administration.

2525. Burns, Richard Dean, ed. *Guide to American Foreign Relations since 1700*. Santa Barbara, Calif.: ABC-Clio, 1983.

2526. Congressional Information Service. *CIS Index to U.S. Executive Branch Documents, 1789-1909: Guide to Documents Listed in Checklist of U.S. Public Documents, 1789-1909, Not Printed in the U.S. Serial Set, Part 1, Commerce and Labor Department, Treasury Department*. 5 vols. *Part 2. War Department*. 4 vols. *Part 3, Interior Department, Interstate Commerce Commission, Justice Department, Labor Department, Library of Congress*. 4 vols. *CIS Index to U.S. Senate Executive Documents and Reports*. 2 vols. Bethesda, Md.: Congressional Information Service, 1987+. Provides access to the edition by the same name.

2527. *Congressional Quarterly's Guide to the Presidency*. Washington: Congressional Quarterly, 1989. A lengthy guide to studies on the presidency.

2528. Coren, Robert W., Mary Rephlo, David Kepley, and Charles South. *Guide to the Records of the United States Senate at the National Archives, 1789-1989: Bicentennial Edition*. Washington: National Archives and Records Administration, 1989.

2529. Cronin, John William, and W. Harvey Wise. *A Bibliography of William Henry Harrison, John Tyler, James Knox Polk*. Washington: Riverford Publishing Co., 1935.

2530. Davison, Kenneth E. *The American Presidency: A Guide to Information Sources.* Detroit: Gale Research Co., 1983.

2531. Duncan, Richard R. *Theses and Dissertations on Virginia History: A Bibliography.* Richmond: Virginia State Library, 1986.

2532. Durfee, David A., ed. *William Henry Harrison, 1773-1841: John Tyler, 1790-1862; Chronology, Documents, Bibliographical Aids.* Dobbs Ferry, N.Y.: Oceana Publications, 1970.

2533. Fehrenbacher, Don E. *Manifest Destiny and the Coming of the Civil War, 1840-1861.* New York: Appleton-Century-Crofts, 1970. A fairly comprehensive bibliography of American historical scholarship for the later antebellum period.

2534. Hart, Lyndon H., III. *A Guide to Bible Records in the Archives Branch, Virginia State Library.* Richmond: Virginia State Library and Archives, 1985.

2535. *An Index to the Presidential Election Campaign Biographies, 1824-1972.* Ann Arbor: University Microfilms International, 1981.

2536. Jacob, Kathryn Allamong, and Elizabeth Ann Hornyak, eds. *Guide to Research Collections of Former United States Senators, 1789-1982.* Washington: Historical Office of the United States Senate, 1983.

2537. Kuehl, Warren F. *Dissertations in History: An Index to Dissertation Completed in History Departments of United States and Canadian Universities, 1873-1960.* Lexington: University Press of Kentucky, 1965.

2538. Library of Congress. *Catalog of Broadsides in the Rare Book Division, Library of Congress, Washington, D.C.* 4 vols. Boston: G. K. Hall & Co., 1972. Divided into geographical, author-title, and chronological catalogs.

2539. Library of Congress. *Library of Congress Catalogs: National Union Catalog of Manuscript Collections.* Washington: Library of Congress, 1962–. 26 vols. to date. Issued by various publishers over the years, the catalog guide lists and briefly describes major collections registered with the Library of Congress since 1959; generally issued annually.

2540. *List of Treaties Submitted to the Senate, 1789-1931, Which Have Not Gone into Force, October 1, 1932.* Washington: Government Printing Office, 1932.

2541. *List of Treaties Submitted to the Senate, 1789-1934.* Washington: Government Printing Office, 1935.

2542. Lord, Clifford L., ed. *List and Index of Presidential Executive Orders: Unnumbered Series (1789-1941)*. Newark: Historical Records Survey, 1943; Wilmington, Del.: Michael Glazier, 1979; Princeton Junction, N.J.: Princeton Datafilm, 1978.

2543. Martin, Fenton S., and Robert Goehlert. *The American Presidency: A Bibliography*. Washington: Congressional Quarterly, 1987. Provides an abbreviated guide to the literature on Tyler and his contemporaries.

2544. McDonough, John J. *Members of Congress: A Checklist of Their Papers in the Manuscript Division, Library of Congress*. Washington: Library of Congress, 1980. Lists and describes collections of papers of 894 individuals.

2545. McPherson, Edward, comp. *Consolidated Index of the Reports of the Committees of the House of Representatives, from the Twenty-Sixth to the Fortieth Congress, Inclusive*. Washington: Government Printing Office, 1869. An older, but useful, index to the House reports.

2546. Menendez, Albert J. *Religion and the U.S. Presidency: A Bibliography*. New York: Garland Publishing, 1986. Contains brief reference to Tyler's religious views.

2547. Miles, William. *The Image Makers: A Bibliography of American Presidential Campaign Biographies*. Metuchen, N.J.: Scarecrow Press, 1979.

2548. Miller, Cynthia Pease. *A Guide to Research Collections of Former Members of the United States House of Representatives, 1789-1987*. Washington: Office for the Bicentennial of the United States House of Representatives, United States House of Representatives, 1988.

2549. Molnar, John Edgar. *Author-Title Index to Joseph Sabin's Dictionary of Books Relating to America*. 3 vols. Metuchen, N.J.: Scarecrow Press, 1974. Useful for accessing Sabin's 29-volume work.

2550. Moser, Harold D., comp. *Daniel Webster: A Bibliography*. Westport, Conn.: Greenwood Press, forthcoming.

2551. Mugridge, Donald H., comp. *The Presidents of the United States, 1789-1962: A Selected List of References*. Washington: Government Printing Office, 1963.

2552. National Archives and Records Service. *Catalog of National Archives Microfilm Publications*. Washington: National Archives and Records Service, 1974.

2553. National Archives. *Microfilm Resources for Research: A Comprehensive Catalog.* Washington: National Archives and Records Administration, 1986.

2554. National Historical Publications and Records Commission. *Directory of Archives and Manuscript Repositories in the United States.* Washington: National Archives and Records Service, 1978.

2555. Poore, Benjamin Perley, comp. *A Descriptive Catalogue of the Government Publications of the United States, September 5, 1774–March 4, 1881.* Washington: Government Printing Office, 1885; New York: Johnson Reprint Corp., 1962.

2556. Prucha, Francis Paul. *A Bibliographical Guide to the History of Indian-White Relations in the United States.* Chicago: University of Chicago Press, 1977.

2557. Remini, Robert V., and Edwin A. Miles. *The Era of Good Feelings and the Age of Jackson, 1816-1841.* Arlington Heights, Ill.: AHM Publishing Corporation, 1979.

2558. Remini, Robert V., and Robert O. Rupp. *Andrew Jackson: A Bibliography.* No. 7 of *Bibliographies of the Presidents of the United States.* Westport, Conn.: Meckler, 1991.

2559. Sabin, Joseph. *Bibliotheca Americana: A Dictionary of Books Relating to America, from Its Discovery to the Present Time* ... 29 vols. 1868-1936. Reprint (29 vols. in 15). Amsterdam: N. Israel, 1961-62.

2560. Salmon, John S. *A Guide to State Records in the Archives Branch, Virginia State Library and Archives.* Richmond: Virginia State Library and Archives, 1985. Essential for accessing voluminous records of the state archives.

2561. Schamel, Charles E., Mary Rephlo, Rodney Ross, David Kepley, Robert W. Coren, and James Gregory Bradsher. *Guide to the Records of the United States House of Representatives at the National Archives, 1789-1989: Bicentennial Edition.* Washington: National Archives and Records Administration, 1989.

2562. Schlacter, Gail, ed. *The American Presidency: A Historical Bibliography.* Santa Barbara, Calif.: ABC-Clio Information Services, 1984.

2563. Streeter, Thomas Winthrop, and Archibald Hanna. *Bibliography of Texas, 1795-1845, with a Guide to the Microfilm Collection, Texas as Province and Republic, 1795-1845.* Woodbridge, Conn.: Research Publications, 1983. Provides access to the 39-roll microfilm publication.

2564. Taylor, George Rogers. *American Economic History Before 1860*. New York: Appleton-Century-Crofts, 1969.

2565. Wilson, Clyde N. *John C. Calhoun: A Bibliography*. Westport, Conn.: Meckler Corporation, 1990.

2566. Wise, W. Harvey, Jr., and John William Cronin, comps. *A Bibliography of Zachary Taylor, Millard Fillmore, Franklin Pierce, James Buchanan*. Washington, D.C., Riverford Publishing Co., 1935.

XIV

Iconography

2567. Bassett, Margaret. *Profiles & Portraits of American Presidents & Their Wives.* Freeport, Me., Bond Wheelwright Co., 1964. Tylers discussed pp. 95-108. Healy portrait; portrait of Letitia Christian; Francesco Anelli portrait of Julia Gardner Tyler.

2568. Blaisdell, Thomas C., Jr., and Peter Selz. *The American Presidency in Political Cartoons, 1776-1976.* Salt Lake City: Peregrine Smith, 1976. Originally published as a catalog of exhibition held at University Art Museum, Berkeley, Calif., January 13-February 22, 1976.

2569. Bowers, Claude Gernade. *John Tyler: Address by Hon. Claude G. Bowers of New York at the Unveiling of the Bust of President Tyler in the State Capitol, Richmond, Virginia, June 16, 1931.* Richmond: Richmond Press, 1932. Contains photograph of bust and assessment of President Tyler as "an honest statesman who refused to be a party to the intolerable treachery."

2570. Brown, William Henry. *Portrait Gallery of Distinguished American Citizens, with Biographical Sketches, and Fac-Similes of Original Letters.* Hartford, Conn.: E. B. & E. C. Kellogg, 1845; [New York: G. A. Baker & Co., 1931].

2571. *Ceremonies of the Unveiling of the Monument to John Tyler, Tenth President of the United States, Hollywood Cemetery, Richmond, Virginia, October 12, 1915.* [Richmond? 1915?]. Program for the ceremonies includes illustration of monument and portrait of Tyler with outline sketch of his life.

2572. *Ceremonies of the Unveiling of the Bust of President John Tyler, Old Hall of the House of Delegates, State Capitol, Richmond, Virginia, Tuesday, June 16, 1931, 3:30 O'Clock, P.M.* [Richmond? 1931?]. Also available in *Pamphlets* [603]. Program for the occasion, includes photograph of bust, photograph of Charles Keck, sculptor, and of Mrs. Alfred I. DuPont, donor.

2573. Christian, George Llewellyn. *John Tyler: Address Delivered Before the Colonial Dames of America in the State of Virginia at Greenway, Charles City County, Va., on Monday, October 27, 1913, at the Unveiling of a Memorial to Mark the Birthplace of President Tyler.* Richmond: Whittet & Shepperson, 1913. Describes Tyler as "a straight and consistent politician, gentleman and patriot."

2574. Cowley, Charles. "The Minority Report of the Electoral Commission." *Magazine of American History* 27 (February 1892): 81-97. Identifies Julia Gardiner Tyler as one of the persons in the picture of the electoral commission of 1877.

2575. Dallas Museum of Fine Arts. *Mr. President: A Pictorial Parade of Presidents from Washington to Eisenhower, 1789-1856: Exhibition at Dallas Museum of Fine Arts for the State Fair of Texas, October, 1956.* Dallas, 1956.

2576. Devitt, George Raywood, comp. *The White House Gallery of Official Portraits of the Presidents.* New York: Gravure Co. of America, 1901, 1907, 1908. Healy portrait of Tyler, with brief sketch.

2577. Dickson, Harold E. *John Wesley Jarvis, American Painter, 1780-1840, with a Checklist of His Works.* New York: New York Historical Society, 1949. Lists Jarvis portraits of Tyler.

2578. Durant, John, and Alice Durant. *Pictorial History of American Presidents.* New York: Barnes, 1955, 1959, 1962, 1964, 1965.

2579. Duyckinck, Evart A. *Lives and Portraits of the Presidents of the United States.* New York: Johnson, 1881. Engraving by Chappel, p. 140.

2580. Duyckinck, Evert A. *National Portrait Gallery of Eminent Americans: Including Orators, Statesmen, Naval and Military Heroes, Jurists, Authors, Etc., Etc., from Original Full Length Paintings by Alonzo Chappel, with Biographical and Historical Narratives.* 2 vols. New York: Johnson, Fry & Co., n.d. Engraving and sketch.

2581. Freidel, Frank, ed. *The Presidents of the United States.* Washington: White House Historical Association, 1975.

2582. Getchell, George H. *Our Nation's Executives.* New York: Getchell, 1885. Engraving by Hall, p. 160.

2583. Gordon, Armistead Churchill. "John Tyler, Son of Virginia." *Confederate Veteran* 24 (January 1916): 4-5. Discusses monument in Hollywood Cemetery, Richmond.

2584. Gordon, Armistead Churchill. *Monument to John Tyler: Address Delivered in Hollywood Cemetery, at Richmond Va., on October 12, 1915, at the Dedication of the Monument Erected by the Government to John Tyler, Tenth President of the United States.* Washington: Government Printing Office, 1916. Also available in *Pamphlets* [603].

2585. Hess, Stephen. *The Ungentlemanly Art: A History of American Political Cartoons.* New York: Macmillan, 1968, 1975.

2586. "Inaugurations of the Past." *Harper's Weekly* 57 (March 8, 1913): 14-22. Includes portrait of Tyler.

2587. Jennings, Janet. "White House Portraits." *Independent* 56 (March 31, 1904): 723-29. Discusses portraits of first ladies.

2588. Jensen, Amy La Follette. *The White House and Its Thirty-Three Families.* New York: McGraw-Hill, 1958, 1962.

2589. Leish, Kenneth W., ed. *The American Heritage Pictorial History of the Presidents of the United States.* 2 vols. New York: American Heritage Publishing Co., 1968. Includes short biographical sketch.

2590. Lorant, Stefan. *The Presidency: A Pictorial History of Presidential Elections from Washington to Truman.* New York: Macmillan, 1951.

2591. Loubat, J. F. *Medallic History of the United States, 1776-1876.* 2 vols. New York: Loubat, 1880.

2592. MacNeil, Neil. *The President's Medal, 1789-1977.* New York: C. N. Potter, 1977.

2593. Milhollen, Hirst Dillon, and Milton Kaplan. *Presidents on Parade.* New York: Macmillan, 1948. Mainly a collection of photographs, reproduced from material in the collections of the Library of Congress.

2594. Musculus, John A. *An Index of State Bank Notes that Illustrate Characters and Events.* Bridgeport, Pa.: John A. Musculus, 1938. Lists banknotes, with name of issuing institution, denomination, and city, for Tyler.

2595. "A National Portrait Gallery, 1837-1849." *Chicago History* 7 (1966): 359-74. Reproduces likenesses by Charles Fenderich from the collections of the Chicago Historical Society.

2596. *National Portrait Gallery of Distinguished Americans.* 4 vols. Philadelphia: D. Rice & A. N. Hart, 1853-54. Volume 4, Plate 23, engraving by Forrest.

2597. National Portrait Gallery, Washington, D.C. *National Portrait Gallery, Smithsonian Institution: Permanent Collection Illustrated Checklist.* Ed. Frances Stevenson Wein. Washington: National Portrait Gallery by the Smithsonian Institution Press, 1980.

2598. Norfleet, Fillmore. *Saint Memin in Virginia: Portraits and Biographies.* Richmond: Dietz Press, 1942.

2599. Oliver, Andrew. *Portraits of John Quincy Adams and His Wife.* Cambridge: Harvard University Press, 1970. Auguste Edouart silhouette and James Reid Lambdin portrait of Tyler discussed.

2600. Oliver, Andrew. *Auguste Edouart's Silhouettes of Eminent Americans, 1839-1844.* Charlottesville: University of Virginia Press for the National Portrait Gallery, 1977. Contains silhouette of Tyler and some of his contemporaries.

2601. Pach, Alfred. *Portraits of Our Presidents: The Pach Collection.* New York: Hastings House, [1943].

2602. Pessolano-Filos, Francis, and Armando de Trevera. *Medals of the Presidents, Secretaries of the Treasury, and Directors of the U.S. Mint, 1789-1981; Also Correspondence between the Author and the Director of the Mint and Other Government Officials.* New York: Eros Publishers, 1987.

2603. Press, Charles. *The Political Cartoon.* Rutherford, N.J.: Fairleigh Dickinson University Press, 1981. Explores the history and influence of political cartoons in the United States.

2604. Rohrbach, Peter T., and Lowell S. Newman. *American Issue: The U.S. Postage Stamp, 1842-1869.* Washington: Smithsonian Institution Press, 1984.

2605. "The Tyler Group." In the Floyd and Marion Rinhart Collection of Daguerreian Art and Other Rare Photographic Images, 1839-1874, Ohio State University, Columbus. Contains seven daguerreotypes and five ambrotypes and includes both John Tyler and Julia Gardiner Tyler.

2606. *Virginia Born Presidents: Addresses Delivered on the Occasions of Unveiling the Busts of Virginia Born Presidents at Old Hall of the House of Delegates, Richmond, Virginia.* New York: American Book Co., 1932. Carries address of Claude G. Bowers on the occasion.

2607. Weddell, Alexander Wilbourne. *A Memorial Volume of Virginia Historical Portraiture, 1585-1830.* Richmond: William Byrd Press, 1930.

2608. Wein, Frances Stevenson, ed. *National Portrait Gallery, Smithsonian Institution: Permanent Collection Illustrated Checklist.* Washington: National Portrait Gallery by the Smithsonian Institution Press, 1980.

2609. Weitenkampf, Frank. *Political Caricature in the United States in Separately Published Cartoons.* New York: New York Public Library, 1953; Reprint: New York: Arno Press, 1971.

2610. Whitney, David C. *The Graphic Story of the American Presidents.* Chicago: J. G. Ferguson, 1972.

List of Serials Consulted

African Repository and Colonial Journal
Alabama Review
American Antiquarian Society
    Proceedings
American Bar Association Journal
American Collector
American Heritage
American Historical Review
American Journal of Legal History
American Journal of Political Science
American Journal of Sociology
American Literature
American Quarterly
Arkansas Historical Quarterly

Bulletin of the Historical Society of
    Montgomery County

Campaigns & Elections
Century Magazine
Civil War History
Collector
Congressional Studies
Current History

Daughters of the American Revolution
    Magazine
De Bow's Review

Fireside Sentinel

Georgia Historical Quarterly
Green Bag

Harvard Journal of Asiatic Studies
Historical Journal of Massachusetts
History in the House

Indiana Magazine of History
International Review
Iron Worker

John P. Branch Historical Papers of
    Randolph-Macon College
Journal of American History (New
    Haven)
Journal of American Studies
Journal of Politics
Journal of Southern History
Journal of Economic History
Journal of the Early Republic

Le Commerce, Journal Politique et
    Litteraire
Leisure Hour
Lippincott's Monthly Magazine
Louisiana History
Louisiana Studies

Magazine of History
Magazine of American History
Maryland History
Michigan Law Review
Mississippi Valley Historical Review
Missouri Historical Review
Modern Age

National Geographic Magazine

National Magazine and Republican
　Review

New-England Galaxy

New-England Magazine

New England Quarterly

New Jersey History

New York History

New Yorker

North American Review

North Carolina Historical Review

Northern Neck of Virginia Historical
　Magazine

Northern Virginian

Northwest Ohio Quarterly

Ohio Archaeological and Historical
　Quarterly

Ohio Archaeological and Historical
　Society Publications

Ohio History

Outlook

Papers of the Albemarle County
　Historical Society

Pennsylvania History

Presidential Studies Quarterly

Proceedings of the American Antiquarian
　Society

Prologue

Publications of the Southern History
　Association

Quarterly Journal of Speech

Quarterly of the Texas State Historical
　Association

Records of the American Catholic
　Historical Society of Philadelphia

Red River Valley Historical Review

Register of the Kentucky Historical
　Society

Scribner's Magazine

Sewanee Review

Social Science Journal

South Atlantic Quarterly

South Carolina Historical Magazine

Southern Communication Journal

Southern Literary Messenger

Tennessee Historical Magazine

Tennessee Historical Quarterly

Time

Transactions of the American
　Philosophical Society

Tyler's Quarterly Historical and
　Genealogical Magazine

U.S. News and World Report

United States Magazine and Democratic
　Review

Vermont Historical Society Proceedings

Vermont History

Virginia Cavalcade

Virginia Genealogist

Virginia Magazine of History and
　Biography

Virginia State Bar Association Reports

West Virginia History

Western Pennsylvania Historical
　Magazine

William and Mary College Quarterly

William and Mary College Quarterly
　Historical Magazine

William and Mary College Quarterly
　Historical Papers

Wisconsin Magazine of History

Yearbook of the Supreme Court Historical
　Society

Index to Authors, Editors, Compilers, and Translators

Note: Numbers refer to entries, not page numbers.

Abbott, John S. C., 782
Abel, Annie Heloise, 431
Abel, Ernest L., 1443
Abell, Alexander G., 203, 1789
Abernethy, Thomas Perkins, 880
Abraham, Henry J., 1210
Adams, Charles Francis, 313, 1817, 2231
Adams, Ephraim Douglass, 432, 433, 1563, 1612, 2144
Adams, George Jones, 434
Adams, Henry, 435, 2359
Adams, Herbert Baxter, 436
Adams, James Truslow, 1211
Adams, John Quincy, 635
Adams, John Wolcott, 1029
Adams, William Harrison, III, 1212, 1213
Aderman, Ralph M., 437, 438
Adkins, Edwin Payne, 2080
Adler, Joseph G., 2099
Agar, Herbert, 783, 2360
Aikman, Lonnelle, 2407
Alexander, Holmes Moss, 2232
Alexander, John Rufus, 440
Alexander, Thomas B., 1030, 1214, 1215
Allen, David Grayson, 312

Allen, George, 441
Allen, Harry C., 1613, 1614
Allen, Stephen, 210
Allis, Frederick S., Jr., 651
Alvord, C. W., 501
Ambler, Charles Henry, 355, 358, 1216-1218, 1564, 2192
American Historical Association, 2523
Ames, Herman V., 96
Ames, William E., 1444
Ammon, Harry, 843, 844, 2233
Anbinder, Tyler G., 2087
Anderson, Burnett, 1289
Anderson, Dice R., 2234
Anderson, James L., 1763
Anderson, John T., 1115
Anderson, Sterling P., Jr., 2193
Anti-Junius, 1795, 1796
Appleton, Nathan, 315-317
Archer, William Segar, 154, 319
Armbruster, Maxim Ethan, 784
Armstrong, Walter P., 2130
Arndt, J. Chris, 1615
Ashley, Evelyn, 443
Ashworth, John, 1219, 1220
Atchison, Theodore, 1928
Atkins, Jonathan M., 994

Index of Subjects

Note: Numbers refer to entries, not page numbers

Abell, Alexander G., 203
Aberdeen, George Hamilton-Gordon, Lord, 2149, 2157
Abingdon, Va., *Banner*, 662
Abingdon, Va., *Little Tennessean*, 663
Abolitionism, 976, 1056, 1111, 1394, 1475, 1484-1486, 1489, 1492, 1494-1496, 1498, 1501, 1504, 1506. *See also* Antislavery, Slavery
Adams, Charles Francis, 481, 2260
Adams, George Jones, 434
Adams, John, 779
Adams, John Quincy, 313, 314, 331, 408, 635, 908, 913; biographies of, 1922-1924; portraits of, 2599
Agriculture and agricultural developments, 1539
Alabama, 170; politics in, 1214, 1344, 1417; presidential campaign of 1836 in, 999; Whig party in, 1307
Albany Argus, 665
Albany Evening Journal, 664
Alexander, John Rufus, 440
Allen, George, 441
Allen, William, 1925
Alvarez, Manuel, 1571

American Colonization Society, 247, 777, 781, 1505
American Peace Crusade, 1453
Amistad (Schooner) Case, 598, 1490, 1494, 1495, 1498
Anderson, John, 531
Anelli, Francesco, 2567
Antimasonic Party, 915, 1027, 1133, 1424
Antislavery, 1313-1315, 1484, 1485, 1501, 1502, 1504, 1821, 2286, 2287, 2309; and presidential campaign of 1844, 1766. *See also* Abolitionism, Slavery
Appleton, Nathan, 315-317; biographies of, 1926, 1927
Apportionment Act of 1842, 1389
Archer, William Segar, 154, 319
Argentina, 1694
Arkansas, 1231, 1426
Aroostook War, 1634, 1656
Arthur, Sir George, 563
Ashburton, Baring, Alexander, Lord, 258, 301, 302, 1632, 2144, 2288
Atchison, David R., 1928, 1929
Attorneys General of the United States,

About the Compiler

HAROLD D. MOSER is currently editor-director of The Papers of Andrew Jackson at the University of Tennessee. He was formerly editor of the Correspondence Series, The Papers of Daniel Webster, at Dartmouth College.

Bibliographies of the Presidents of the United States

Series Editor: Mary Ellen McElligott